THE SACRAMENTS

RITES OF CONVERSION

WILLIAM J. O'MALLEY, S.J.

TABOR ®

PUBLISHING

Allen, Texas

NIHIL OBSTAT
Rev. Glenn D. Gardner, J.C.D.
Censor Librorum

IMPRIMATUR
† Most Rev. Charles V. Grahmann
Bishop of Dallas

May 8, 1995

The Nihil Obstat and Imprimatur are official declarations that the material reviewed is free of doctrinal or moral error. No implication is contained therein that those granting the Nihil Obstat and Imprimatur agree with the contents, opinions, or statements expressed.

Design: Davidson Design

Illustrations: Pin Yi Wu

Acknowledgments and photo credits are found on page 254.

Send all inquiries to:
Tabor Publishing
200 East Bethany Drive
Allen, Texas 75002–3804

Printed in the United States of America

ISBN 0–7829–0472–6 (Student Text)
ISBN 0–7829–0477–7 (Resource Manual)

1 2 3 4 5   99 98 97 96 95

To all the students
who made me
think of
these things . . .

CONTENTS

INTRODUCTION

Probably no student opening this text said, "Oh, goody! Another course on the sacraments!" Understandable.

What makes this approach to the sacraments different is that it admits that fact and starts from there. It shows students who are disenchanted with the celebration of the sacraments—and perhaps also with the Church and religion and even the soul itself—how empty the soulless life really is.

Life without the Sacred

Years ago, Peggy Lee sang a song: "Is that all there is?" What is the "that" she sings of? Money, nightclubs, raises, grades, trophies, working fifty weeks a year for a two-week vacation.

A world where "anything goes," where there is nothing sinful and nothing sacred, with no dimension to our lives that lasts when our time runs out, gets its inescapable comeuppance from the fact that one day it will all simply stop.

Without God, at the moment of death we suddenly stop being real: all our struggles for dignity, our triumphs, our battle scars are simply wiped out, like a computer file in a power outage. Grim, yet inescapable. Without God, we spend our days killing time, till time ultimately kills us. Without God, we are all headed in only one direction.

Is that all there is?

Without a map, a sense of direction, trustworthy landmarks, and the conviction that there is in fact a real destination, we are lost. A child waking from a nightmare is surrounded by darkness, nothing familiar, and she cries out in terror. But her mother comes into the room, turns on the light, wraps the child in her arms and says, "Everything's all right, honey. It's okay." And the child feels "at home" again, safe.

In our confusing lives, we all still need that sense of being "at home," knowing that—no matter how baffling our days become—it all does make sense; there is a direction and a destination. Otherwise, our lives are lived in terror of the faceless unknown.

There are some men and women, however, who believe there is no God—and in fact feel there is no need of God, that we can get along quite well without a God, thank you. We are rational animals who can pretty well figure out most problems with hard-nosed logic. Empirical science shows clear, this-world explanations for phenomena that preceding centuries attributed to spirits and demons, prayers answered and denied. Not magic, but cause-and-effect: reason.

Yet there are moments in our lives that defy that reduction of human beings to no more than rational animals, competitors and consumers. We stand under a summer sky ablaze with light that began its journey toward us before humans existed, and we say, "Oh, my God!"

An infant curls his whole fist around our pinkie finger and grins, and we say, "Oh, my God!" We walk away from a near-fatal accident, hearts thundering, and we say, "Oh, my God!"

Ritualizing Belief

Falling in love, marrying, having children are not rational acts. But they are not irrational. Those urges and life commitments arise not from the body or from the brain but from the human soul. Most times we can avoid the needs of our souls, distracting its hungers with busyness. But there are times when the soul "catches up" with us, when (even without our knowing the cause) we are soul-weary, quicksanded in trivia and routine—a directionless endurance. Then we need God.

Perhaps you yourself feel no need of reconciliation; "I can take care of myself, thank you." Perhaps you feel no need for the Eucharist, especially when it is embedded in a ritual incapable of moving the human soul. Beyond doubt there are moments in your life when there is not only a need but a demand for a context larger and richer than the everyday, the here-and-now.

Marriage in the office of a justice of the peace is legal. But there is something "missing," something important, too meaningful to be hidden away like a secret. For the two people entering this union, this is

an enormous part of their meaning, of their being "at home." It begs for celebration, and not merely in the presence of their friends but in a context that assures them that even death cannot end it.

Something within us simply cannot rest content that the birth of a child merely is recorded in some county office. It begs for celebration, and not merely in the presence of friends but in a context that assures the infant's parents that even death can never end their love and this life.

There is an emptiness in our souls where once a loved one lived. That life cannot simply be erased. It begs for celebration in a context that assures us life has more value than merely enduring, year after year, and then ceasing to be real.

Sacrament as Rites of Conversion

Each of the sacraments celebrates, ritualizes, those moments of our lives. Each is a rite of conversion in an ongoing relationship—not merely a once-for-all rite but a high point in a lifelong process, a celebration of change, a rite of conversion.

The purpose of this book is to attempt to revivify those symbols. Which, whether successful or not, is a very Christian enterprise. The whole message of Christianity is about resurrection and rebirth: a more abundant life!

The Meaning
of
Sacrament

Chapter 1

Animating the Human Soul

I am a part of all that I have met; / Yet all experience is an arch wherethrough
Gleams that untraveled world, whose margin fades / For ever and for ever when I move.
How dull it is to pause, to make an end, / To rust unburnished, not to shine in use!
As though to breathe were life!
Alfred Lord Tennyson, "Ulysses"

CONVERSION TO HUMANITY

Survey

This survey is not an exercise for a grade, but a means to stir up interest and get an idea of varying opinions in your group. Some of the statements are matters of objective fact; others are merely subjective opinions. On the rating scale under each statement circle the number that best reflects your current opinion about that statement.

 +2 = strongly agree,
 +1 = agree,
  0 = cannot make up my mind,
 −1 = disagree,
 −2 = strongly disagree.

Then share the reasons for your opinion.

1. Humans are the only species free *not* to live up to their nature.

 +2 +1 0 −1 −2

2. The body is more important than the mind.

 +2 +1 0 −1 −2

3. The mind is more important than the soul.

 +2 +1 0 −1 −2

4. No reasonable person would say he or she does not want a better life.

 +2 +1 0 −1 −2

5. Everyone has a personality; not everyone has character.

 +2 +1 0 −1 −2

6. The soul holds the mind and body together in a coherent whole.

 +2 +1 0 −1 −2

7. All humans have souls, but many do not activate that potential.

 +2 +1 0 −1 −2

8. If you have a *reason* to live, you can put up with just about anything.

 +2 +1 0 −1 −2

9. No one can take your soul away from you without your cooperation.

 +2 +1 0 −1 −2

10. An extroverted personality is better than an introverted one.

 +2 +1 0 −1 −2

A Puzzlement

Am I the bulb that carries the light, or am I the light of which the bulb is the vehicle?   Joseph Campbell

■ *What do think Campbell means?*

The Human Soul

Now what I want is Facts [Mr. Gradgrind told the teacher, Mr. McChoakumchild, and his quavering pupils]. Teach these boys and girls nothing but Facts. Facts alone are wanted in life. Plant nothing else, and root out everything else. You can only form the minds of reasoning animals upon Facts: nothing else will ever be of service to them. This is the principle on which I bring up my own children, and this is the principle on which I bring up these children. Stick to Facts, sir!"

Charles Dickens, *Hard Times*

No room in Mr. Gradgrind's school for fancy, imagination, intuition, the unquantifiable, the "sense" of something larger than "Fact." In his school, a horse was not a noble beast, a snorting steed with flaring eyes, Bucephalus-Rocinante-Silver; it was "an equine quadruped." His students were not human spirits yearning for greatness, dreaming dreams, envisioning the unheard-of, exulting in the circus. They were "reasoning animals," to be sorted by his school into those capable of being managers and those destined to be no more than "the hands" in his mills. No sin in Mr. Gradgrind's school or world, except for sloth and lack of productivity. Nothing sacred except financial profit.

We are free to treat one another—and ourselves—as if we were nothing more than mere animals with computers implanted in our heads. But that is self-evidently *not* all that we are.

We know we are not angels, but we also know we are not sharks or spinach or stepping-stones. There is something in each of us that is *more* than the physical hungers of the body for food, exercise, sex, sleep, and *more* than the mental hungers of the mind for facts, gossip, definitions, causes-and-effects, distractions.

There are hungers that simply cannot be reduced to the physical or mental. There is unselfish love, honor, imagination, music, dreams, awe, trust, freedom, dignity—none of which is "rational," none of which is taught in most schools. Nor is our concern with the soul and religion, just with the soul and *humanity*. Until the human soul begins to evolve, religion has no chance.

What separates humans from even the most intelligent animals is not the body or brain (which they share). What separates us—by a quantum leap—is the soul. No matter where it is "located," it is undeniably there. And we experience extensively what happens when an individual or society *denies* it is there.

But what *is* the soul?

It may come as a bit of a shock, but no one sees you! Not that you are invisible. The only thing others really can see of you is your body. They do not see who-you-are; they do not see your *self*. Other people can look at the way you use your body, what you wear; they can assess what you talk about and make educated *guesses* about the "you" inside. But that is all they are, guesses.

THE TRUE SELF

Even we ourselves would be hard-pressed to "capture" in words who we really are. The reasons for this are:

- First, that the soul—the "me"—is elusive. It is incapable of showing up on an X-ray plate.

- Second, and more importantly, finding one's soul requires effort. And most of us have more important things to do than to make the effort to find out who we are, where we have been, where we are going. We just . . . go on.

Which is a good reason to write an autobiography, no matter how painstaking the task, because without a sense of "self," our days are nothing more than odd beads without a string to tie them together.

*There is something
in each of us
that is more than
the physical hungers
of the body.*

You know someone is alive when a person's breath fogs a mirror. That breath is a sure sign that at least the body is alive. In Hebrew, Greek, and Latin, the word for "breath" is the same as the word for "spirit," "soul": *ruah, pneuma, anima*. Soul is the "aliveness" in each of us.

When someone dies, something that was there before is gone. The body is there, but the *person* is not. Either the person is "somewhere else" or the person no longer *is*. Even hundreds of thousands of years ago, neanderthals buried their dead with weapons and provisions, because they believed the soul—the person—was on a journey into another way of existing.

The soul is the whole scheme of *values* that give a sense of rootedness to life. It feeds on the outer world and digests what it finds to form wisdom and character. "Personality" is on the outside: a defense; "character" is on the inside: the true self.

The soul holds together body and mind into a coherent whole. But the soul—the self—is not a destination to be attained and conquered once for all; it is a *process* of becoming, a journey. The soul is not a map; it is a compass. Activating one's soul is a decision, a *conversion*, a new way of seeing. It is not just the rational left brain counting the costs, figuring the odds, guarding the self. It is also the intuitive right brain "sensing" the rightness of one's choices, one's direction, one's whole life.

THE TRUE LIFE WISH

Sigmund Freud enunciated what he called "The Pleasure Principle." Each of us, he claimed, is in tension between two inner forces: *Eros*, the life wish, and *Thanatos*, the death wish. Eros craves challenge, commitment at risk, the journey—as with Tennyson's "Ulysses." Thanatos craves security, being unbothered, a return to the womb.

The healthy psyche (soul, self) can be drawn by the life wish, in even the smallest challenges of living, to hazard the good we have in the hope of something better. The true life wish is the urge to become a better *self*, to be fully conscious of oneself as a *human* being. In Nazi prison camps, under the most antihuman conditions, women and men kept hold of their souls because they had a *reason* to: a loved one, a religious faith, a commitment to a cause—anything larger than the limits of their skins. Others "sold their souls," licked boots in order to survive, and died inside themselves—even though their bodies continued to move.

A soul can be surrendered, but it can never be *taken* away. But without that inner compass, life is "a tale told by an idiot, full of sound and fury, signifying nothing."

Personality vs. Character

We often see or read about what happens to individuals who merely "react" to life, letting life "happen to" them; for example: Gogo and Didi in Samuel Becket's *Waiting for Godot*, Gregor Samsa and his family in Franz Kafka's parable "The Metamorphosis," Janis Joplin, Jimi Hendrix, River Phoenix, Kurt Cobain . . . and the beat goes on. One is tempted to believe that such people did not "lose" their souls or "sell" them. Rather they never really *had* their souls in the first place.

Such *soulless* people (however successful they appeared to be) each had a surface "personality," and often a very marketable one at that. But they lacked the inner "character" to deal with life with both feet planted on the ground. They lacked the ability to refuse to be treated—or treat themselves—with less dignity than a human being deserves.

It is easy to see the difference between "personality" and "character." The description "She has a lot of personality" means the person has the ability to charm, beguile, engage attention. "She has a lot of character" is something quite different. This person has a kind of rootedness, self-confidence, the ability to weather whatever comes.

Personality is on the outside; character is on the inside.

Personality is a set of habits that we unconsciously and reactively develop (usually before the age of four). It is our personality that helps us cope with the challenges of living in our particular family. Personalities have been described in various ways: aggressive or defensive; introverted or extroverted; shy, confident; vain, humble; sensitive, coarse; and so on.

Woodstock II (1994).

They develop in response to the family's being warm or chilly, demanding or yielding, caring or indifferent, and so on.

Each of us is invited to form a personally validated self—a character, a soul, a self.

No particular personality type is "better" than any other; each has its assets and liabilities. Nor are we "responsible" for our personality type—at least in the sense that we "chose" it. The habits of our personality *were formed,* in a small child, without any reasoned choice.

But when we come into adolescence, able to reason and ponder, capable of taking charge of our own life, then we do become responsible for what we *do with* the personality we have developed. That is the time when each of us is "invited" to form a personally validated self—a character, a soul, a self.

But many people refuse that invitation. And many—perhaps most—potential human beings somehow content themselves with getting by on personality, image, making a living and then dying, without ever finding out what living was for.

That invitation to form a personally validated self is rooted in the human soul. You are free to refuse it, and the daily newspapers indicate many people who do: murderers, child molesters, drive-by shootists, drug lords, pimps. But those who refuse—or even scorn—the invitation to activate their human potential, their souls, are not limited to such dramatic cases. There are also workers grimly enduring dull jobs only to get the paycheck, grinding numbly along.

There are prisoners in "rehabilitation" centers corraled like animals, scheming for dominance like animals, herded from task to task like animals. Students tolerating the opportunity to learn, to open their horizons, as if learning were an unjust sentence, drudging for five days and coming alive only for a part of the weekend.

Reflection

Probably no reasonable person would say he or she does *not* want a better life. Yet the actual decision to set out on the journey requires a *conversion,* a turnabout from one's comfortable former habits. ("Habit is the great deadener.") Conversion demands a conscious effort and commitment to read more widely in order to explore greater horizons. It involves taking more time out of the rush of the day to reflect.

■ *Ask yourself if you honestly do want to commit yourself to activating the human potential—the soul—within you. The inertia we share with animals does not take readily to change and effort.*

■ *If you draw back from the invitation to live a more fully human life, what are the obstacles that root your resistance? How could they be overcome? Would that be worth it?*

The soul is the whole scheme of values that gives rootedness to life. Personality is on the outside; character is on the inside.

EVOLVING A HUMAN SOUL

Survey

This survey is not an exercise for a grade, but a means to stir up interest and get an idea of varying opinions in your group. Some of the statements are matters of objective fact; others are merely subjective opinions. On the rating scale under each statement circle the number that best reflects your current opinion about that statement.

+2 = strongly agree,
+1 = agree,
 0 = cannot make up my mind,
−1 = disagree,
−2 = strongly disagree.

Then share the reasons for your opinion.

1. Human beings have a fully activated conscience . . . from birth.

   +2 +1 0 −1 −2

2. "Conscience," "character," "psyche," "ego" are all names for the human soul, seen from different angles.

   +2 +1 0 −1 −2

3. One can be human but act less than human.

   +2 +1 0 −1 −2

4. Math and science are objectively more important in human development than art and music.

   +2 +1 0 −1 −2

5. Sometimes I have a sense of a supernatural "presence" in nature.

   +2 +1 0 −1 −2

6. The most important result of a good education is credentials for a well-paying job.

   +2 +1 0 −1 −2

7. The most important result of a good education is forming a personal philosophy of life.

   +2 +1 0 −1 −2

8. An appealing personality will get you further in this world than genuine character.

   +2 +1 0 −1 −2

9. One of the elements of being "popular" is self-confidence.

   +2 +1 0 −1 −2

10. Male souls have "feminine" qualities, and female souls have "masculine" qualities.

   +2 +1 0 −1 −2

Bringing the Soul Alive

There are (at least) five processes needed to evolve a human soul—and we are not speaking of religion yet. That goes much further. Even nonbelievers must evolve their souls, just in order to be fully human beings; and many have. The five processes are:

- *Admitting that,* beyond the mind and body, *one even has a soul.* We must acknowledge that our soul—our humanity—is only a potential that need not be activated, and we must commit ourselves to the effort to bring that potential into actuality. (We have already discussed that need.)

- *Activating the imagination*—all the right-brain human powers denied in a society based solely on "the empirical, this-worldly, secular, pragmatic, contractual, hedonistic, disenchanted."

- *Developing a sense of the numinous*, that is, a sense of the sacredness (again, not yet religious) of nature. This is what the ancients called the *anima mundi*, "the soul of the earth."

- *Evolving a personal philosophy of life,* the priorities that show what is essential to human life and what is superficial, a pattern that gives order, significance, and a sense of wholeness.

- *Evolving a personally validated conscience* that knows not only *that* a given act is generally considered immoral but *why* it is—and yielding to that truth.

IMAGINATION

The right-brain potential of the human mind is given short shrift in our schools. In a budget crunch, it is axiomatic that the first cuts must be to art and music so that the

"real" subjects like math and science suffer no harm. Even English becomes an opportunity not to *feel* and *experience* what the great writers have experienced—to "taste" the juice of an author's verbs, to feel wonder at the possibilities of human dignity and depravity—but to *analyze*, develop SAT verbal skills, and pass objective tests.

Winston Churchill once wrote, "My education was interrupted only by my schooling." Learning yields too often to an arbitrary process that has nothing whatever to do with "real life."

It is endured as the price of achieving work credentials. It has little, if no, interest whatever in the common humanity and common environment all education's disciplines scrutinize.

And of course when schooling is over, there are far too many more "important" elements in life to engage our attention: work, bills, taxes, family squabbles, neighborhood problems, finicky automobiles. And of course mind-numbing television. Little wonder we have a soulless society.

The soul's instrument is the imagination. Unused, the imagination atrophies and dies, and with it the human soul. Learn to sketch, write a story, make music, rather than merely listening. Your soul will waken.

> *Until the human soul*
> *begins to evolve,*
> *religion*
> *has no chance.*

THE NUMINOUS

The word *ecology* comes from the Greek *oikos*, which means "home." We share life with everything on this planet; we share the *anima mundi*. Native Americans feel that profoundly. When the government wrote to Chief Seattle in 1852 with an offer to buy the land of his people, he wrote back:

> The earth does not belong to man, man belongs to the earth. All things are connected like the blood that unites us all. Man did not weave the web of life, he is merely a strand in it. Whatever he does to the web, he does to himself.

Today when we sit down to eat, some of us thank God for the food. But more *primitive* people prayed to thank the animal they hunted and to ask that its spirit would return—as one would thank a friend for cooperating in a mutual relationship. For them, nature was not mute; it "spoke," I to Thou, not I to It.

Today in our cities, as the asphalt spreads and the foliage recedes, we become tougher-souled. Fewer and fewer notice heaps of garbage, noise, old tires, rusty appliances, broken furniture, rusty cars, weeds, unless they are especially blatant. Fewer and fewer feel the smothering, soulless rage that sprayed the graffiti.

Opportunism, enlightened self-interest have freed us from superstition, but we have lost our souls. We do not turn to devils but to anesthesia. The "Earth Mother" is demythologized into nothing more than dirt, under which may lurk oil or uranium. We are so weakened by spiritual anemia that we have lost even our sense of evil.

Every soul needs a walk in the park at least once a week.

PHILOSOPHY OF LIFE

The psychiatrist Carl Jung observed:

> A sense of a wider meaning to one's existence is what raises a person beyond mere getting and spending. If they lack that sense, they are lost and miserable.

Of course the primary concern of every human being is staying alive, and thus also the concern to secure what allows us to live: food, clothing, and shelter. But if that concern occupies our lives *exclusively,* then as Chief Seattle wrote, it is "the end of living and the beginning of survival."

The root of people with character—as opposed to those to whom life's disjointed events merely "happen"—is that they have found at least a tentative answer to that most important and profound (and ironically seldom posed) question: What are people *for?* Or, to put that same question in other forms:

- What does "success" *really* mean?

- What does a totally fulfilled human being look like?

- What must I do, or have, or achieve to be happy?

We have been conditioned (brainwashed, actually) by the media to believe that the key that unlocks all those questions is simple: money. But money (and the means to it) is a reductionist answer to a quite complex question. Food, clothing, and shelter are indeed indispensible to human life and therefore essential to human fulfillment. But does fulfilling this need have to include filet mignon, Armani, and condominiums?

Many "successful people" who have had their share—and more—of those luxuries have overdosed. That does not mean those who have money cannot be happy. But if they are happy, it is not the money that has caused their happiness.

What is the secret, then? What do people who "have it all" possess *within* themselves that allows them to be rich yet still buoyant, hopeful, generous, high on life? Answer that question and you will have begun to have a personal philosophy of life, a soul. Once you uncover that secret, all your priorities will line up in order.

The human person, created in the image of God, is a being at once corporeal and spiritual. The biblical account expresses this reality in symbolic language when it affirms that "then the LORD God formed man of dust from the ground, and breathed into his nostrils the breath of life; and man became a living being." Man, whole and entire, is therefore willed by God.

In Sacred Scripture the term "soul" often refers to human life or the entire human person. But "soul" also refers to the innermost aspect of man, that which is of greatest value in him, that by which he is most especially in God's image: "soul" signifies the spiritual principle in man.

Catechism of the Catholic Church, 362–363

CONSCIENCE

When each of us is born, we are little different from animal cubs: what Freud called the Id. But sometime during our second year of life, we begin to develop muscle control and teeth—through no fault of our own. It is just in the natural way of things. Before that transition, that conversion from infancy to childhood, everything we did was acceptable to our parents and care-givers—no matter how inconvenient. Wet the diaper, toss the pureed vegetables, in fact toss everything, and they cleaned it up. If an infant is inconvenienced, wail and it will be taken care of.

But once nature has given you the means to control yourself, at least in some measure, you begin to hear for the first time ever words you will hear in various forms thenceforth for the rest of your life: *good* and *bad*. That is the time when your parents begin taping on your innocent mind a Superego: a series of do's and don'ts that you have no way to comprehend or critique but that you simply accept as the price of your parents' approval.

Then comes the radical conversion of adolescence. You finally begin to achieve a mental sophistication capable of dealing with Shakespeare and trigonometry. The nature of human development invites you to develop an Ego, your own personally validated conscience. You begin to critique all those do's and don'ts and find which ones square with objective reality and which do not.

But once again there is an invitation that you can refuse, or ignore, or even be totally unaware of. Adolescents who fail to rise to that challenge end up victims either of their taped Superegos or, rejecting those stric-tures, their own moody Ids. Or more likely, they live a life jerked around by both: "I really shouldn't do that . . . But I *want* . . . But . . . Still . . ."

Reflection

The ironic result of passively adapting to another people's needs, demands, and goals in the effort to gain their approval is that one ends up less valuable, less inter-esting, less desirable. Begin to evolve a personal answer to the most important and profound (and seldom posed) questions.

- *What are people for?*
- *What does "success" really mean?*
- *What does a totally fulfilled human being look like?*
- *What must I do, or have, or achieve to be happy?*

True happiness is not found in riches or well-being, in human fame or power, or in any human achievement—however beneficial it may be— such as science, technology, and art, or indeed in any creature, but in God alone, the source of every good and of all love.

Catechism of the Catholic Church, 1723

Jose Ferrer and Ingrid Bergman in *Joan of Arc*, 1948.

A Balanced Soul

The key to a healthy soul is seeing, affirming, and accepting the world *as it is* and not as we wish it were: accepting the good and bad, dark and light, the expectability of the unexpected. Wisdom begins when we come to peace with the unchangeable, which means surrendering all the self-defeating "if only's."

We also must beware of a reductionism in values. We must avoid focusing our quest on the pursuit of any one virtue unbalanced by its opposite. Love, for instance, unchecked by hard-nosed common sense can devolve into enslavement; purity becomes prudery; devoutness turns into fanaticism; charity becomes gullibility.

The healthy soul has to have an openness to the activities and values of both the right brain and the left brain. Without that balance, we become coldly rational apes or sentimental dreamers: "There is no such thing as an unjust profit" or "Nothing must stand in the way of love!" Unless the two radical powers of the mind have a healthy relationship, we end up acting half-wittedly.

In their "being-man" and "being-woman," they [man and woman] reflect the Creator's wisdom and goodness.

Catechism of the Catholic Church, 369

Carl Jung established that the healthy soul is *androgynous*, that is, both masculine and feminine. The healthy soul is a wedding of those "masculine" qualities associated with the left brain (and wrongly stereotyped as belonging only to males): rationality, decisiveness, seeing values in a strict vertical line of importance, and those "feminine" qualities associated with the right brain (and wrongly stereotyped as belonging only to females): intuition, inclusiveness, seeing problems in a horizontal plane which judges them not in isolation but in the context of other significant factors.

The masculine potential in a woman, Jung called the *animus;* the feminine potential in a man, he called the *anima*. Both are powers that need not be activated in everyone. One's talent for football or dancing or the violin may be ignored, as can one's human soul. But we ignore them to the soul's peril.

To be fully human, a man must not be afraid that tenderness, compassion, and compromise make him somehow effeminate. And a woman must not fear that rationality, determination, and resolution make her somehow a kind of predatory "she-male." It is perfectly healthy for a man to weep when there is a reason; perfectly healthy for a woman to stand up and be heard.

The "man-within-a-woman" is the invitation to initiative, courage, objectivity. The "woman-within-a-man" is the invitation to vulnerability, personal love. It is an openness to the nonrational (as opposed not only to the rational but to the irrational).

The undeveloped *animus* needs to read *Joan of Arc* and see *My Fair Lady*. The undeveloped *anima* needs to read *A Separate Peace* and see *Ordinary People*.

Reflection

The first step toward making peace with the unchangeable is surrendering all the frustrating, self-defeating "if only's." Any statement that comes after those two words is, ipso facto (by the fact itself), impossible.

■ *What "if only's" plague your thoughts at times: the ill-focused resentments about what the world and life and family and work and school have dumped on you? Take some time and list them.*

■ *Now, what is the only sensible thing to do with that list—and with all the impossibilities on it?*

Marriages do not just "happen." Marriages take work: reflection, creativity, effort.

■ *What is the state of the "marriage" between the "masculine" and "feminine" in your soul?*

■ *There is no problem in being genuinely proud of areas where your soul is quite balanced. But without getting nervous or self-protective about it, how could that balance be improved? What does your soul need in order to be healthier?*

What are people for?

Once you uncover that secret,

all your priorities

will line up in order.

Understanding the Human Soul

Review

1. How are humans different from even the most "intelligent" animals?

2. What does it mean to be "centered"? What is the soul? What activities does it engage in that cannot be reduced to body or brain? Why did ancient languages use the same word for "soul" as for "breath"?

3. What is the difference between personality and character?

4. What is the difference between Eros and Thanatos? What does each crave?

5. Explain: Anyone with a *why* to live for can endure just about any *how*.

6. Explain: The first step in activating the human soul is admitting that you even *have* one.

7 What is the role of the right-brain human potential—imagination, intuition, seeing things in context—in the full development of a human being? Why is that potential given such little attention in schooling? Explain: "My education was interrupted only by my schooling."

8. What does the word *numinous* mean? What is the *anima mundi?*

9. Explain: The root of people with character is that they have found at least a tentative answer to the question: What are people for?

10. Explain: The healthy soul is androgynous.

Discuss

1. Imagine that you and your best friend in school are not exactly models of virtue; nothing serious, but constant detention for little things. Your friend comes to you and says. "I have been molested by a teacher and am too afraid to tell anyone." Given your reputations, what would you do?

2. How many of your peers would you guess routinely cheat on quizzes, tests, homework? What does that say about the health of their souls? Can you routinely cheat and legitimately claim to be "okay," to have real character?

3. None of us is a mobster. Most of our "crimes" are petty. But rather than embarrass us, that pettiness seems to *absolve* us. Why is that a cop-out?

4. What concrete evidence do you have from the way you do your job (getting an education) that your life is motivated more by Eros, the life wish, rather than by Thanatos, the death wish?

5. In a given week, other than passively listening to someone else's music, what do you do to keep your imagination alive?

6. Have you ever had the experience of "sensing" the hugeness of creation? What was it like?

7. What does Carl Jung mean by "a sense of a wider meaning to one's existence"? Quite honestly, what is really your motivation for going to school? Is it getting a well-paying job or evolving a personal philosophy of life? If it is the former, what concrete evidence is there in your *present* life on which to ground the hope that you will begin to evolve a personal philosophy of life in college?

8. Although each of us is unique, we all have gone through the same process of having our Id controlled by others imposing a Superego. Was the process for you too strict? Too lenient? What has been the effect of that on the way you face problems now? Are you honestly ready to take control of your own Id, to critique all the elements in your Superego, to reason to your own Ego?

Activities

1. Role-play this scenario. You are in a Nazi concentration camp. You are forced to work a ten-hour day on nothing but two wads of bread and a cup of watery soup. Your rotten clothes hang off your skinny shoulders like a scarecrow. The guards are inhuman. You have the opportunity to give up your religion for a good meal.

2. Choose two people you know who have character. Ask them to rank each of these qualities in its order of importance for their lives.

    ___ Trustworthiness   ___ Hard work

    ___ Good looks   ___ Success

    ___ Creativity   ___ Honesty

    ___ Friendships   ___ Sexuality

3. Read through a magazine or a daily newspaper. List all the ways society rewards the "masculine" more than the "feminine"— even in a woman. Why?

Scripture Readings

Skim the passages. Pick one that appeals to you and (1) summarize its main point, (2) tell how it relates to the chapter, and (3) list one or two thoughts that entered your mind as you read it.

- Genesis 1:27   Creation of humans
- Ezekiel 36:26   New heart
- Matthew 10:28   Whom to fear
- Matthew 16:25–26   Saving one's life
- Luke 1:48   Mary's song of praise
- 1 Corinthians 15:44–45   The resurrected body
- 1 Peter 2:11   War against the soul

Journal

Prayerfully reflect on these words:

There is something in each of us that is more than the physical hungers of the body.

Name and describe those hungers in us that are deeper than the "physical hungers of the body." Describe how each of those "deeper hungers" enriches your life.

A sense of a wider meaning to one's existence is what raises people beyond mere getting and spending. If they lack that sense, they are lost and miserable.

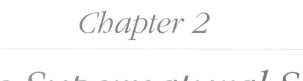

Chapter 2

The Supernatural Self

What is that which gleams through me and smites my heart
without wounding it? I am both ashudder and aglow.
Ashudder insofar as I am unlike it, aglow insofar as I am like *it.*
Saint Augustine

THE BEYOND IN OUR MIDST

Survey

This survey is not an exercise for a grade, but a means to stir up interest and get an idea of varying opinions in your group. Some of the statements are matters of objective fact; others are merely subjective opinions. On the rating scale under each statement circle the number that best reflects your current opinion about that statement.

> +2 = strongly agree,
> +1 = agree,
> 0 = cannot make up my mind,
> −1 = disagree,
> −2 = strongly disagree.

Then share the reasons for your opinion.

1. It is quite likely God is pursuing us more eagerly than we are pursuing God.

   +2   +1   0   −1   −2

2. The one undeniable future event that puts all values into perspective is death.

   +2   +1   0   −1   −2

3. Conflicting ideas can cause more suffering and death than AIDS.

   +2   +1   0   −1   −2

4. There are human needs more important even than going on living.

   +2   +1   0   −1   −2

5. Imagination is not at odds with factual knowledge; in fact it is a way of *illuminating* factual knowledge.

   +2   +1   0   −1   −2

6. Religion is about theology, not about communicating with God.

   +2   +1   0   −1   −2

7. You don't see any person; you see only the person's body.

   +2   +1   0   −1   −2

8. If there were a reality faster than light, it would be everywhere at once.

   +2   +1   0   −1   −2

9. Hope is ultimately a defiance of death.

   +2   +1   0   −1   −2

10. The greatest soul problem we have today is the triumph of triviality.

    +2   +1   0   −1   −2

A Puzzlement

Speaking of Herman Melville's novel *Moby Dick,* in which an obsessed sea captain named Ahab is in pursuit of a white whale that has maimed him and torn off his leg, the British journalist Bernard Levin writes:

> The whale itself, perhaps the most gigantic symbol in all literature (it is a white whale, remember) no less certainly represents something greater than the greatest of sea beasts. Probably Moby Dick meant to Melville what the Hound of Heaven meant to Francis Thompson ("I fled Him down the nights and down the days"), for surely the whale is pursuing Ahab even as Ahab is pursuing the whale.
>
> *The Listener,* 12 August 1982

■ *Have you ever felt that God was pursuing you? Explain.*

The Sacred, Holy, Supernatural

Frequently we have encounters with the numinous, the "sacred" in nature. For example: the summer sky at night, the crackling thunderstorm, the vastness of the sea, the immensity of the universe, the sudden felt awareness of one's own inevitable death, and therefore of the preciousness of everything.

In these encounters with nature, when we experience the "numinous," we come in contact with "Something More," with the mystery we call God.

The awe we feel in those encounters with the numinous—those moments when we say, "Oh, my *God!*"—truly are encounters with God. They are moments of ecstasy—*ek-stasis*—when we "stand outside" the everyday, and even outside of ourselves. A flash of eternity in the present.

The world is charged with the grandeur
  of God.
  It will flame out, like shining from
    shook foil;
  It gathers to a greatness, like the ooze
    of oil
Crushed. Why do men then now not
    reck his rod?
Generations have trod, have trod,
    have trod;
  And all is seared with trade; bleared,
    smeared with toil;
  And wears man's smudge and shares
    man's smell: the soil
Is bare now, nor can foot feel, being shod.
And for all this, nature is never spent;
  There lives a freshness deep down
    things;
And though the last lights off the black
    West went
  Oh, morning, at the brown brink
    eastward, springs—
Because the Holy Ghost over the bent
    World broods with warm breast and
    with ah! bright wings.

Gerard Manley Hopkins, S.J.,
"God's Grandeur"

There is a genuine difference in our encounters with the "sublime," as in a first viewing of the Sistine ceiling, and our encounters with the numinous, or the sacred, in nature, as with the star-strewn sky. The awe we feel at seeing the Sistine ceiling is a tribute to the artist, Michelangelo. The awe we feel at seeing the "firefolk sitting in the air" is—whether we are aware of it or not—a tribute to the Creator.

God, who through the Word created all things and keeps them in existence, gives [us] an enduring witness to Himself in created realities.

Vatican II, *Dogmatic Constitution on Divine Revelation*

We need to clarify a few words that we often use—or at least hear—and believe but that we vaguely understand: *sacred, holy,* and *supernatural.* The word *sacred* does not merely mean "set aside from the secular" or "precious." It means "holy." And *holy* does not mean "completely good," in the moral sense of "being sinless, unblemished, faultless." It means, in fact, "the presence of the transcendent—the supernatural—*in* our immanent world," the Beyond in our midst.

Pictures we see in church, cartoons about people in heaven, religion classes, have led us to believe—wrongly—that *supernatural* merely means "physically *above*," as in *superstructure* or *supervise:* "above" the clouds, "over the rainbow." Rather *super-natural* means "highly intensified," as in *supercharged* or "a *superhuman* feat." It means an infusion of aliveness from the Beyond, from another dimension of being real, a dimension that permeates and

enlivens *the nature which was already there.* In fact that supernatural infusion—grace—does make us truly "superhuman."

The premise of the profane world is that no one who uses electrical appliances and computers and X-ray machines can believe in a dimension of reality that defies computation, left-brain dissection, rigid scientific analysis. Yet those very valuable instruments of the mind are also incapable of coping with love, honor, dignity, dreams—which are nonetheless not only *real* but very important elements of living a fully human life. Such a stance does, in fact, place limits on what we *allow* to be real.

What's more, since 1933, when Heisenberg was awarded the Nobel Prize for Physics for the creation of quantum physics, we have known that even the models of *physics* are no more than approximate *metaphors* (right brain) for realities we cannot see. As Jung wrote, "It is almost ridiculous prejudice to assume existence can be only physical." And in the end, the secular world's denial of the supernatural becomes the triumph of the trivial, since all the medals, profits, condominiums, and skyscrapers shrivel into Lilliputian perspective in the face of the ultimate Gulliver, Death.

SENSE OF THE SACRED

Money is no guarantee of happiness, fulfillment, or success. If some wealthy people *are* happy, what do they possess *within* themselves that allows them to be rich yet still buoyant, hopeful, generous, high on life? When we have gone beyond all needs—beyond food, clothing and shelter, the need to belong, money, fame, sex, power—we find human beings are at the very core (potentially) religious beings. We find that there is no wholeness in us till we make our spiritual hunger more important than all the others.

Michelangelo Buonarroti (1475–1564).
Overall view of ceiling of Sistine Chapel, Vatican Palace.

Wealthy people who are genuinely happy may not call that dominant inner need "spiritual hunger" or "soul." Perhaps they view it as "integrity" or "self-esteem" or "honor." But it is the same thing, just as awe at the numinous is a tribute to God, whether one realizes it or not.

The sense of the sacred cannot be taught. It is only evoked, awakened—in the sense that *Buddha* means "the one who woke up." Nor is imagination at odds with knowledge. It is indeed a way of *illuminating* facts. But insights through imagination will be more ambiguous, more open-ended than strict formulas and definitions. When asked what a dance meant, the great choreographer Martha Graham said: "Mean? Darlings, if I could *tell* you, I wouldn't have *danced* it!"

If you want to "understand" Handel's *Messiah*, I don't hand you the score. If you want to know why fans love baseball, it will be of little help to study the physics and geometry of the game. In all those cases—and in the case of the sacred—you have to experience them. You have to develop a sensitivity to the sacred to evolve the *potential* within you, in order to apprehend the holy.

THE EXPERIENCE OF THE UNSEEN

That experience of God is often lost in theologizing: in studying *others'* experience of the numinous, or the holy, only with left-brain analysis and formulas. Thus, for instance, sacraments might be understood as mere conduits by which grace is "put into us," like gas into a car. We might miss the insight that they are vulnerable *connections* to the Energy that enlivens all reality. If you want to understand the sacraments, you have to be as vulnerable to them as Martha Graham's audience was to her movements and the fans to a baseball game.

If you really want to *understand* God, I do not merely hand you a catechism. A book like this one may intrigue you to make yourself vulnerable to experience God, but it is no substitute for the experience.

It is difficult to deal with an entity like God, immanent yet transcendent, real but unseen. And yet, surprisingly, most of reality around us we do not see. This is true not just in the endless depths of the universe, but even in our very own rooms. We do not see others' thoughts, their lunches digesting, the blood pumping through their bodies.

We do not see their fears, their hopes, their dreams. Yet they are real. And very important.

We do not see the alpha rays, gamma rays, muons and gluons and quarks whizzing all around us. We do not see most of the light spectrum, and yet it is there. We do not see the television and radio signals pulsing all around us. Yet, they are real. We do not see the air, yet it keeps us alive.

Couple that modern insight with the insight of Exodus. When Moses asked, "When I go to the Israelites and say to them, 'The God of your ancestors sent me to you,' they will ask me, 'What is his name?' So what can I tell them?" (Exodus 3:13). Moses was asking for much more than a label. For a Hebrew like Moses, one's name designated his or her role in the community. And God's reply was, "I am who I am" (Exodus 3:14).

> *The secular world's denial of the supernatural becomes the triumph of the trivial.*

THE EXPERIENCE OF GOD

Science says there can be no reality faster than light. Well, what if there *were* a light, an energy, faster than light? It would be moving so fast that it would be everywhere at once. Like God. So dynamic that it would also be utterly at rest. Like God. And science now believes when it cracks open the last building block of matter, what it will find is nonextended energy. Like God. $E = mc^2$ means matter is energy. There is an insight there.

What is God's role in the community? Existence.

God is the pool of existence out of which anything that *is* gets its "is." At least in that sense, insofar as the power of God is immanent, God *is* the *anima mundi,* "the spirit of the earth." When we react in awe and reverence to the numinous in nature, we are reacting to the Source of its aliveness and energy. "The world is charged with the grandeur of God" (Gerald Manley Hopkins, S.J.).

RUMORS OF GOD

The philosopher Thales of Miletus (640?–546 B.C.) said that "everything is full of gods." All round us, if we are aware, we find rumors of God. The Letter to the Hebrews says, "Remember to welcome strangers in your homes. There were some who did that and welcomed angels without knowing it" (13:2). Anyone we meet on the street could be a messenger, a signal of God's presence in the world. Finding these signals (much less recognizing them) depends primarily on our *openness* in our perceptions of reality. But

this openness depends also on overcoming TRIVIALITY—and even before that we need to *recognize* that much of what we think really important in life is, against the background of the transcendent and death, actually trivial.

How can we be sure our perceptions of the Beyond in our midst are not self-deceptions? The answer is simple: we cannot, any more than we can be certain of the other discoveries of the intuitive right brain—love, faith, hunches. But the undeniable hungers to find answers and to survive death argue to a God who can fulfill them. Peter Berger in his book *A Rumor of Angels* (Doubleday, 1970) argues for several signals within human beings, of all times and cultures, that validate our apprehensions of the Beyond in our midst.

■ First, the argument from the inner human need for *order,* for the "mother" to come in at night and assure us "Everything is all right," not just within this home, but everywhere. But if the supernatural is a delusion, and all we have is a time-space reality, then what the mother lets her child believe is a lie: there is sickness "out there," dopers, DWIs, child abusers. If Freud is right, religion—the mother, a Parent God that will "make everything right"—is a fantasy. Ultimately (in the face of death) life makes no sense if this life is the only reality and not just a foreground of another transcendent reality in which love and suffering are not annihilated by death.

■ Second, the argument from the inner human need for *play.* Play sets up its own universe. In the "serious world," it may be 2:34 P.M., June 15, 1995, but in that world of play it is the third quarter, the second act, the fifth round. It is the moment when Thomas More makes a joke to his hangman, a band plays on the deck of the *Titanic.* It is marked by acts of faith that this reality is not really as important as it seems.

Third, the argument from the inner human need for *hope*. We *count* on the future, even when things look impossible, as we see in courage in the face of death, getting married, having children. Somewhere within us is rooted an inner need to say "NO" to death. Freud considered that need also a childish self-delusion. But why are we the only ones who have it? Animals can recoil from danger, but we have no evidence they anticipate the reality of death and yearn to outwit it.

Fourth, the argument from the inner human need for *damnation*. That might sound somewhat sinister, as opposed to the inner need for salvation. But there is something ineradicable in us that demands a fitting punishment for deeds monstrous beyond the imagination, like the despicably casual indifference to the sacredness of human life and death in Nazi extermination camps. There must be justice. And even death is not punishment enough.

Oh, morning,

at the brown brink eastward, springs—
Because the Holy Ghost over the bent
World broods with warm breast and
with ah! bright wings.

Gerard Manley Hopkins, S.J., "God's Grandeur"

Fifth, the argument from the inner human need for *humor*. We are not merely *animal rationale*, "the animal who reasons"; we are also *animal risible*, "the animal who laughs." There has to be something more than Gradgrind! The very depth of our seriousness demands that we dance!

Reflection

This reflection will take about fifteen minutes. In the Lilliputian perspective that may seem a lot of time, but it is not. We are dealing here with the most important thing in your life: your self, your soul, your meaning. It is the most important reflection in this book.

First, find a place where you can be relatively undisturbed: no phone, no sirens, no TV, a room where you can shut the door on the world for a few moments, or a secluded part of a park. Sit quietly, eyes closed. Roll your head around your neck and get rid of all the tensions, all the obligations. Let them drain down from your head into your shoulders, into your back, then down your back into your seat and away. Peace.

Then focus on your breathing, but really deep breaths, in for five full counts, out five full counts. Over and over until you feel a soothing rhythm. Then consider your breath. That air keeps you alive. We have no idea where it has been, but we use it and pass it on. Ponder that for as long as it "feeds" you.

Then expand your awareness—and your self—beyond the little circle of peace where you sit, out into the surroundings, beyond the walls or the trees. In your imagination move gradually beyond where you are, this county, this state, this country. The air that enlivens us moves eastward across the country, across the Atlantic, Europe, Asia, the Pacific, and back to us. There you are, focused, at the center of that enormous enlivening reality.

Finally, realize that the word for breath is ruah, pneuma, anima: spirit. That is your true meaning. That is your true "home."

THE OVERWHELMING MYSTERY

Survey

This survey is not an exercise for a grade, but a means to stir up interest and get an idea of varying opinions in your group. Some of the statements are matters of objective fact; others are merely subjective opinions. On the rating scale under each statement circle the number that best reflects your current opinion about that statement.

> +2 = strongly agree,
> +1 = agree,
> 0 = cannot make up my mind,
> –1 = disagree,
> –2 = strongly disagree.

Then share the reasons for your opinion.

1. Without the revelation of Jesus, we would be lower than dirt in contrast to God.

   +2 +1 0 –1 –2

2. A "mystery" is nothing more than a problem for which we have yet to find a rational solution.

   +2 +1 0 –1 –2

3. The "fear" before God is at least remotely comparable to fear before a nuclear reactor.

   +2 +1 0 –1 –2

4. The root of all religion is not theology but personal contact with God.

   +2 +1 0 –1 –2

5. Like a true love commitment, contact with God is a matter of both exaltation and humility at being so loved.

   +2 +1 0 –1 –2

6. Jesus did not save us from sin but from meaninglessness.

   +2 +1 0 –1 –2

7. Before baptism, an infant is invincibly corrupted.

   +2 +1 0 –1 –2

8. Because of original sin, God was so angry that God could never love human beings till the Crucifixion.

   +2 +1 0 –1 –2

9. When we receive the sacraments, grace is something "pumped into" us, like gas, whether we want it or not.

   +2 +1 0 –1 –2

10. The people who met Jesus during his life knew exactly who and what he was.

    +2 +1 0 –1 –2

Contacting the Holy

Our experience of the Beyond in our midst is the experience, our contact, with the *mysterium tremendum,* "the overwhelming mystery." Such an experience is a sense of awe at something objective, really there, outside ourselves, that causes an involuntary feeling of smallness.

When Abraham dares to plead with God for the citizens of Sodom, Abraham's instinctive reaction is to doubt his worthiness:

> *"I am bold indeed to speak like this to my Lord, I who am but dust and ashes."*
> Genesis 18:27 *(The Jerusalem Bible)*

After the miraculous draught of fishes, Peter begins to have some dim insight into an awesome power in Jesus and he says:

> *"Go away from me, Lord! I am a sinful man!"*   Luke 5:8

These responses are not the same as being "humiliated," as by a bully, but rather in the sense of being "humbled," as by unexpected love. One has the sense (not a concept) of being so small in the face of something so powerful and enormous yet loving. We feel, at one and the same time, submissive yet elated. "Ashudder insofar as I am unlike it, aglow insofar as I *am* like it."

MYSTERIUM TREMENDUM

A mystery is always "beyond words," but not because it cannot be understood. One can understand a mystery only by going through the process oneself. Herman Hesse's Siddhartha found he had to leave the Buddha, because wisdom cannot come from listening to words about someone else's wisdom but only in *contemplation.* The same is true of comprehending the reality of the holy—not just as an external *rite* but as a felt experience.

Abraham and the Three Angels
Gaudenzio Ferrari (1471–1546)

The root of the word *tremendum* is *tremens*, "quivering," a quivering not from fear but from astonishment. Nor is it the same as "eerie, weird, dreadful," as listening to stories of ghosts or demons. It is, rather, awe. Today, we overwork the word *awesome*. Now it means to many nothing more than "rather good." But it really means "breathtaking, wondrous, in*spirit*ing." This is fear only in the sense of fear before stored-up Energy, daunting and yet fascinating, intoxicating, urgent, compelling, alive. Humbling and exalting at the same time, honored for the privilege. At such moments we have come in contact with the living God rather than merely with the *idea* of God. *This is the root of all religion.*

In revealing his mysterious name, YHWH ("I AM HE WHO IS," "I AM WHO AM" or "I AM WHO I AM"), God says who he is and by what name he is to be called. This divine name is mysterious just as God is mystery. It is at once a name revealed and something like the refusal of a name, and hence it better expresses God as what he is—infinitely above everything that we can understand or say: he is the "hidden God," his name is ineffable, and he is the God who makes himself close to men.

Catechism of the Catholic Church, 206

OLD TESTAMENT

When Abraham receives three shining visitors, he feels honored, falls with his face touching the ground, and says, "Please do not pass by my home without stopping; I am here to serve you" (Genesis 18:3). When Jacob emerges from a vision of God, he is afraid and says, "What a terrifying place this is! It must be the house of God; it must be the gate that opens into heaven" (Genesis 28:17). When Moses encounters Yahweh speaking from within the burning bush, he "covered his face, because he was afraid to look at God" (Exodus 3:6).

At his call to be a prophet, Isaiah has a vision of the Lord, "sitting on his throne, high and exalted" (Isaiah 6:1) and he cries out:

> *"What a wretched state I am in! I am lost, for I am a man of unclean lips and I live among a people of unclean lips, and my eyes have looked at the King, Yahweh Sabaoth."*   Isaiah 6:5 *(The Jerusalem Bible)*

Not "unclean" in the sense of sinful, but in the sense of unworthiness in such a presence. The psalmist puts it well:

> *I praise you because you are to be feared; all you do is . . . wonderful.*
> Psalm 139:14

NEW TESTAMENT

In the New Testament, too, you find the same admixture of intimidation and exaltation in the presence of the truly holy. When the Baptist speaks of Jesus, he says:

> *"I am not good enough even to bend down and untie his sandals."*   Mark 1:7

Chapter 2   The Supernatural Self

When a centurion asks Jesus to heal his servant, the centurion—a pagan—says:

"Sir, . . . I do not deserve to have you come into my house, neither do I consider myself worthy to come to you in person. Just give the order, and my servant will get well."   Luke 7:6–7

At the Transfiguration, the divinity in Jesus burns through the limits of his flesh, and the three disciples see for an instant who he really is:

When the disciples heard the voice, they were so terrified that they threw themselves face downward on the ground. Jesus came to them and touched them. "Get up," he said. "Don't be afraid!"
Matthew 17:6–7

Saul—who had held men's cloaks while they stoned the Christian, Stephen, and persecuted the renegade community—was walking along the road to Damascus to seek out and arrest the followers of Jesus. Suddenly Saul was overwhelmed by a great light and he heard the voice of Jesus say:

"Saul, Saul! Why do you persecute me?"
Acts 9:4

And in that moment, Saul was blinded and he could not see for three days. But seeing that blinding light, he was converted. His whole life and way of seeing things turned around. The Letter to the Hebrews captures the idea:

It is a terrifying thing to fall into the hands of the living God!   Hebrews 10:31

This reaction to the presence of the holy is not reasoned but instinctive. Nor is it the result of some kind of *moral* unworthiness because "I have done such and such sins." Rather it flows from a feeling of absolute profaneness in the presence of the holy, a sense of being "shadows in the Light."

Jesus came to ransom us from that sense of utter abasement, from that sense of unworthiness before God. Because the core of his message is that this *mysterium tremendum* is also our Father.

Reflection

Job, the perfect and upright man, suffered incredible torment, and he racked his mind trying to find some *reason* to justify his suffering. But his friends insisted he must have done some wickedness, since God does not punish the innocent. Finally, after nearly fifty pages of debate, back and forth, the Lord himself appears in a whirlwind and says, "Where were you when I made the world? If you know so much, tell me about it." It is an overwhelming utterance; read it: Job 38–41. Then try to explain Job's response to it.

I know, Lord, that you are all-powerful;
   that you can do everything you want.
You ask how I dare question your wisdom
   when I am so very ignorant.
I talked about things I did not
   understand,
   about marvels too great for me to know.
You told me to listen while you spoke
   and to try to answer your questions.
In the past I knew only what others had
   told me,
   but now I have seen you with my
   own eyes.
So I am ashamed of all I have said
   and repent in dust and ashes.
Job 42:2–6

Salvation

It is difficult at a baptism to understand how, as the result of two not overly bright naked people eating *one* piece of fruit, this gurgling little bundle of new life, with perfect tiny fingers and beautiful eyes, is somehow "tainted" with original sin and thus "apart from God." If God were that vindictive, how do we explain God's indefatigable solicitousness for wayward Israel in book after book of the Bible?

IMAGES OF GOD

Such a metaphor of a vindictive God springs too easily to mind when we hear the words *redemption, reparation, atonement.* Such words can too easily associate the actions of God and Christ with the workings of pawnbrokers, process servers, and international tribunals after cessation of hostilities. Becoming locked into such an inadequate metaphor, we turn God into a Banker, and not a kindly Banker either. Rather, one who refused to relent until every last penny of the debt was paid in the blood of Jesus, a God who apparently nursed a grudge far longer than Jesus allowed us to. If we are about to sacrifice, Jesus says, and we realize that we still have a grudge against someone, we should leave our offering on the altar and first go and become reconciled with that person.

> *"So if you are about to offer your gift to God at the altar and there you remember that someone has something against you, leave your gift there in front of the altar, go at once and make peace with that person, and then come back and offer your gift to God."*   From Matthew 5:23–24

The image of a vindictive God goes directly counter to the image Jesus himself gave us in the father of the prodigal son (Luke 15:11–32). When the wayward boy headed for home, the father saw him while "he was still a long way from home," which means the father was out there every day looking for him.

And the father "was filled with pity, and he ran, threw his arms around his son, and kissed him"—*before* the boy even apologized!

The father had probably forgiven his son before the boy was off the property. But his forgiveness could not be activated until the boy admitted he needed it. But *all* the son had to do was come home! Even before the young man finished his memorized speech, the father interrupted him: "This son of mine was dead, but now he is alive!" And the father didn't give him a retaliatory penance: the father gave him a party!

That is the image of God Jesus gave us. Clearly not of a God who holds grudges, demands restitution, forgives "under certain conditions." Jesus told us we must forgive "not seven times, but seventy times seven, because the Kingdom of heaven is like this" (Matthew 18:22). So we can expect at least as much forgiveness from God. God is not just one for second chances; God is one for four hundred and ninety chances!

ORIGINAL SIN

What, then, is original sin? Whatever the cause, the effects of whatever-original-sin-is are undeniable. There is no doubt that human beings refuse to act human. Read the daily newspapers; watch the evening news broadcast.

Within each one of us, there is a self-absorption that refuses to admit we have made a mistake. There is an inertia that—even though we feel vaguely guilty—finds it too much effort to go back to the first wrong turn and start over. "Original sin" balks at conversion. Even saints like Paul were afflicted with it:

> *I do not understand what I do; for I don't do what I would like to do, but instead I do what I hate.*   Romans 7:15

That is the effect of original sin. That little infant about to be baptized does have both the potential to be intensely more human than she or he is at that moment and the potential to atrophy as a human being. Baptism is an invitation to the infant—and perhaps more so to the infant's parents and godparents—to encourage her or him continually to accept it.

"Salvation"—redemption from a sense of meaninglessness, ultimate purposelessness, validation of one's suffering—is a value sought by *all* religions. It is too narrow to say Jesus died only to "save us from sin," since his sacrifice did not eradicate our tendency to sin. And surely he did not offer himself up to save us only from some future hell—which, like the economic metaphor for original sin, makes God want vindictive punishment.

Indeed, the Letter to the Philippians shows God's response to the sacrifice of Calvary was not wiping out a debt but exaltation:

For this reason God raised him to the highest place above and gave him the name that is greater than any other name. And so, in honor of the name of Jesus all beings in heaven, on earth, and in the world below will fall on their knees, and all will openly proclaim that Jesus Christ is Lord, to the glory of God the Father.   Philippians 2:9–11

A WELCOMING HOME

Just as the father of the prodigal jubilantly welcomed his son back from his disgrace and bedecked him in the best garments and threw him a feast, God the Father welcomes Jesus back to heaven to be glorified. And if God sent Jesus as a model for our lives, that is what God is preparing for each of us as well—membership in the family of the Trinity. We are Peers of the realm of God. That is what happens when we are baptized. We are welcomed "home" and glorified.

The "sin" that the sufferings of Christ atoned for was not merely eating a piece of fruit. It was not even to "wipe from God's mind" the enormities human beings have perpetrated against one another since the beginning—much less to wipe out the secret nastinesses of which each of us has been guilty. It was to heal the *estrangement* between humankind and God, to welcome us "home."

The Bible gives us a better metaphor to understand what "original sin" and "salvation" meant all along. The Covenant that Yahweh swore with Israel on Sinai was like a marriage to which Yahweh (unlike a grudge-bearing God) was never unfaithful, yet which Israel deserted again and again. This metaphor is clearest in the book of the prophet Hosea, where God says of the people:

"Like a woman who becomes a prostitute, they have given themselves to other gods."   Hosea 4:12

Again and again Yahweh's response is similar to that of the prodigal's father. Yahweh comes after that prostitute people, just as Jesus came to us, to heal the estrangement:

So I am going to take her into the desert again; there I will win her back with words of love. I will give back to her the vineyards she had and make Trouble Valley a door of hope. She will respond to me there as she did when she was young, when she came from Egypt. Then once again she will call me her husband—she will no longer call me her Baal.   Hosea 2:14–16

That image of God—so consistent with the image of the father of the prodigal—shows how sin and salvation are connected: forgiveness, for all those willing to avail themselves of it. Every one of the sacraments is precisely that: a second chance, a welcoming "home," where everything is right again.

After his temptations in the desert (Luke 4:1–13), Jesus came to the Nazareth synagogue, opened the scroll of Isaiah, and read:

"The Spirit of the Lord is upon me,
    because he has chosen me
        to bring good news to the poor.
He has sent me to proclaim liberty
        to the captives
    and recovery of sight to the blind,
to set free the oppressed
        and announce that the time has come
    when the Lord will save his people."
                                    Luke 4:18–19

That is Jesus' statement of purpose, of his mission, of the meaning of the "salvation" he brought us! It is good news, liberty, clear-sightedness, liberation from oppression.

Luke 4:19 is better translated "to announce the Year of Grace," which is much clearer about what "when the Lord will save his people" means. That year, that Jubilee Year, which is outlined in Leviticus 25:8–55, occurred every fiftieth year. It was the *Year of the Amnesty of God*: all is forgiven, no strings. A time when all debts were forgiven unconditionally.

But to receive that unconditional forgiveness we first have to admit that our idols, our Baals, have led us to poverty, captivity, blindness, oppression. Even God does not force us to accept that forgiveness and freedom until, like the prodigal, we admit we need them and head for home.

Reflection

Consider what the poet says about his relationship to God—and God's relationship to him.

Batter my heart, three personed God;
    for you
As yet but knock, breathe, shine,
    and seek to mend;
That I may rise and stand,
    o'erthrow me and bend
Your force to break, blow, burn
    and make me new.
I, like an usurped town, to another due,
Labour to admit you, but Oh, to no end;
Reason, your viceroy in me,
    me should defend,
But is captived and proves weak
    or untrue.

Yet dearly I love you and would be
    loved fain,[1]
But am betrothed unto your enemy:
Divorce me, untie or break that
    knot again,
Take me to you, imprison me, for I,
Except you enthrall[2] *me, never shall*
    be free,
Nor ever chaste, except you ravish me.
                                    John Donne

■ *How does what the poet says give you insight into the God-you relationship?*

[1] Gladly.
[2] Enslave.

Conversion

The process of conversion is a complete turnabout. It is a radical changing of priorities. It is an admission—against the forces of original sin that I need to take a completely fresh look at . . . everything.

One way to begin to make this turnabout is to consider the highly successful method of the so-called Twelve-Step programs, which began with Alcoholics Anonymous:

The Twelve Steps of Alcoholics Anonymous

1. We admitted we were powerless over alcohol[1] and that our lives had become unmanageable.

2. Came to believe that a Power greater than ourselves could restore us to sanity.

3. Made a decision to turn our will and our lives over to the care of God *as we understood Him.*

4. Made a searching and fearless moral inventory of ourselves.

5. Admitted to God, to ourselves, and to another human being the exact nature of our wrongs.

6. Were entirely ready to have God remove all these defects of character.

7. Humbly asked Him to remove our shortcomings.

8. Made a list of all persons we had harmed, and became willing to make amends to them all.

9. Made direct amends to such people whenever possible, except when to do so would injure them or others.

10. Continued to take personal inventory and when we were wrong, promptly admitted it.

11. Sought through prayer and meditation to improve our conscious contact with God as *we understood Him,* praying only for knowledge of His will for us and the power to carry that out.

12. Having had a spiritual awakening as a result of these steps, we tried to carry this message to alcoholics and to practice these principles in all our affairs.

[1] One could insert almost any problem for "alcohol."

The physical conversion of adolescence is out of our hands, like the emergence of a butterfly. But as the psychological conversion of a child into an adult is an invitation we can refuse or accept, so is the spiritual conversion from a life focused unflinchingly on buying and selling, beating the system, getting out of school, proving ourselves by one-upping everyone else, and so on. Even further, our spiritual conversion is a major conversion to surrender our need to "control it all" to the One who truly controls it all.

Athletes may come to a point where all the bits and pieces, all the practice, no longer mean anything. They "lose themselves" in the game, and the game "plays itself," or rather the game plays itself *through* them. The same happens sometimes with musicians: the music "plays them." So too with religious, spiritual conversion:

> *It is no longer I who live, but it is Christ who lives in me.*   Galatians 2:20

Spiritual conversion comes from ceasing to resist, to try to do it alone, letting the Larger Power surge up from within. The key to such conversion is self-surrender: "Let go! I'll catch you!" Just as I stand, I am *accepted* by God. Acquiescence and assurance. But such a conversion is not solely a matter of accepting God, or even of being accepted *by* God. It is also inviting that Power—and its power—into myself, into my life.

This endeavor of conversion is not just a human work. It is the movement of a "contrite heart," drawn and moved by grace to respond to the merciful love of God who loved us first.

Catechism of the Catholic Church, 1428

Grace

Grace is the aliveness—the power—of God in us, the indwelling of God; that *is* salvation. Jesus said:

"I have come in order that you might have life—life in all its fullness."   John 10:10

It is God's will for us that, in Jesus Christ, we become not only fully human but *super-human*, supernatural.

Mary Fisher (1948–1994).

Grace is a *participation in the life of God.* It introduces us into the intimacy of Trinitarian life.

Catechism of the Catholic Church, 1997

In *The Varieties of Religious Experience* (Longmans, Green, 1902), the psychologist William James wrote that the grace of God operates "through the subliminal door," through the intuitive potential of the undervalued right brain. Some of the effects of opening oneself to grace are:

- a feeling of being in a wider context than the world's selfish interests;

- a friendly continuity with an ideal Power and a surrender to it;

- elation and freedom;

- a shifting of the emotional center to "Yes"; openhandedness, openheartedness, open-mindedness.

As Clare Booth Luce asked, "Can I see your freedom? Can I feel your joy?" Anyone connected to the grace of God ought to be more graceful, more gracious, living more abundantly, living life to its fullness. There are channels of grace everywhere, not only in nature and in the sacraments, but in people. When Hindus greet one another, they place their palms together (as they do when praying) at the center of their foreheads. That gesture "says" that the god in me bows to the god in you.

When Jesus speaks of the Last Judgment (Matthew 25), he says that the one question that will determine whether the life you lived was worth it will not be how much money you made or how often your name was in the newspapers. There will be only one question: "*I* was hungry. *I* was thirsty. *I* was imprisoned. *I* was lonely. What did you do about that?"

In *Sleep with the Angels* (Moyer Bell, 1994) Mary Fisher speaks of such graceful, grace-filled moments:

> This is grace: When your child tries and fails, and ruins your family name; when he tells you secrets you hope the neighbors never uncover; when he says, "I've been arrested," when she blurts out, "I had an abortion," when full of fear they, trembling, stammer, "I wanted to die. . . ." When at that moment neither pride nor reputation slow you down on your rush to lift them up, cradle them in your arms, kiss their tears and tell them you love them—this is love undeserved. Grace.
>
> This is grace: The high school senior was undergoing cancer therapy. On top of the crushing fear and daily nausea, he suffered the added indignity of losing all his hair. Still, when the day came that the therapy ended, he headed back for school. When he walked through the door that first morning, there were all his friends with shining bald heads. They had, every one of them, shaved their scalps clean. They could not take his cancer, but they could relieve his shame.

Grace is that same solicitousness, a self-communication of God to us, if we are willing to receive God. And as we will see more extensively later, each of the sacraments is a mutual vulnerability between God and ourselves, each one a conversion, each one a welcoming home.

Sacraments of Initiation

- *Baptism*, of course, is the first step of our initiation into the body of Christ. It is the "gateway to life in the Spirit, and the door which gives access to the other sacraments" (*Catechism of the Catholic Church,* 1213).

- At *Confirmation* we solemnize the beginning of our living with the power and gifts of the Spirit. It celebrates the process by which we learn and live the new role we have as members of the body of Christ.

- The *Eucharist* is the "meal" that celebrates our at-homeness. It is an opening to the eternal each week, in which the false promise of Satan in the Garden comes true: "Eat this and you *will* become like God." "The holy Eucharist completes Christian Initiation" (*Catechism of the Catholic Church,* 1322).

Sacraments of Healing

- *Reconciliation* celebrates our returning to the Father, to be welcomed—forgiven unconditionally—home.
- The *Anointing of the Sick* puts life and death before that far larger background of the eternal so that we can see death as it really is. It unites the sick person to the passion of Christ, giving strength, peace, and courage to deal with the suffering of illness or old age.

Sacraments at the Service of Communion

- In *Matrimony* two people *become* a new home, a sign of the covenant of Christ and the Church. It celebrates an exchange of selves that is a conversion of two lives into one life, and a promise of new human and superhuman life.
- *Holy Orders* is the sacrament of apostolic ministry. It converts an individual from the service that all baptized Christians are called to, to the service of the servants who mediate the prayers of the people to God and the grace of God to the people.

Reflection

All of us, at least in our more reflective moments, want to live the one life we have to its fullest.

◼ *What are the obstacles (not from outside but from inside)—the idols—that keep you from complete possession of what Jesus said he had come to bring—more abundant life?*

◼ *In what ways are you poor, captive, blind, oppressed—again, not by others, but by self-imposed enslavements that bar the grace of God?*

The sacraments are "of the Church" in the double sense that they are "by her" and "for her." They are "by the Church," for she is the sacrament of Christ's action at work in her through the mission of the Holy Spirit. They are "for the Church" in the sense that "the sacraments make the Church," since they manifest and communicate to men, above all in the Eucharist, the mystery of communion with the God who is love, One in three persons.

Catechism of the Catholic Church, 1118

Understanding the Supernatural Self

Review

1. What is the difference between "sublime" and "numinous"? Why is "sacred" more than merely "set aside from the secular"? What does the word *transcendent* really mean? *Supernatural* doesn't mean "physically above." What does it mean?

2. Explain: One cannot explain the sacred in any meaningful way to someone who has not experienced it.

3. Explain: What is essential is always invisible.

4. What does *mysterium tremendum* mean? What is the mystery, and what is so scary about it? How is "humiliating" different from "humbling"?

5. Explain: The root of all religions is not theology but contact with God.

6. Explain: Like a genuine love commitment, contact with God is both exhilarating and humbling. Why do people who believe they have contacted God say it makes them feel like "shadows in the Light"?

7. From what does the Crucifixion and the Resurrection "save" us? How does Jesus' story of the father of the prodigal son help us understand that?

8. What does "conversion" mean? What does "grace" mean?

Discuss

1. There are people who are poor, hungry, and homeless who still have pride and a sense of dignity. How do you explain that?

2. How much "Wow!" is there in your life? How many things make you lose your breath in awe? If there are very few occasions like that, what does that say about the state of your soul?

3. Has most of your religious education gone to understanding and communicating with God or to studying doctrines? What's the difference?

4. If Thales is right and "everything is full of gods," why do we sense the Beyond in our midst so seldom? What gets between us and the numinous?

5. What would happen if this country, like ancient Israel, had a Jubilee Year, a year of amnesty, every fifty years during which all financial debts were cancelled, domestically and internationally? What would be the effect on families living in poverty?

6. We have all been baptized, but how many of us have been converted? Read over the Twelve-Step program again. Would you say you are ready for that kind of decision and program in regard to your own soul?

7. Who do you know whose freedom you can see and whose joy you can feel? Talk about them.

8. What do you think of when you hear the word *salvation?* Do you feel in need of "saving"? From what? Can people see your freedom, feel your joy?

44

The Meaning of Sacrament

Activities

1. Interview several faculty members or a member of your parish staff. Ask the person, Do you agree or disagree with the statement: Money, fame, sex, and power cannot assure human fulfillment? Record their responses and report back to your group.

2. Check the library for accounts of people who have encountered the *mysterium tremendum*. You might want to check accounts of people who have had near-death experiences.

3. Have members of your group divide into teams and debate Peter Berger's arguments to substantiate our experience of the presence of God in our lives (pages 28–29).

4. Create a work of art—a drawing, a dance, a poem, a song, and so on—to relate a personal experience of the *mysterium tremendum*.

5. Read through a daily newspaper. Are there more stories about people's encounters with "sin" than about their encounters with "salvation"? Why is that? How does that affect what we "see" in the world?

6. In small groups, review "The Twelve Steps of Alcoholics Anonymous" listed on page 38. Substitute several problems for alcohol. List the reasons these twelve steps can help young people make a radical change in their priorities, a spiritual conversion.

Scripture Readings

Skim the passages. Pick one that appeals to you and (1) summarize its main point, (2) tell how it relates to the chapter, and (3) list one or two thoughts that entered your mind as you read it.

- Exodus 13:17–22 — The pillar of cloud and the pillar of fire
- Psalm 8 — God's glory and human dignity
- Isaiah 6:3 — Glory to God
- Matthew 17:5–7 — Transfiguration of Jesus
- Mark 1:15 — Call to conversion
- Acts 2:38 — Turn your life around
- Romans 3:23 — Salvation

✎ Journal

What have been your experiences of the numinous, or the sacred? Where do you discover the sacred each day in your life? How do these experiences keep your life focused on the road to true human fulfillment?

*God is higher than my highest
and more inward
than my innermost self.*

Saint Augustine, *Confessions*

Holy Days of Obligation

Dec. 25 Christmas, the Nativity of the Lord,

Jan. 1 Solemnity of Mary the Mother of God.

40 days after Easter - Ascension of the Lord

Aug. 15 - Assumption

Nov. 1 - All Saint's Day

Dec. 8 - Immaculate Conception.

Chapter 3

Symbolic Rituals

What is essential is always invisible.
Antoine de Saint-Exupéry, *The Little Prince*

SYMBOLS

Survey

This survey is not an exercise for a grade, but a means to stir up interest and get an idea of varying opinions in your group. Some of the statements are matters of objective fact; others are merely subjective opinions. On the rating scale under each statement circle the number that best reflects your current opinion about that statement.

+2 = strongly agree,
+1 = agree,
 0 = cannot make up my mind,
−1 = disagree,
−2 = strongly disagree.

Then share the reasons for your opinion.

1. If we rely *only* on the left brain *or* the right brain, we search for truth half-wittedly.

   +2   +1   0   −1   −2

2. Definitions are much more reliable than symbols for understanding the truth of things.

   +2   +1   0   −1   −2

3. There are realities that actually exist but are not in any way physical.

   +2   +1   0   −1   −2

4. When advertisers try to associate cars with sexiness, they are using symbols.

   +2   +1   0   −1   −2

5. Even without thinking about it, we deal with symbols and symbolic language all day.

   +2   +1   0   −1   −2

6. The pictures we see of atoms are pretty accurate depictions of what an atom really looks like.

   +2   +1   0   −1   −2

7. The pictures we see of God are pretty accurate depictions of what God really looks like.

   +2   +1   0   −1   −2

8. Some symbols of ancient cultures are still meaningful thousands of years later.

   +2   +1   0   −1   −2

9. If we always communicated with scrupulous left-brain accuracy, human speech would be deadly dull.

   +2   +1   0   −1   −2

10. Dreams are symbolic stories our unconscious tells about ourselves when our guard is down.

   +2   +1   0   −1   −2

A Puzzlement

It is a holy thing to clean a toilet very well.   Hindu Adage

■ *Why is that true?*

Left Brain vs. Right Brain

In trying to understand the world and ourselves better, the mind has at hand two quite different functions of the brain. The left lobe deals primarily in clear-cut rational definitions; the right lobe deals primarily in less precise but often more illuminating symbols.

One meticulously rational dictionary takes forty-two finely printed lines to define *love*. And at the end one understands little more about real loving than if the definition had been printed in Mandarin. On the other hand, a little girl's carefully corn-rowed hair or a little boy spruced up in Sunday best "says" love, too, and a lot better than forty-two lines of prose.

Definitions best isolate realities that are cut-and-dried, literal, clearly-this-and-nothing-else: aardvark, electromagnetism, monarchy, cranium, zygote. Symbols suggest, rather than isolate, in order to provoke a better *understanding* of more elusive realities: love, loyalty, courage, justice, the spirit of a society.

Similarly, a carefully reasoned philosophical treatise gives us a clear skeletal *explanation* of, say, atheism. But two hours watching the symbolic story of Didi and Gogo, in Samuel Beckett's absurdist tragicomedy *Waiting for Godot,* struggling to keep busy gives us a less clear but more profound *understanding* of what atheism really is, how it "feels."

The story of Luke Skywalker not only entertains but helps us understand better what we must do in order to fulfill our humanity. Parables are like parabolas; they come at the truth "around the corner."

—————

Everything has its spiritual meaning, which is to the literal meaning what the soul is to the body.

Nathaniel Hawthorne

—————

Again, it is important not to approach symbols with the literalism of the left brain. If someone says, "Let these roses show you how much I love you," the literalist has to say that when the roses wilt the love has died. If Jesus literally ascended "up" into heaven, even traveling at the speed of light, he would still be inside the Milky Way galaxy.

Earth, Moon, and Milky Way.

We resort to symbols simply because there *are* realities—honor, the human soul, the afterlife, God—that truly exist but are not visible or physical. Yet we human beings are physical, and our ability to apprehend external realities begins in our physical senses. Even our experience of the numinous in nature begins with our eyes and ears and skin.

As we saw before, no one really sees *you*—your real inner self, your soul—but only your body. And they can begin to understand you only *through* the actions and words of that body.

Somehow, we want to understand the invisible-yet-real *as if* it were visible. In H. G. Wells's story "The Invisible Man," the hero had discovered a way to make himself unseen. And in order to get into situations undetected, he had to go naked. But when he *wanted* to be seen and communicate with someone, he had to put on an overcoat and hat and wrap his face in a bandage. That is what symbols do for ideas and nonphysical realities: they wrap them up in "clothes" so that we can see them better.

SIGNS VS. SYMBOLS

Like so many other words, the word *symbol* is often used slap-dash—like the words *love, value, awesome*. Companies use logos to isolate immediately their product as being different from some other company's. After all the ads, each of us can tell the Cadillac "symbol" from that of Ford.

But those pictures—which immediately identify—are not strictly speaking symbols. Rather, they are "signs," idea-pictures, that denote (separate from all others) rather than connote (suggest a value). If a picture of a fish, for instance, means "Buy fish here," it is no more than a straightforward sign. But if a fish sign in a catacomb means "We are Christians," then it is a symbol. Not just a designation, but a declaration of *values*.

To make the distinction clearer. Efficient mass production demanded a revolution in the art of selling: consumerist advertising. This was a shift from a rational style of selling that focused on the product's demonstrable, objective *qualities* (a sign) to an emotional appeal to the consumer's psychological, subjective *needs* (a symbol).

For instance, when Ford first brought out the Model-T, its advertising focused on the inherent value of the car itself: transportation, economy, ease of repair (a straightforward sign).

But then the market became saturated; everybody who could afford a car already *had* a Model-T, which, as advertised, took a great deal of time to wear out. But who was going to buy the new cars coming off the assembly line? The advertisers and salespeople had to find a motivation for customers to want to buy a *new* Ford (even though the one they had was still good for years). So they began advertising a "newer, improved, better" car, "sleeker, more aerodynamic," and ultimately "sexier."

The connotations surrounding cars no longer were principally objective (maintenance, mileage, durability) but rather the car was an *ego-enhancer:* freedom, mobility, sexual prowess, rising social status. You can see that difference in the gap between the dull "Model-T" and the muscular "Mustang."

We resort to symbols simply because there are realities— honor, the human soul, the afterlife, God— that truly exist but are not visible or physical.

WORDS AS SYMBOLS

Words are symbols, too. They not only denote—"light," "female parent," "equine quadruped." But they also connote— "moonbeam," "Mom," "steed." It is the connotations that give the words *power*— "I have a dream!" "I absolve you from your sins." "This is my Body."

Symbols are a means to convey not only an idea but the *value* of the idea. They are "charged," like a battery ready to deliver power when it is grounded in a ready receiver. A symbol is a channel that somehow "connects" the viewer with the power of the value. It is like an acorn unfolding itself into the roots and branches of a great oak, far bigger than its apparent self.

Much of what we say is not literal but figurative (without our even realizing it): "She's got a brick for a heart." "I came out of there walking six inches off the ground!" And in dealing with the transcendent—that is by definition not visible—we can only use symbols.

On the one hand, we know that God is in a dimension of reality beyond time and space. Therefore, God is not male, does not sit on a throne, or have hands or a voice. On the other hand, God is not some mere abstraction, like fidelity or mathematics or the Uncaused First Cause. Therefore, it helps us understand and deal with God if we act *as if* God were not everywhere but sitting right next to us in the passenger seat. Some combine the insights of science and Exodus into light and think of God as "One made of light."

Jesus made it even easier. The Son of the Invisible God did put on clothes to walk among us, to show us how to live and die well. But Jesus did not just "put on" humanity, like a tunic; he fused divinity into humanity so we could understand God better.

NATURAL SYMBOLS VS. CULTURALLY CONDITIONED SYMBOLS

Symbols are words, objects, places, and actions that evoke more than their literal meaning: value. There are some symbols that evoke value simply by what they are, in any culture or society. These are natural symbols. Other words, objects, places, actions are culturally conditioned and evoke a particular value only within a particular culture.

Natural Symbols

Roses make us readily think of fragility and beauty. Birds call to mind freedom, in any culture. Thus some other creature with wings suggests throwing off constraints: Icarus, Pegasus, Hermes with winged helmet and sandals, angels. The phoenix rising from its ashes and a butterfly emerging from an ugly caterpillar are obvious symbols of resurrection and rebirth. In any culture, bread means food and wine means celebration.

Primitive tribes fixed a totem pole carved with faces of its guardian animal spirits at the center of the village, the focus of the people, anchored in the earth and yet reaching up into the heavens. The same is true of the cross on Calvary and the medieval cathedral.

The winter solstice is meaningful in all cultures. At that time of the year the nights are longest, and the skies have been gray for weeks, saturating our souls with gloom. And no matter where we are, we yearn for a rebirth that seems so far away. So we remind ourselves of the rhythm of nature and celebrate the promise of new life on the darkest night of the year—in the Mithraic cults, the Day of the Unconquered Sun; in Christianity, Christmas. Then when spring begins to seem more than just a faint hope, we have Passover and the escape from Egypt, Easter and the Resurrection. We have the symbols of eggs, which are a natural symbol of birth; and bunnies, the essence of fertility.

Though he was not of our culture, that young man standing in Tienanman Square, arms at his sides and head bowed before two gigantic tanks, "says" dignity and courage under oppression to anyone, in any culture. And far better than any dictionary.

Our dreams (like Dorothy's in *The Wizard of Oz*) are filled with natural symbols, what Jung called "archetypes." For example, a girl dreams her mother is backing the car out of the driveway in anger, and she runs after her through air like lucite, soundlessly crying, "Mommy!" (her fear that, no matter what she does, she can never get her mother's approval).

Dreams are symbolic stories our unconscious tells us about ourselves.

Saxman native village totems in Ketchican, Alaska.

Culturally Conditioned Symbols

Because of its shape, a sphere—self-contained, whole, a surface around which anything could travel forever, and its association with the global earth and planets—is a natural symbol for perfection. But though you may know a horseshoe, a four-leaf clover, and a rabbit's foot are symbols of good luck, there is no way you could deduce that from their shape.

Some symbols have meaning only within a matrix hallowed by tradition. They evoke a sense of value only in those who are aware of that tradition and revere it. An American flag is just a piece of cloth, but it has been made "sacred" by its association with our past: the Revolution, the Civil War, Iwo Jima. The Liberty Bell is just a cracked antique; the Bill of Rights, just a piece of paper ornately penned. Voting seems an ineffectual act when there are so many other voters; Monticello is just a well-preserved old plantation. But not to those who cherish the tradition behind these symbols. For them all these symbols radiate a very real value.

Similarly, clothes "speak." Why do judges wear robes and not just appear in pin-striped suits like the lawyers? Because the robe "says" authority. A varsity jacket is nothing more than a coat, but within that small society of a school it has been "charged" by a season of shared blood, sweat, and tears. "Grunge" clothes make no statement at all unless the majority of the society wants button-down collars and long skirts. Ethnic costumes from "the old country"—kilts, pajamas, saris, dashikis, turbans—give a value and sense of identity only to those who revere them.

A couple might want to be married in the Navajo rite because the words are nice and the ritual very attuned to nature. But the rite itself will not make a Navajo marriage or suffuse their lives with the Navajo mysteries. Similarly, you may want to be married in a Catholic church or have your child baptized or your parents buried "in the Church." But there is at least something "untoward" about making use of those symbolic rites of the Catholic Church when they have less meaning to you than choosing the bridesmaids' dresses, the music, and the limousine. When those are the only three occasions in your adult life you are ever in a church, it is like coming "home" only to "use the facilities."

Culturally conditioned symbols have meaning only for those who are "in on" the society's code. Apocalyptic books in the Bible (such as Ezekiel and Revelation) are filled with bizarre symbols like monsters with many horns and eyes, flying wheels, mammoth statues made of different materials. These biblical books were written during times of persecution as "underground" messages to give hope to the oppressed that the invaders would be defeated. The symbols are meaningful only to those "oppressed" and not to the persecutors.

Tossing a pinch of incense on smoldering coals would seem an insignificant act. But when the coals were at the feet of a statue of the "divine" emperor, that act took on an entirely different meaning for an early Christian. A signature is nothing more than a configuration of ink on a paper. But Thomas More refused to sign his name—which was his "word"—because signing meant far more than just lines on a page. It would symbolize his denial of the primacy of the papacy in religious matters.

Reflection

Look around your room. List all the things you see that have more meaning to you than they would have to the audience at a public auction.

- *Why are they meaningful, "charged"?*
- *Then say what each of them—one by one—tells about who the invisible inner "you" is.*

RITUALIZING BELIEF

Survey

This survey is not an exercise for a grade, but a means to stir up interest and get an idea of varying opinions in your group. Some of the statements are matters of objective fact; others are merely subjective opinions. On the rating scale under each statement circle the number that best reflects your current opinion about that statement.

+2 = strongly agree,
+1 = agree,
 0 = cannot make up my mind,
−1 = disagree,
−2 = strongly disagree.

Then share the reasons for your opinion.

1. When two people truly are in love, they have to externalize it, celebrate it, make it public.

   +2   +1   0   −1   −2

2. People in love who have to hide that love feel cramped, frustrated, impoverished.

   +2   +1   0   −1   −2

3. The extravaganzas surrounding presidential elections are completely phoney and no one is taken in.

   +2   +1   0   −1   −2

4. Professional sports are no longer "sportive" but merely a branch of show business.

   +2   +1   0   −1   −2

5. Shopping malls are "temples" to the Myth of Progress and Conspicuous Consumption.

   +2   +1   0   −1   −2

6. If there is no "connection" to God, all religious rituals are self-delusive.

   +2   +1   0   −1   −2

7. Rituals can be an *obstacle* to communication with God.

   +2   +1   0   −1   −2

8. Most people would just as soon avoid the consequences of a direct relationship with God.

   +2   +1   0   −1   −2

9. If the Mass does not "work" for someone, quite likely it is as much the person's fault as the liturgy's.

   +2   +1   0   −1   −2

10. Jesus was not just a symbol of God but the real thing.

   +2   +1   0   −1   −2

Secular Rituals

We need to *express* our beliefs, to externalize our private convictions, just as we need to express our love.

Something in us also hankers for ritual to break the deadening routine and put our lives into a bigger context. When the New York Rangers won the Stanley Cup in 1994 after fifty years, there *had* to be a parade. Without the fireworks, the Fourth of July would be just another day. The Olympics have to begin with the torch. No one wants to finish high school or college and just walk away; there has to be some kind of ceremony.

There are three moments in life, even for people who "don't need Church," when they definitely do need Church: birth, marriage, and death. These moments are too *important* to be solemnized in some civil office.

The Democratic and Republican presidential campaigns are a whole series of ritual extravaganzas to elicit *belief* in the candidates. There are primaries, conventions, campaigns, culminating in the final ritual when the president is inaugurated.

Decked out with balloons and bunting, orchestrated speeches and responses, past heroes trotted out, processions, noisemakers, signs, and so on.

On election night, TV anchor people sit before electronic maps like Druid priests, explaining where it's all going. And finally the inauguration takes place amid hymns like "Ruffles and Flourishes" and "Hail to the Chief," formal oaths, a rousing sermon on American values and purposes. It gives us a sense of being a democracy.

Sports, too, have their rituals, cathedrals, "sacred" objects. Trips to the Super Bowl and the World Series are to sports fans what visits to Mecca are to Muslims and trips to Jerusalem are to Jews and Christians. Sports stadiums—temples to competition—are "holy" places set aside from the everyday, most of them bigger than the Roman Colosseum.

The ritual begins with the national anthem, which makes it very "American," and there is often a goddess-queen. Costumed cheerleaders and bands act like acolytes and choirs. Mascots, like the idols of primitive tribes, embody the *spirit* of the team—Eagles, Rams, Buccaneers, Tigers.

Presidential inauguration of Bill Clinton, swearing-in ceremony (January 20, 1993).

For each sport, there is a Pantheon, a Hall of Fame, where the great heroes are enshrined like Odysseus and Hercules. The game ball has a special meaning within the culture, and fans (from the word *fanatic*) take home souvenirs like relics. Some follow the season as scrupulously as a liturgical calendar. But when the fans are at the game, they are out-of-the-ordinary, hyperalive yet self-forgetful, "charged up." People talk with total strangers with ease. They feel a sense of loyalty and community. It is a "devotion" one need not be ashamed to speak about at the water cooler or in a taxicab.

Sacred Rituals

The difference between secular and religious rituals is that a sacred liturgy goes not only beyond every day but beyond time itself. The object of such rituals is the *mysterium tremendum*.

The word *religion* comes from the root word *ligare*, which means "to bind together," and the prefix *re*, which means "over and over." Prayer is religion in action; the words of a prayer are only a means of putting oneself in union with God, open and expectant. Prayer is a *CONNECTION* with the power and energy of the "overwhelming mystery."

For primitive societies the root of magic was that the "soul"—the *anima mundi*—permeates the universe. It gives everything its purpose and meaning, and one can relate to it I to Thou. Thus the whole universe is a sacrament, a vehicle of holiness.

Native American medicine men, Eskimo shamans, Druid priests were trying not to manipulate the gods but, as Wordsworth put it, "to see into the heart of things." They were trying to put themselves in accord with the gods' messages through nature and achieve the wisdom to accept and trust them.

Today we are no less gullible in our belief that technology, the new magic, can control "the gods of nature"—provided it does not destroy nature first, as it did its gods.

Ironically, especially in sophisticated societies such as our own, rituals can often be an *obstacle* to religious experience. This can be true not only when rituals are poorly celebrated, but even when they are scrupulously carried out as if they were a "performance" or the coronation of a European monarch.

Formal religious rites can become a *substitute* for genuine religious experience, often because many would prefer it that way, rather than risk the uncertainties of contact with the Unknown. Rituals are not intended to produce belief. Rather, they intend to provoke a response to the numinous. But if they are going to work a change within the participants, they have to count on religious belief *beforehand*. In none of the four Gospels does Jesus ever perform a miracle to elicit belief but only in *response* to it:

> *"Your faith has saved you."*   Luke 7:50

Nor can one expect to walk into a church "cold," not having had any other contact with God during the week, and expect to get "zapped"—any more than one would expect to fall in love forever on the first date. It would be a rare Sunday when everyone in the congregation is "up" at the same time. What we bring to the celebration of the sacraments—especially the Eucharist—is not our momentary selves but our *true* selves. If both the presider and the people are "genuine," then the celebration will "work."

Ritual is never individualistic or private. Rather, it is a public expression of one's beliefs, buoyed by the presence of others into realizing I am not alone. Yoga, for instance, is not strictly speaking "worship." It could be merely communication with the inner self.

Ritual is effective only if there is that "connection"—not with the words—but with the transcendent God present in immanent reality. Religion *means* "connection."

Reflection

Consider your own participation in the eucharistic ritual at Mass.

■ *How does it "work" for you?*

Many say they stopped "going to Mass" because they "didn't get anything out of it." Is that really the purpose of the Mass? Other than showing gratitude, it surely is, because any sacrament is intended to be a channel of grace, a greater aliveness, celebrating the "connection" to God. Part of the reason some stop "going to Mass" might be that the Mass is poorly celebrated—an ill-considered and inconsiderate homily, lackluster music, a graceless "performance." But that is not all of it. You could have a "script" by Shakespeare or Arthur Miller, a priest with all the charisma of Robin Williams, music ministers as talented as a Broadway cast of *Damn Yankees*, but if the members of the assembly are uptight and loath to open up, nothing will happen. No battery can charge anything when the receiver is turned off.

Jesus never worked miracles to provoke faith but only in *response* to it.

■ *How is it possible that the failure of the ritual to provoke a felt inner change in you has something to do with you, as well?*

Any ritual is an attempt to externalize one's beliefs. But one cannot externalize a belief that is hardly there.

> *"I do have faith, but not enough. Help me have more!"*   Mark 9:24

SACRAMENT

Survey

This survey is not an exercise for a grade, but a means to stir up interest and get an idea of varying opinions in your group. Some of the statements are matters of objective fact; others are merely subjective opinions. On the rating scale under each statement circle the number that best reflects your current opinion about that statement.

    +2 = strongly agree,
    +1 = agree,
     0 = cannot make up my mind,
    −1 = disagree,
    −2 = strongly disagree.

Then share the reasons for your opinion.

 1. Jesus died *so that* the Church might be born.

    +2   +1   0   −1   −2

 2. Priests are ordained to serve the Church, but baptism ordains every Christian to serve the world.

    +2   +1   0   −1   −2

 3. People too often sell themselves short and say, "Oh, I'm nobody."

    +2   +1   0   −1   −2

 4. Most mental patients are unable to face life as it is and have lost a sense of personal meaning.

    +2   +1   0   −1   −2

 5. Grace—the superaliveness of God—is restricted to the sacraments of the Roman Catholic Church.

    +2   +1   0   −1   −2

 6. The sacraments work like magic, transforming even the unwilling.

    +2   +1   0   −1   −2

 7. Although we take them for granted, human eyes are a truly miraculous pair of machines.

    +2   +1   0   −1   −2

 8. The Protestant Reformers went too far in "disenchanting" the sacraments.

    +2   +1   0   −1   −2

 9. The celebration of each sacrament is a special moment, but only one moment in an ongoing process of conversion.

    +2   +1   0   −1   −2

10. The more estranged we are from nature, the less meaningful the sacraments will be.

    +2   +1   0   −1   −2

Jesus, the Sacrament of God

Some views of God, like paganism and pantheism, make God too immanent, too locked within nature and therefore controllable. At the opposite extreme other views, like Platonism and Deism, make God too transcendent, too aloof and unreachable. Both are right, and both are wrong, because neither is corrected by the truths within the other. God is both the immanent God of Hosea, who seeks out the wayward, and the transcendent God of Job, who is not answerable to us.

The ancient heroes of Israel, like Moses, stood as a kind of focal point, a lightning rod, where the power of God intersected with the people. Like the priests, they passed the needs of the people on to God and mediated God's answers back to them.

But in Jesus, the hero *is* God *and* the people, at once. Jesus is God offered to humankind and humankind offered to God.

> *He always had the nature of God,*
> *but he did not think that by force he*
> *should try to remain equal with God.*
> *Instead of this, of his own free will*
> *he gave up all he had,*
> *and took the nature of a servant.*
> *He became like a human being*
> *and appeared in human likeness.*
> *He was humble and walked the*
> *path of obedience all the way*
> *to death—*
> *his death on the cross.*
> *For this reason God raised him*
> *to the highest place above*
> *and gave him the name that is*
> *greater than any other name. . . .*
> *And all will openly proclaim that*
> *Jesus Christ is Lord.*
>
> Philippians 2:6–9, 11

Christ on the Cross
Rembrandt Harmensz van Rijn
(1606–1669)

Carl Bindhammer (1940–   ).

This does not mean that the Son stopped being God when incarnated into the man Jesus. Jesus was "of divine status," the Word—the Self-expression—of the Father, who did not treat the status of divine dignity as a privilege to be clutched at. Instead, he "gave up all he had." He did not empty himself of divinity but of the privileges of it to become just like us, finding his way step by step without any exceptional privileges. Jesus did that out of obedience to the Father, even to the humiliation of death on a cross. As a result God "raised him to the highest place above and gave him the name that is greater than any other name": *Kyrios*, "Lord," a word Jews used as a substitute for the unspeakable name of God, *YHWH*.

Jesus was not a "symbol" of God; he was the Real Thing, truly God and truly human.

The controversies in the early Church about the God-Man nature of Jesus, oddly enough, are mirrored in today's biblical movies. One set of heresies held that Jesus was only human—but raised to near-divine status, a human being but not fully divine. That view is reflected in *Jesus Christ, Superstar* and *The Last Temptation of Christ.*

At the other extreme, a set of heresies held that Jesus was always God and only "appeared like" a human being. That view is reflected in even very fine films like *Jesus of Nazareth*. Jesus looks almost totally unworldly, somehow distressed at having to be with these "worldly" people.

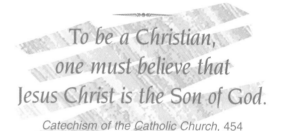

To be a Christian, one must believe that Jesus Christ is the Son of God.

Catechism of the Catholic Church, 454

Both extreme views base themselves on the antagonism between the sacred and the secular, spirit and matter, transcendent and immanent. Both views cannot cope with the fact that Jesus was *both*, the unspeakably holy Son of God and yet also human accused of eating and drinking with a relish unbecoming a holy man. Filmmakers ought to look at Mother Teresa's face. They will see an almost otherworldly serenity coupled with the unstoppable determination of a runaway train.

A sacrament is a visible symbol of an inward grace, and Jesus is grace made visible. Jesus *is* the sacrament of God, God not only present but visible, filled with grace and ready to enliven souls with the super-aliveness of God.

"I am the real vine" (John 15:1). As sap rises out of the roots through the vine into the branches, so the aliveness of the Father—grace—rises into Jesus and into us. The risen Jesus—the glorified Christ—is a *dialogue* between God and the community, the channel through whom the enlivening Spirit of God comes to us.

The Church as the Sacrament of Christ

Just as the Spirit of God was embodied in Jesus, now after Jesus' exaltation as the Christ, that same Spirit is embodied in the Church. As Jesus was the sacrament of God, the Church is the sacrament of Jesus Christ.

THE BODY OF CHRIST

When we enter, or are initiated into, the Church, we enter Christ. This does not mean only the "official" Church, which we mean when we say things like "When is the Church going to . . . ?" It means *all* of us: pope and peasant, baroness and bag lady, king and cabdriver. We now are the body of Christ, who has no hands but ours, no voice but ours, no heart but ours.

The Church's first theologian, Paul, describes it for us:

> *Christ is like a single body, which has many parts; it is still one body, even though it is made up of different parts. In the same way, all of us, whether Jews or Gentiles, whether slaves or free, have been baptized into the one body by the same Spirit, and we have all been given the one Spirit to drink. . . .*

> *So then, the eye cannot say to the hand, "I don't need you!" Nor can the head say to the feet, "Well, I don't need you!" On the contrary, we cannot do without the parts of the body that seem to be weaker; and those parts that we think aren't worth very much are the ones which we treat with greater care. . . . And so there is no division in the body, but all its different parts have the same concern for one another. If one part of the body suffers, all the other parts suffer with it; if one part is praised, all the other parts share its happiness.*
> *All of you are Christ's body.*
> 1 Corinthians 12:12–13, 21–23, 25–27

Mother Teresa of Calcutta (1910–   ).

Just as the whole planet is a body with a soul, the *anima mundi*, so the Church is a body with a soul, the Holy Spirit. We are all interrelated parts. If the individual body has a toothache, it affects all the rest of the body's parts. If some people violate the ecology of the planet for their own profit, all of us—as Chief Seattle said—are violated. If part of the Church is suffering, we all suffer, at least in our compassion. Conversely, just as the leg or elbow has life only when it is connected to the body and its heart, so the Christian life is possible only in connection to the body of Christ.

CALLED FORTH TO SERVE OTHERS

Each of us has a place in the workings of the Church. We are all ministers, not merely sheep waiting to be ministered to:

There are different kinds of spiritual gifts, but the same Spirit gives them. There are different ways of serving, but the same Lord is served. There are different abilities to perform service, but the same God gives ability to all for their particular service. The Spirit's presence is shown in some way in each person for the good of all.   1 Corinthians 12:4–7

The point, obviously, is service—not the "importance" or even the "effectiveness," just serving. Priests' service is administering the sacraments and the care of souls, but the care of souls is not *solely* for priests. The root of the word *minister* is *ministrare*, not to rule, but "to serve."

■ Parents care not only for the souls of their children, but also for those of their neighbors and fellow workers. Which ones are not living life as abundantly as they could?

■ Students serve by studying in order to be of greater service later on, not merely as wage earners but as healers. The life of service for students does not begin when they "get out into the real world." But where are they now? Everywhere they look there are souls. Which ones are not living life as abundantly as they could?

■ Business people must serve, not merely negatively by their lack of dishonesty, but positively in their solicitousness for those who will be affected by their decisions. Which ones are not living life as abundantly as they could?

■ Managers must have concern for their workers. Which ones are not living as abundantly as they could?

The Greek word for "Church" is *ek-klesia*, "called forth." We are thus not just a group of Jesus' admirers. We are engrafted into the One Who Was for Others.

Jesus was the perfect respondent to God's call. He showed us a divine way to be human, a human way of being God. In Christ, divinity and humanity fuse, interpenetrating one another. Thus, the saving acts of the "man," Jesus, were and are performed by a *divine* person, the Son of God. Those actions were and are sacramental—a sacrament is a bestowal of divine aliveness in an outwardly visible form.

Because the acts of Jesus were the acts of a *timeless* God, those acts are not restricted to the time-limited historical Jesus. They go on, now.

> *Jesus Christ is the same yesterday, today, and forever.*   Hebrews 13:8

The actions of the risen Christ in the Church today are as effectual as the actions of Jesus, working visibly among the people of Palestine. The sacraments are actions of Christ, working visibly among his people.

We too are "called forth" to be sacraments wherever we go, channels of grace for others to more abundant life.

Reflection

Think of all the people you come in contact with every week—not just family, friends, next-door neighbors, but plumbers, mechanics, cafeteria workers, secretaries, managers. List them if it helps.

■ *Which ones are not living life as abundantly as they could? How might you at least try to change that? Choose just one—and it needn't be the most difficult one.*

■ *Is it possible that you sell yourself short, or avoid the challenge, or concentrate on your shortcomings rather than—like Peter walking on the water—keeping your eyes only on Jesus? Explain.*

■ *How do you serve as an alive, active member of the body of Christ?*

In our dealings with God, through Jesus Christ, each of us stands somewhere along the spectrum stretching between the two extremes: transcendent and immanent, the distant and unapproachable God of the Deists and the intimate gods of the pagans.

■ *In your own "connection" with God, is God perhaps too far away and judgmental? Or perhaps too buddy-buddy, a pushover, with very little of the "overwhelming mystery"?*

■ *Describe your relationship with God.*

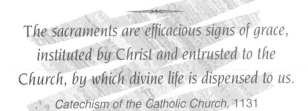

The sacraments are efficacious signs of grace, instituted by Christ and entrusted to the Church, by which divine life is dispensed to us.
Catechism of the Catholic Church, 1131

The Sacraments of the Church

Carl Jung said that most of the patients he had treated in a lifetime as a psychiatrist had lost their faith and therefore had no religion or Church to help them live a *symbolic* life. "There had not been one whose problem in the last resort was not that of finding a religious outlook on life."

ACTIONS, NOT THINGS

The symbol system of the Catholic Church is embodied principally in the seven rituals called sacraments. The original meaning of *sacramentum* was "a pledge" of good faith that bonded two people together. A sacrament, therefore, can be seen as a pledge on God's part, through Jesus Christ, to honor a commitment to Christ's body, the Church, to "be with" the Church.

We have seen that the whole world, in one sense, is a "sacrament," the physical vehicle through which we apprehend the *anima mundi*. We have also seen that Jesus is the sacrament of God, the visible presence of God living and acting among us. And since the exaltation of Jesus Christ, the Church is the visible "body" through which God honors Jesus' promises of grace: the super-aliveness of the Trinity. If the analogy is not too clumsy: the Energy is the Spirit of Christ, the Church is the storage place, and the sacraments are seven special outlets.

The sacraments are different from other symbols because what they connect us to is the *mysterium tremendum*. They are encounters with the glorified Christ. They celebrate *changes*, rites of conversion, in one's relationship with God through the body of Christ.

The love of God for us is always there, even for those who have run away, even for those who have never felt at home in the Church. The sacraments do not bring into existence something that was never there. Rather, they celebrate our new *awareness* that God's love and aliveness are there, for us.

It is important to understand that the seven sacraments are not *things*. They are encounters, through the physical symbolic actions, with the risen Lord who was and is *the* sacrament of God. They are *actions*, not things, that the assembled Church celebrates and is enriched by. They are not things we "receive" or things "done to us."

The sacraments are not magic—manipulating the gods of nature with incantations, and yet they *are!* They are *magic*, at least in the sense that the human eye is magic, that the mystery of love is magic, that the stirring in my heart at a summer sky ablaze with stars is *magic!*

The sacraments are not "automatic." No sacrament changes anyone unless the person has a genuine feeling of a *need* and a desire to be changed. Reconciliation is not a car wash; Eucharist is not a vitamin pill; Anointing of the Sick is not a painkiller. Like the forgiveness of the father of the prodigal, no sacrament changes us unless we want it to work.

But the Church declares that a sacrament works *ex opere operato*, that is, "merely by the fact that the operation has been performed." No matter how sinful the minister, if the recipients are open to the grace, the sacrament effects a real change within them. Contrary to the accusations of the Reformers, the Church does not hold that sacraments are magic, in the strict sense: laying an obligation on God.

The Reformation taught us lessons, many of which we did not "hear" until four hundred years later. Its leaders called attention, rightly, to the role of *personal* faith and involvement in order for sacraments to be fully effective. This view was contrary to the official Church's defense of *ex opere operato*, the sacrament effects a change no matter what.

But the Reformers went too far. They "disenchanted" the presence of God in our symbolic lives. They took all the "mystery" out of the Christian life.

The Resurrection
Titian (1477–1576)

RITES OF CONVERSION

A sacrament is *Christ's* act, an act of grace, an act of love undeserved. Christ has freely chosen to give grace—an intensity of inner aliveness—when the recipient genuinely wants it, just as the father of the prodigal gave forgiveness when his son asked for it, just as Jesus gave healing in response to faith. When a priest, deacon, or layperson baptizes, as Saint Augustine said, "It is really Christ who baptizes." When the sick person is anointed, it is Christ himself who is present.

Jesus promised:

> *"Where two or three come together in my name, I am there with them."*
>
> Matthew 18:20

And this is the Jesus who could work miracles with mud and spittle.

Each sacrament is, as this book's title suggests, a *rite of conversion,* a privileged moment, but only one moment in a *process.*

Each sacrament is a celebration of a rite of conversion, of change, in an ongoing *relationship.*

Each of the sacraments is a rite of conversion in an ongoing relationship; not merely a once-for-all rite but a high point in a lifelong process.

The focal, core sacrament is the Eucharist. It is at the heart of the Church's life, the central act of gratitude, the Body and Blood of Christ enlivening the body of Christ. Branching from that central "heart" are the other sacraments of *Christian initiation* (Baptism and Confirmation), the sacraments of *healing* (Reconciliation and Anointing of the Sick), and the sacraments *at the service of communion* (Holy Orders and Matrimony)—all of which have their roots in the heart: the Eucharist.

Sacraments of Christian Initiation

■ *Baptism* is only the beginning of membership in this family—the Church, the body of Christ.

■ *Confirmation* strengthens and "confirms" us in our relationship with God through the body of Christ, to be more than a mere passive member but, sealed with the Spirit, to become a minister of the more abundant life.

■ The *Eucharist* is a coming-home as a family, to be reminded of who we are and what we are for, the recharge of the Spirit in us.

Sacraments of Healing

■ *Reconciliation* heals that relationship in the encounter with the forgiving Christ. It is a reminder that we too often sell short our dignity as daughters and sons of God.

■ *Anointing of the Sick* heals the soul who feels abandoned by God, putting this suffering *into* the body of Christ on Calvary, which paradoxically was the doorway to rebirth.

Sacraments at the Service of Communion

■ *Holy Orders* quite obviously is a radical change in an individual's relationship with the body of Christ.

■ *Matrimony* creates a bond between spouses. "Authentic married love is caught up into divine love" (*Church in the Modern World*).

Each of the sacraments is not merely a once-for-all rite but a high point in a lifelong *process*. In every sacrament, we tend to focus only on the isolated *act* when the sacrament is publicly solemnized. But a *marriage,* for instance, is not restricted to the time of the wedding. It is a process of *becoming* married, which began long before the rite and will continue to grow long after the celebration of the rite. Couples in their fifties are far *more* married than they were on their wedding day.

The more we are estranged from nature, the less meaningful the symbols of the sacraments become. Water is trivial, something you wash in, swim in, hidden away in pipes. We have lost the taste of bread unless it is slathered with peanut butter. Wine is nothing unless you have had too much. Oil is for salads and suntans. The purpose of the rest of this book is to attempt to revivify those symbols. Which, whether successful or not, is a very Christian enterprise. The whole message of Christianity is about resurrection and rebirth: a more abundant life!

Reflection

■ *Very honestly, how much "magic" is there in your life?*

■ *Where does it really manifest itself?*

■ *If there is little or none, do you feel impoverished? Missing something very important in a fully human life?*

■ *What is your sensitivity to the numinous in nature? To the symbols of the Church? If you have little or none, is it possible you are missing something?*

The great religions . . . witness, often impressively, to this cosmic and symbolic meaning of religious rites. The liturgy of the Church presupposes, integrates and sanctifies elements from creation and human culture, conferring on them the dignity of signs of grace, of the new creation in Jesus Christ.

Catechism of the Catholic Church, 1149

Understanding Symbolic Rituals

Review

1. What is a symbol and what are its purposes? In what ways can symbols illuminate strictly rational understanding? What is the difference between a "sign" and a "symbol"?

2. What is the difference between natural symbols and culturally conditioned symbols? Why can symbols and stories from long-lost cultures nonetheless evoke in us the same response as for people long dead?

3. Why is it natural to celebrate at the winter solstice and at the beginning of spring? What does such celebration do for the soul?

4. What do symbols do to bind a people together? What is missing in the soul when cultural symbols are drained of their meaningfulness?

5. What is the reason humans have to ritualize—externalize—their firmly held beliefs? Why can't they just keep them to themselves?

6. What makes sacred rituals different from secular rituals like the World Series or a political convention? What is the "connection" involved in religion that is more important than the connection one has to the game and to one's fellow fans?

7. What did Jesus give up at the Incarnation? How did that action blur the clear distinction between sacred and secular?

8. Jesus performed no miracle except in *response* to faith. What insight does that provide regarding the efficacy and felt meaningfulness of the sacraments?

9. Explain: The Church is the prolongation of the body of Christ. What is the aliveness in that body? In what ways does that super-aliveness animate the members of the body?

10. Explain: The sacraments are not "things" but effective *actions* of the entire Church. What does *ex opere operato* mean? Explain: It is really Christ himself who baptizes, forgives, transforms the bread and wine.

11. Explain: The sacraments are not magic, yet in a very real way they are "magical." How did the Reformers go too far in "disenchanting" the sacraments?

Discuss

1. Why have humans consistently associated heaven with "up"—Mt. Olympus, Mt. Sinai, angels flitting through clouds? Now, we know "up" has meaning only relative to where you happen to be standing at the moment. Yet we still think of heaven as "up." Why?

2. In time of drought, a Christian or Muslim might pray to God for rain. On the contrary, the Navajo pray to restore harmony between themselves and the drought, to recognize what is beyond the human capacity to change. What insight does that give into how we might alter the way we pray for favors?

3. Consider your own participation in the eucharistic ritual at Mass. Does it "work" for you? Many say they stopped going because they "didn't get anything out of it." Is that really the purpose of the Mass? Other than showing gratitude, it surely is, because any sacrament is intended to be a channel of grace, a greater aliveness, the "connection" to God.

4. Why are we less sensitive to the real value and the symbolic value of water, bread, wine, oil?

5. How do you serve as an alive, active member of the body of Christ?

6. In your imagination, try to expand your awareness beyond yourself to all the people with you at Mass on a Sunday. What is going on inside all the people—singly and together?

7. Expand your awareness even further to the Church all over the world—not just good works like hospitals and missions, but as if all the Catholics in the world were together at a *single* Mass. What is going on?

8. Finally, break beyond the limits of time and space and sense the Church expanding to all the Christians who have ever lived, countless billions of souls in heaven, all somehow present with you at that Sunday Mass. What is going on?

Activities

1. Interview several members of your family and the faculty. Ask each to name several "symbols" that express their beliefs and convictions. Report your research to the group.

2. Look around the classroom and pick out all the objects that have a greater value than their literal value, say at a garage sale. Look in your purse or wallet, your jewelry, your tote bag. What value does each of those objects evoke?

3. Everyone in the room belongs—at least remotely—to some kind of ethnic group. Have those who are only one generation from the "mother" country tell what customs the old people in their families still practice. What does celebrating those customs *add* to the spirit of the family? What are those who have drifted away from their ethnic heritage missing?

4. Divide your group into two teams. Debate this statement, Technology has become "the new magic."

5. What is the root meaning of "*ek-klesia*," the Church? As a group list the ways the members of your group are called to be a sacrament to the secular world. Are you effective "sacraments"? Why or why not?

6. List all the items you can think of in your parish church. You may not even know what some are or what they are for. Pool your knowledge. What values is each trying to convey? For instance, to put the focus at Mass on the altar table, the tabernacle has been removed to the side somewhere.

What difference does that make for people who drop into the church daily to make a visit?

7. Reread Saint Paul's description of the Incarnation. Try to imagine Jesus' life as it might have been as an ordinary Jewish boy. Then try to describe the impact on his soul at his baptism when he realized that "You are my own dear Son!" Then imagine what happened when the Spirit "led" him into the wilderness to have that realization tempted: "If you are God's Son, order these stones to turn into bread."

Scripture Readings

Skim the passages. Pick one that appeals to you and (1) summarize its main point, (2) tell how it relates to the chapter, and (3) list one or two thoughts that entered your mind as you read it.

• Wisdom 13:1	Recognizing the living God
• Psalm 148:3–10	A call for the universe to praise God
• Matthew 13:34–35	Use of parables
• Mark 7:33–34	Symbolic act of Jesus
• Luke 8:4–8	Parable of the sower
• John 13:1–11	Jesus washes his disciples' feet
• Acts 14:17	Evidence of God's action
• Romans 1:19–20	God's invisible qualities can be seen

✎ Journal

When we enter, or are initiated into, the Church, we enter Christ. We are all interrelated parts of one body, the body of Christ.

Think of all that has been part of your life today. How have you experienced the truth of the above statements?

Sacraments
of
Initiation

Chapter 4

Baptism: Incorporation into the Body of Christ

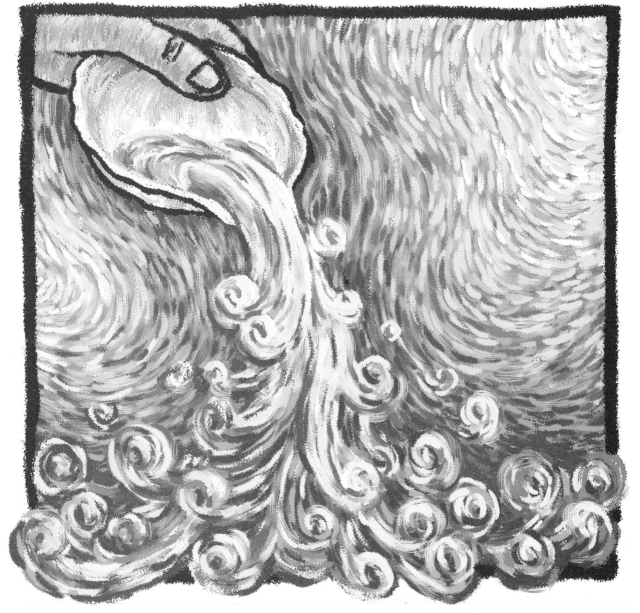

As soon as Jesus was baptized, he came up out of the water.
Then heaven was opened to him, and he saw the Spirit of God
coming down like a dove and lighting on him. Then a voice said from heaven,
"This is my own dear Son, with whom I am pleased."
Matthew 3:16–17

INITIATION

Survey

This survey is not an exercise for a grade, but a means to stir up interest and get an idea of varying opinions in your group. Some of the statements are matters of objective fact; others are merely subjective opinions. On the rating scale under each statement circle the number that best reflects your current opinion about that statement.

+2 = strongly agree,
+1 = agree,
 0 = cannot make up my mind,
−1 = disagree,
−2 = strongly disagree.

Then share the reasons for your opinion.

1. Rites of initiation are a "graduation" from one state and "commencement" into another.

 +2   +1   0   −1   −2

2. If baptism is an initiation into a group the parents do not frequent, it is a sham for show.

 +2   +1   0   −1   −2

3. In the earliest days of the Church, most candidates for baptism were adults.

 +2   +1   0   −1   −2

4. Far more vividly than we, newly baptized early Christians knew they were "different" from nonbelievers.

 +2   +1   0   −1   −2

5. Our culture today is almost as pagan and irreligious as the culture of ancient Rome.

 +2   +1   0   −1   −2

6. Like all sacraments, the celebration of Baptism is only one focal step in a lifelong process.

 +2   +1   0   −1   −2

7. Before baptism, an infant is literally a child of Satan.

 +2   +1   0   −1   −2

8. Baptism is a "gift" only in the sense one has been judged worthy of a challenge.

 +2   +1   0   −1   −2

9. Water is a natural symbol of both life and death.

 +2   +1   0   −1   −2

10. Baptism removes from the human soul all tendencies ever to sin again.

 +2   +1   0   −1   −2

A Puzzlement

Saint Paul wrote:

For surely you know that when we were baptized into union with Christ Jesus, we were baptized into union with his death. By our baptism, then, we were buried with him and shared his death, in order that, just as Christ was raised from death by the glorious power of the Father, so also we might live a new life.

Romans 6:3–4

■ What does this passage mean?

Christian Initiation

Each of us has been initiated more than a few times. The first days of grade school, high school, college, the people who have been there longer go out of their way to ease the embarrassment and the disorientation, to make us feel "at home." They help us fit in—when we do not feel at home at all and feel we are sticking out like a skunk at a garden party. It is called "orientation," getting our bearings against a whole new background. When each of those levels of education is over, a ritual celebrates not only that we have graduated *out of* the past stage but also that we have entered *into* a new stage of our life, "a commencement."

Some people have been inducted into the military services, the National Honor Society, the scouts, a fraternity or sorority. With the sponsorship of a full member and after a period of probation, the group holds a ceremony to signify that the person is no longer just one of "them" but one of "us." The ceremony embodies a change in status, a *conversion*.

CONVERSION: DEATH AND REBIRTH

Baptism is also an initiation. The celebration of baptism is an orientation against a whole new background. It is a "graduation" from one way of looking at life and the "commencement" of a new one. It is the ritualization of a person's conversion. In the very early Church, Baptism, Confirmation, and first Eucharist were celebrated in an integrated single process. This celebration, usually only for adults, took place only once a year at the Vigil of Easter. It was a fitting, highly symbolic moment.

The whole imagery of baptism recaptures Jesus' death and rebirth (resurrection), which is the core of Christianity. The church community gathered with the bishop in a large home, singing, meditating on Scripture, praying for the elect who waited outside, praying with their sponsors and deacon. It was an all-night vigil.

Just before dawn, those who had completed the catechumenate—a process of instructions, exorcisms, works of charity, and praying, which sometimes lasted three years—gathered outside around the baptismal pool. There their sponsors attested to their good conduct, especially their works of charity. The elect, those about to be baptized, removed all their clothing, symbolizing putting off their old lives. (Quite likely, out of modesty, men and women were baptized separately, therefore the need for women deacons.)

The deacons invited the elect to foreswear paganism, then anointed them with ordinary olive oil, a symbol of the "everyday" the elect were leaving behind. Then deacons led them, naked as Adam and Eve, down the steps into the flowing water. Standing before the elect, a priest asked the three baptismal questions:

- *Do you believe in the Father?*
- *Do you believe in the Son?*
- *Do you believe in the Holy Spirit?*

The elect responded to each, "I do believe." And at each response the deacons submerged the person under the water, a ritual drowning into the body of Christ's death. Each time they emerged again and breathed life.

The newly baptized came out of the water, dried themselves, and were anointed once again, but this time with the perfumed oil of thanksgiving, the chrism, to symbolize their new life. They put on new white garments. And, each holding a lighted candle, filed into "the Church," where the bishop laid his hands on each one in turn, praying they might be worthy receptacles of the Holy Spirit.

Then the bishop anointed each again with the same perfumed oil of thanksgiving, signifying their acceptance into the People of God (this anointing, confirmation, later became celebrated separately), kissed them, and welcomed them into the body of Christ, the Church. Then the celebration concluded with the new Christians' first Eucharist.

CHRISTIAN FREEDOM

That ritual at dawn on Easter Sunday morning was only the final, culminating moment in a long process of gradual but total *conversion* to Christ. It celebrated in ritual a complete turnabout from a life of self-absorption to a life of self-giving. Why did a person choose such a turnabout? At first, the person might have been puzzled by the otherworldly serenity of a Christian neighbor, or the person was puzzled by the neighbor's kindness to the most unpleasant people.

Redemption means "liberation, setting free." People around could see a change of attitude, a conversion, from apprehension to serenity. The newly initiated now lived differently from the way they had before and from the way most people lived. They were no longer harried, offering one another support, consolation, funds when they were in

need. Even in times of persecution, of personal failure, of bereavement, they now had a totally different perspective: the Resurrection.

This of course is why the Church grew so quickly. ("Can I see your freedom? Can I feel your joy?") People saw what liberation from the chaos of life meant, not in theory but in the everyday lives of Christians. Others wanted to understand such a life, experience it, share it. So, inquisitive neighbors made inquiries and, after a period of scrutiny—to be sure they were not spies looking to report Christians—these "inquirers" were introduced into a first understanding of the gospel message. Then, after a long period of instruction, they were enrolled among those to be baptized at the Easter Vigil.

After such a long process and such a vivid ceremony, newly baptized Christians had no doubt whatever that they were "completely new." They had no doubt they were beginning a totally different way of looking at life, and of dealing with their neighbors, their work, their families. And they knew they were completely "different" from their pagan neighbors because of that.

Holy Baptism is the basis of the whole Christian life, the gateway to life in the Spirit. . . . Through Baptism we are freed from sin and reborn as [children] of God; we become members of Christ, are incorporated into the Church and made sharers in her mission: "Baptism is the sacrament of regeneration through water in the word."

Catechism of the Catholic Church, 1213

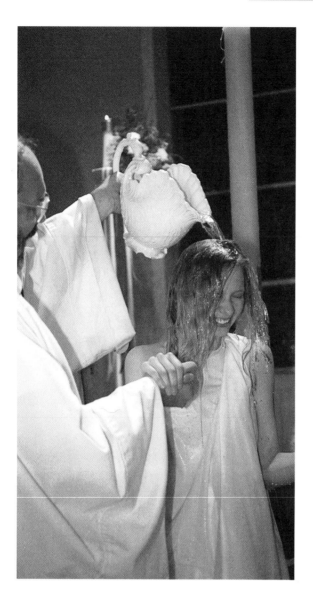

Like each of the other sacraments, Baptism is about achieving a newer, richer *freedom*. Freedom in the Christian sense means that we have courage and self-confidence (or Christ-confidence) enough that we can put ourselves at the disposal of others. The hippest, most arrogant have not that kind of courage and self-confidence. That sort of freedom seemed "foolishness" to the Greeks, who classical culture thought were the epitome of how human beings should live:

> *By means of the so-called "foolish" message we preach, God decided to save those who believe. Jews want miracles for proof, and Greeks look for wisdom. As for us, we proclaim the crucified Christ, a message that is offensive to the Jews and nonsense to the Gentiles; but for those whom God has called, both Jews and Gentiles, this message is Christ, who is the power of God and the wisdom of God. For what seems to be God's foolishness is wiser than human wisdom, and what seems to be God's weakness is stronger than human strength. . . .*
>
> *But God has brought you into union with Christ Jesus, and God has made Christ to be our wisdom. By him we are put right with God; we become God's holy people and are set free.*
>
> 1 Corinthians 1:21–25, 30

Most Christians today were baptized as infants when they were unaware of the symbolism that points to the meaning of the sacrament. And although many of the symbolic actions that are part of the celebration of Baptism have been thinned by propriety (no nakedness, no total immersion, no complete change of clothing) and further thinned by our culture's detachment from natural symbols like water, fire, oil, being a genuine Christian should still make one feel dramatically "different."

To be genuinely Christian means that our self-absorption and self-protectiveness are "disabled," in order that we can be free to serve others.

Baptism *introduces* us to a community *through which* we can be outfitted to face the tasks of life in a more dignified way than others do. But, as we have seen so often before, Baptism is an invitation. We can refuse this invitation, even though in infancy others accepted it for us. Being free, we may choose *not* to be free.

> Baptism not only purifies
> from all sins,
> but also makes the neophyte
> "a new creature" . . .
> who has become a
> "partaker of the divine nature,"
> member of Christ
> and co-heir with him,
> and a temple
> of the Holy Spirit.
>
> *Catechism of the Catholic Church, 1265*

SYMBOLIC ACTIONS

In Greek, *bapto* means "to dye a garment to change its color," and the more intensive form, *baptizo,* means "to cause to perish," as in drowning. When speaking of more commonplace ritual cleansings, Greeks used less dramatic words like *wash, rinse, sprinkle.* Thus, by choosing the word *baptizo,* the early Church did not think of this baptismal action as an everyday ritual. It was life-changing.

Immersing in Water

Water is a very positive symbol. It is a symbol for life. Our planet is the only planet we know of that is blue. All human life came out of those blue waters. Each one of us lived nine months in the water in our mother's womb; our bodies are 70 percent water. Water quenches thirst; we can go a full month without much food, but only five days without water. We use water to cleanse our bodies and our homes, to water lawns, fill pools, extinguish fires. Without water and the sun, we could grow no food. Perhaps young city people have no felt understanding of the "sacredness" of an oasis to a desert nomad, but the toughest city kid knows the joy of opening a fire hydrant in July and frolicking in water.

Yet, like human nature, water has its dark side too. Floods destroy homes, crops, human lives; polluted water carries disease; storms can wipe out whole coastlines. Anyone used to swimming in calm lakes knows the terror of water when swimming in the ocean the first time and being caught and hurled head over heels in the breakers. Anyone caught at sea in a storm, as the apostles were, understands the panic water can raise in us. It was out of the chaos of the primeval waters that God brought cosmos, and the two forces have been in conflict ever since.

Water is an equivocal symbol, suggesting new life on the one hand, and death on the other. Saint Paul finds in baptism a death to the world ruled by evil powers (the self-absorption that impoverishes others and oneself on the one hand or seeks *self-justification* through the Law on the other). But Paul also sees the possibility of rising up from the waters of chaos into the cosmos of Christ. When we "enter" Christ—the Church—there is no more fragmentation:

It is through faith that all of you are God's children in union with Christ Jesus. You were baptized into union with Christ, and now you are clothed, so to speak, with the life of Christ himself. So there is no difference between Jews and Gentiles, between slaves and free people, between men and women; you are all one in union with Christ Jesus.

Galatians 3:26–28

Father, you give us grace through sacramental signs, which tell us of the wonders of your unseen power.

In baptism we use your gift of water, which you have made a rich symbol of the grace you give us in this sacrament.

Roman Missal, Easter Vigil: Blessing of Water

At the opening of Genesis, God's Spirit hovered over the chaos of the waters and, with a word, brought forth all living things (Genesis 1:1–31). Entering the ark by Noah and his family (as entering the Church) was making a commitment to a new, special relationship with God; they were reborn out of the waters to begin again. The terms of acceptance? A new respect for life (Genesis 7:1–9:29).

The Israelites went through the tumult of the Red Sea and came out the other side a new nation, while the Egyptian slavers perished (Exodus 14:1–31). And finally they passed through the River Jordan into the Promised Land. But ever after that they kept falling back into "the slave mentality," worshiping idols, returning to chaos.

John the Baptist appeared by that same Jordan, preaching conversion and entry into the new Promised Land. And though sinless himself, Jesus underwent a baptism, going down into the water and emerging renewed in the Holy Spirit (Matthew 3:13–17). This Jesus, who identified himself with the sinners he came to save, leads us from the waters of chaos by going to the very bottom of them himself and coming out. During his life, Jesus calmed the storm on the lake (Matthew 8:23–27) and walked on the waters without fear (Matthew 14:22–33). And to Peter Jesus said:

"I have a baptism to receive, and how distressed I am until it is over!"

Luke 12:50

For Jesus, his second "baptism" *was* his death and resurrection. And the early Christian communities believed that they too had died and been reborn completely new because of Christ's death-resurrection.

For surely you know that when we were baptized into union with Christ Jesus, we were baptized into union with his death. By our baptism, then, we were buried with him and shared his death, in order that, just as Christ was raised from death by the glorious power of the Father, so also we might live a new life.

Romans 6:3–4

Baptism "recaptures" that whole series of events. In baptism we are "plunged into" that experience of Jesus, and are born again as daughters and sons of God.

> *For through the living and eternal word of God you have been born again as the children of a parent who is immortal, not mortal.*   1 Peter 1:23

Anointing with Chrism

In our culture, oil has a very commonplace, domestic, undramatic meaning: salads, suntans, lubrication. It also has strongly negative associations: crude oil spills and the death of the ecology. But at the time when the sacraments were taking concrete form, oil—like water and wine—was an important element of daily life.

Oil was what bound together the elements of bread, and therefore it symbolized the healing of fragmentation. Wrestlers anointed their entire bodies to make it more difficult for an opponent to get a hold on them, and Saint Ambrose (A.D. 340?–397) claimed that that was precisely one of the functions of anointing at Christian initiation.

In the Bible, priests, monarchs, and prophets were anointed with oil when they assumed their new roles (1 Samuel 10:1; 16:1–13). As the first public act of Jesus' ministry:

> *he came to Nazareth, where he had been brought up, and went into the synagogue on the sabbath day as he usually did. He stood up to read, and they handed him the scroll of the prophet Isaiah. Unrolling the scroll he found the place where it is written:*
>
> > "The Spirit of the Lord has been given to me,
> >
> > for he has *anointed* me. . . ."
>
> *He then rolled up the scroll, gave it back to the assistant and sat down.*
>
> Luke 4:16–18, 20 (*The Jerusalem Bible*)

The word *messiah* means "the Anointed One." Thus, in the oil of baptism, each of us is anointed a "messiah"—priest, monarch, prophet:

> God the Father of our Lord Jesus Christ has freed you from sin, given you a new birth by water and the Holy Spirit, and welcomed you into his holy people. He now anoints you with the chrism of salvation. As Christ was anointed Priest, Prophet, and King, so may you live always as members of his body, sharing everlasting life.
>
> *Rite of Baptism for Children*

In his first letter Peter is not speaking to officials of the church community but to ordinary people like you. He writes:

> *You are the chosen race, the King's priests, the holy nation, God's own people, chosen to proclaim the wonderful acts of God, who called you out of darkness into his own marvelous light.*   1 Peter 2:9

It makes no difference if Christians speak Greek or Hebrew, whether they are male or female, old or young. They—you—are priests, prophets, peers of the realm of God.

But—with that ever-present Christian irony—to be anointed as priest-prophet-peer means precisely the opposite of what it means in "the world": not to rule but to serve.

> *I appeal to you to be shepherds of the flock that God gave you and to take care of it willingly, as God wants you to, and not unwillingly. Do your work, not for mere pay, but from a real desire to serve. Do not try to rule over those who have been put in your care, but be examples to the flock.*   1 Peter 5:1–3

Exorcism/Satan/Sin

No one can deny there is a dark side to human nature. That element in us is symbolized by the Mr. Hyde in Dr. Jekyll, Wolfman, Dracula. Although our brains have a cerebral cortex capable of writing *King Lear* and sending rockets to Jupiter, at its core is the brainstem we share with reptiles. Just as one can have no understanding of resurrection without a felt understanding of death, or an understanding of freedom without a felt understanding of slavery, so one can have no understanding of baptism (or the whole Christian Church) without a felt understanding of evil.

In the last half century of our culture, we have been effectively and affectively anesthetized to evil. There is hardly a day when the papers and television do not announce a new civil war in some country whose name we have never heard. Pictures of starving human beings, ribs thrusting through their skins, eyes huge with hunger, are so commonplace we quickly turn the page without asking, "Why? Who?"

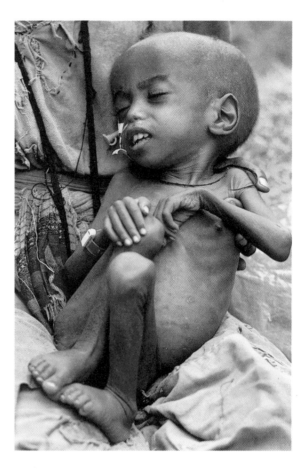

Exploitation of people who are living in poverty, hatreds, rivalries, greed, manipulation of the minds of the young, drugs sold in schoolyards, drive-by shootings, families living under bridges, sexually abused children, battered and murdered wives—never get the three-inch headlines in the daily tabloids. We give as little notice to them as we do to the Kiddie Komix, unless they are especially blatant or done by a celebrity. For most, they are not even news.

For earlier cultures, even up to as recently as the '50s, evil was not an abstraction. It was concretized, even for the most sophisticated and educated, in the symbolic figure of Satan. Today, except for a few fringe Satan cults, that embodiment of pure evil is ludicrous to anyone who routinely flies in a plane or uses a computer or has taken even elementary

psychology, the stuff of "Far Side" cartoons. Which, if there is in fact a Devil, would probably be just dandy with him.

But then for a while there was the uncanny phenomenon of *The Exorcist*. That film was different from other horror movies, such as *The Omen,* and *Nightmare on Elm Street,* and even the sequels to *The Exorcist*, all of which gave no more real scare than the momentary terror on a roller coaster. But that film was quite different. In the first place, people were lined up for blocks (and weeks) to see it. Second, it triggered all kinds of bizarre responses. Third, it frightened a great many people back to some practice of religion—perhaps not for long. But at least for a while these people were aware that evil does exist because they had seen it unmasked and almost palpably terrifying.

the mountain to *see* that it was a dead parachutist. And when he ran down the mountain with the truth, they savaged him to death.

Generations of young people have reacted to *The Lord of the Flies* in a way less dramatic but similar to the way millions responded to *The Exorcist*. There is something indefinable but *true* in there somewhere. Simon was right: "Maybe it's only . . . us." No matter how inadequate the symbol that connects us to it, moral evil exists: Auschwitz, Medellin, the South Bronx, South Central L.A., Bosnia, Rwanda, Haiti. Those are only some few places where the more dramatic explosions of evil have taken place in our world today.

> *The reality Satan symbolizes*
> *is corrosively real,*
> *furiously active*
> *in every corner of our lives,*
> *and as easily ignored*
> *as the pollution in our rivers*
> *and the poison in our air.*

There is wholesale evil in our world today that we simply take for granted:

- a million and a half abortions,
- millions of unwed mothers every year,
- fathers deserting the results of a half-hour's self-absorbed pleasure,
- wholesale divorce.

These are all inhumanities that rarely make the front page or headline a newscast. All indignities that we now take as merely "given."

The cause of both the panic in susceptible people and the sneering condescension in sophisticated people was a literalism, where the symbol *becomes* the reality. Just as it did for the marooned boys in *The Lord of the Flies* (which is a translation of the Hebrew word for demon: *Beelzebub*). The marooned boys invested all the evil in themselves—the savages they became once they had shucked the veneer of society along with their clothes onto the pig's head on a stick and onto the mysterious entity flapping and groaning on the mountaintop. Only impractical Simon, the visionary, said, "Maybe it's only . . . us." Only he had the courage to shake off the boys' ignorant beliefs and climb

There also are those tinier evils, which are nonetheless evil:

- lying to people we claim to love,

- cheating on a quiz that in a week we will forget we even took,

- savaging the reputation of another human being in order to be "in,"

- sneering at other people's skin color,

- spitting gum in the drinking fountain because the basket is too far away.

And their very pettiness, rather than embarrassing us, seems to exonerate us.

Whether there is a literal Satan, a disembodied force that roams the world seeking to seduce us, is not the question. What need would we have for such an unneeded tempter when we have a perfectly adequate one within each of us? There is no doubt that whatever the reality Satan symbolizes, evil is corrosively real, furiously active in every corner of our lives. And it is as easily ignored as the pollution in our rivers and the poison in our air.

Simon was right.

Many today are uneasy with the exorcisms of Baptism and any mention of "Satan" in celebration of the ritual. The seeming literalism of the word *Satan* is a bit of an embarrassment even to less sophisticated people. The problem could probably be alleviated—since it is a matter not of sacrosanct symbols but of an undeniable reality—if the celebrant substituted for "Satan" some other formula less associated with superstitious literalism, such as "the powers within us that lead us to harm others and ourselves."

But there is no doubt that Baptism, for adults or for infants, is a declaration that the purpose of the Church and all those genuinely within it is directly counter to that inner force.

Reflection

Consider the question posed in this chapter about the radical difference between the attitudes, priorities, and actions of early Christians and their pagan neighbors.

- *Over and above taking part in the celebration of Mass, how are your concrete choices different from a nonbeliever's?*

We have discussed three quite broad manifestations of evil in the world today to which we have, maybe without realizing it, hardened ourselves: the monstrous evils that overwhelm whole peoples, the utter inhumanities to which the day-to-day reportage has toughened our sensitivities, and the petty everyday indignities that we have come to regard as simply irritating "givens."

- *Make three columns on a sheet of paper and label them* Monstrous, Inhuman, Mean-Spirited. *Spend some time—perhaps more than you had originally planned—and fill in the columns. Is there more evil in the world than you suspected?*

In Baptism, those about to be baptized renounce evil.

Do you reject sin, so as to live in the freedom of God's children?

I do.

Do you reject the glamour of evil, and refuse to be mastered by sin?

I do.

Do you reject Satan, father of sin and prince of darkness?

I do.

- *List the ways you reject "evil."*

RENEWED INITIATION PROCESS

Survey

This survey is not an exercise for a grade, but a means to stir up interest and get an idea of varying opinions in your group. Some of the statements are matters of objective fact; others are merely subjective opinions. On the rating scale under each statement circle the number that best reflects your current opinion about that statement.

> +2 = strongly agree,
> +1 = agree,
>   0 = cannot make up my mind,
> −1 = disagree,
> −2 = strongly disagree.

Then share the reasons for your opinion.

1. Baptism is an invitation from self-absorption to self-giving.

   +2   +1   0   −1   −2

2. If infants are baptized without preparation, adults should be baptized when they request it.

   +2   +1   0   −1   −2

3. Today, adult candidates for Baptism may stay at Mass only to the end of the homily.

   +2   +1   0   −1   −2

4. The primary reason for early infant baptism is that infants will go to heaven if they die.

   +2   +1   0   −1   −2

5. Infants (or anyone) who die without baptism are kept from heaven.

   +2   +1   0   −1   −2

6. Adam and Eve were a literal, historical couple whose sin twisted all human souls thereafter.

   +2   +1   0   −1   −2

7. After that sin, God abandoned humans until the debt for it was suitably paid.

   +2   +1   0   −1   −2

8. The burden of original sin is passed on through the degrading act of sexual intercourse.

   +2   +1   0   −1   −2

9. God loves everyone born into the world, before or even without baptism.

   +2   +1   0   −1   −2

10. To ask how infants can be legitimately committed to a religion asks the wrong question.

    +2   +1   0   −1   −2

Restored Catechumenate

The overwhelming majority of those baptized today are infants. But since Vatican II the Church has—rightly—focused primarily on the initiation of adults into the Church. This renewed emphasis is the norm by which we are to understand the meaning of Baptism—and its connection to Confirmation and Eucharist, the other two Sacraments of Initiation.

RITES OF CONVERSION

The restored rites of initiation are a historically more accurate reenactment of what the early Church intended Christian initiation to be. Its prayers beg freedom from the power of darkness and from sin. With adults the obvious focus is on conversion of heart and entrance into the body of Christ. The symbolism of drowning and coming back to life—of a complete conversion of values and priorities—is far clearer to an adult capable of seeing the two radically different options of self-absorption or self-giving, and making a reasoned choice for one rather than the other.

Anthropologists have found that (in all societies) conversions—changes in the state of one's life—move in three stages.

■ First, a *separation* from one condition.

■ Second, a *transition* phase where one is neither in the old "way" or yet in the new one.

■ Finally, an *incorporation* into a new status and an external ritualization of that internalized new view of human life.

The dominant metaphor for the *restored catechumenate*, another term used to describe the process of initiating adults into the church community, is that of a journey between opposite extremes: darkness and light, slavery and freedom, falsehood and truth, death and life. At the end of their initiation journey, like the Hebrews arriving in Canaan, the catechumens experience a new birth into a community.

RITE OF CHRISTIAN INITIATION OF ADULTS

The Rite of Christian Initiation of Adults is a spiritual journey made up of four "Periods." It is also marked by three "Steps" or "doorways" that lead to the next "Period" of the journey.

Period of Evangelization and Precatechumenate

First Step: Acceptance into the Order of Catechumens

Period of the Catechumenate

Second Step: Election or Enrollment of Names

Period of Purification and Enlightenment

Third Step: Celebration of the Sacraments of Initiation

Period of Postbaptismal Catechesis or Mystagogy

The initiation of catechumens is a gradual process that takes place within the community of the faithful. By joining the catechumens in reflecting on the value of the paschal mystery and by renewing their own conversion, the faithful provide an example that will help the catechumens to obey the Holy Spirit more generously.

From *Introduction to Rite of Christian Initiation of Adults.*

During Lent as the catechumens prepare more intensely for the sacramental celebration of their initiation, the celebrant prays:

Lord God,
source of unfailing light,
by the death and resurrection of Christ
you have cast out the darkness
    of hatred and lies
and poured forth the light of
    truth and love
upon the human family.

Hear our prayers for these elect,
whom you have called to be
    your adopted children.

Enable them to pass from
    darkness to light
and, delivered from the
    prince of darkness,
to live always as children of the light.
              (Second Scrutiny,
        Liturgy of the Word, R.C.I.A.)

But we must remind ourselves again not to let our metaphors run away with us and inflate our expectations. As we saw earlier, we draw such dramatic oppositions between differing values in order to understand each alternative better.

But no catechumen will find those ideals fully realized in a church community, which is made up of human beings. At the end of the catechumen's preparation, there will still be areas of darkness, slavery, falsehood, and death in the lives of the newly baptized. But if the initiation process has been reasonably successful, those areas should be fewer and less intense. Like the North Star, all ideals—light, freedom, truth, and life—are guides to a better life, not a destination.

R.C.I.A.

The Rite of Christian Initiation of Adults (R.C.I.A.) is rather a process of orientation consisting of several rites culminating in the celebration of the Sacraments of Initiation at the Easter Vigil. Throughout the initiation process, several rites are celebrated that are an external acknowledgment of the inner conversion that takes place over an extended period of the initiation process.

Period of Evangelization and Precatechumenate

The first phase, or period, of the initiation process is quite natural and unstructured. Men or women have a "hunch" that their lives are less fulfilling than they could be, a "hunch" that they might be missing out on a very important dimension of human life: the Spirit. They "inquire," they talk with a Christian or Christians they know who seem to have something they do not have, someone clearly committed to living a religious life.

Once the sponsors are convinced the inquirers are sincerely searching and not merely casually interested, they approach the Church to ask that the inquirers might take the "first step," the celebration of the Rite of Acceptance into the Order of Catechumens.

At this rite, the candidates' first acceptance of the Gospel is celebrated, and the sponsors and assembly affirm the candidates' worthiness. Next the celebrant invites the sponsors and candidates to come forward, saying:

> Come forward now with your sponsors to receive the sign of your new way of life as catechumens.
> *Rite of Christian Initiation of Adults*

Tracing the sign of the cross on the forehead of each of the catechumens, marking them as belonging to Christ, the celebrant says:

> [Name], receive the cross on
>   your forehead.
> It is Christ himself who now
>   strengthens you
> with this sign of his love.
> Learn to know him and follow him.
> *Rite of Christian Initiation of Adults*

Christ Pantocrator
El Greco (1541–1614)

Then the sponsors may be invited to mark the five senses of each catechumen with the sign of the cross. This action symbolizes that all means of human perception and response are claimed as members of Christ's body:

- their ears, that they may be attentive to the word of God and the ways God "speaks" through those they meet;

- their eyes, that they may perceive as Christ perceives and see the "numinous" presence all round them;

- their lips, that they may learn to speak in the place of the risen Christ;

- their hearts, "that Christ may dwell there in faith";

- their shoulders, that they may "bear the gentle yoke of Christ";

- their hands and feet, that they may know Christ in their work and walk as he would.

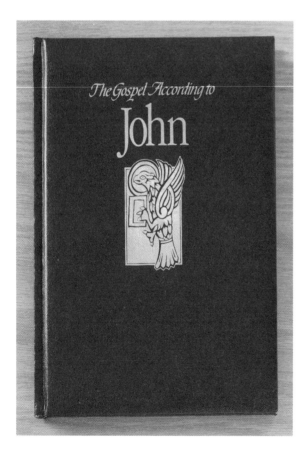

Then the celebrant makes the sign of the cross over all the catechumens, sealing their commitment of their entire selves to Christ, saying:

I sign you with the sign of eternal life in the name of the Father, and of the Son, and of the Holy Spirit.
Rite of Christian Initiation of Adults

The catechumens respond, "Amen."

Period of the Catechumenate

The second phase, or period, of the renewed initiation process is the time of formation, or the catechumenate. It may last several years (in the United States, at least a year), because the candidates or catechumens are involved in a great many other affairs. It is a time of reading, discussing, probing, relying on the support not only of the sponsor but of other candidates or catechumens and their sponsors and the whole parish team. It is also a time of a real commitment to active service: mission.

Conversion to faith in the Gospel requires a knowledge of what that Gospel is—intellectual acquaintance, to be sure. But it is much more than that. Converts need a growing awareness that this revelation about the meaning of human life is true. They also need an *internal* appreciation of what its truth means for themselves as individuals and for the church community into which they are being initiated. Further, in order to keep growing in the faith, converts must undergo a complete transformation of their perceptions and priorities. They must learn to see things as God sees them.

At the end of this second period comes the moment of choice that is solemnized in the Rite of Election, which is usually celebrated at Mass on the First Sunday of Lent. This rite is a very moving event, not only for the catechumens and candidates and their sponsors but for everyone in the parish taking part in it. The celebration of this rite serves as a reminder of their own baptism, and of the kind of changes in attitude and behavior that should be manifest in their own lives because of their baptism.

The celebrant addresses the sponsors, or godparents:

> Have they [the candidates] faithfully listened to God's word proclaimed by the Church?
>
> Have they responded to that word and begun to walk in God's presence?
>
> Have they shared the company of their Christian brothers and sisters and joined with them in prayer?
> *Rite of Christian Initiation of Adults*

After each question the sponsors affirm the candidates by responding, "They have."

The celebrant then addresses the assembly:

> Are you ready to support the testimony expressed about these catechumens and include them in your prayer and affection as we move toward Easter?
> *Rite of Christian Initiation of Adults*

All express their support, saying, "We are."

The candidates then inscribe their names in the Book of the Elect and the celebrant declares:

> I now declare you to be members of the elect, to be initiated into the sacred mysteries at the next Easter Vigil.
> *Rite of Christian Initiation of Adults*

The candidates respond, "Thanks be to God."

We must undergo a complete transformation of our perceptions and priorities. We must learn to see things as God sees them.

After the intercessions for the elect, they leave the assembly, since they are not yet fully members of the body of Christ. Some might find this odd, since any unbeliever off the street could come in and witness the rest of the liturgy without receiving communion. But most catechumens do not seem to mind this dismissal at all, since it makes their First Communion all the more meaningful.

Period of Purification and Enlightenment

In the liturgy and liturgical catechesis of Lent the reminder of baptism already received or the preparation for its reception, as well as the theme of repentance, renew the entire community along with those being prepared to celebrate the paschal mystery, in which each of the elect will share through the sacraments of initiation.

Rite of Christian Initiation of Adults

The next phase, or period, coincides with the season of Lent and the Easter Triduum. This period is a kind of extended spiritual retreat, culminating at the Easter Vigil. At that time the elect celebrate the three Sacraments of Initiation—Baptism, Confirmation, and Eucharist—in the same integrated rite and in much the manner of the initiation of adults into the early Church.

We ask you, Father, with your Son
to send the Holy Spirit upon the waters
    of this font.
May all who are buried with Christ
    in the death of baptism
rise also with him to newness of life.

Blessing of the Water

Every culture since the Cro-Magnons has rejoiced in the birth of a new child. That joy is celebrated over and over in folktales about the birth of a new princess or prince, in which fairy godmothers show up to bestow gifts on this precious child, gifts beyond the inestimable gift of birth, gifts to defend against evil. So at baptism we, the Church, offer the gifts of the Holy Spirit.

The baptism of infants is an *invitation* in which the church community takes on the obligation to the baptized to offer help, understanding, forgiveness whenever these are needed. The words "heir to the Kingdom of God" pick up the meaning perfectly, because an heir is someone who feels "at home," and has a right to feel at home. After the blessing of the baptismal water, the celebrant says:

> Dear parents and godparents: You have come here to present this child for baptism. By water and the Holy Spirit he (she) is to receive the gift of new life from God, who is love.
>
> On your part, you must make it your constant care to bring him (her) up in the practice of the faith. See that the divine life which God gives him (her) is kept safe from the poison of sin, to grow always stronger in his (her) heart.
>
> If your faith makes you ready to accept this responsibility, renew now the vows of your own baptism. Reject sin; profess your faith in Christ Jesus. This is the faith of the Church. This is the faith in which this child is about to be baptized.   *Rite of Baptism for Children*

Parents presenting their infant child for baptism make the responses, not answering for their child, but speaking of their own faith and their commitment to form the child in the faith:

■ They ask that the child be baptized;

■ they sign the child with a cross;

■ they renounce Satan and profess the faith;

■ they carry the child to the font;

■ they hold the lighted candle; and

■ they are blessed by the celebrant.

Even though the child has no way of understanding, experiencing, or choosing liberation, it is a profoundly important gift to the child's parents. And, in their eyes, it would be actually *unkind* of them to withhold it from their child. It has given them a sense of meaning and peace they hope their child will grow into.

The "freedom" of infants is not violated by the fact they are co-opted into the "company of the saints" without their reasoned consideration. In countless ways parents make choices for their children according to their own view of the purposes and needs of human life: citizenship, insurance, inoculations, nutrition, manners, schooling, and so on. In doing so parents hope to communicate the best they have been able to figure out about what life is for.

For the grace of Baptism to unfold, the parents' help is important. So too is the role of the godfather and godmother, who must be firm believers, able and ready to help the newly baptized—child or adult—on the road of Christian life. . . . The whole ecclesial community bears some responsibility for the development and safeguarding of the grace given at Baptism.

Catechism of the Catholic Church, 1255

Reflection

The words of the Rite of Baptism for Children are not addressed to the children about to be baptized but to the small cell of the church community gathered together to witness the Baptism. The question is, What happens to all of *us* taking part in the celebration of the sacrament when the sacrament—as all symbols do—attempts to remind us of what our own baptism means?

- *Do we remember that we are indeed surrounded by real evil—monstrous, inhuman, mean-spirited?*

- *Do we remember again that our deepest orientation is directly in the other direction from the prevailing force? That we have converted from its direction?*

- *Do we realize that we who have been baptized have been anointed priests-prophets-peers and are committed to rescue as many as we can from evil, no matter how petty?*

- *Do we realize that, no matter how we have submitted to evil ourselves, we belong to a community, the People of God, who is willing to welcome us "home" if we merely make the effort to come back?*

- *Finally, "can they see our freedom? Can they feel our joy?"*

Understanding Baptism

Review

1. What is the purpose of all the rites of initiation? How do they reorient the candidates?

2. Why were early Christian baptisms celebrated only at dawn on Easter?

3. Does one need to believe in a literal Satan in order to understand and value Baptism? Of what human tendency is "Satan" a rather adequate symbol? How is he/she/it captured in a similar way in *The Lord of the Flies?*

4. Name some of the events in Scripture that the waters of Baptism "recapture."

5. In the baptismal anointing with chrism, each of us is signed a messiah: priest, monarch, prophet. What are the duties of such offices?

6. Why is the baptism of adults now considered the norm by which we are to understand the Sacraments of Initiation? Describe the three phases of the adult rite: exploration, formation, and election.

7. What are the real reasons for baptizing infants fairly soon after they are born?

8. Explain the meaning of "original sin" and why the literalist "economic metaphor" is not sufficient to explain the undeniable human tendency to harm self and others. How is "blameworthy" as a *cause* different from "responsible" for the *effects?*

9. Explain: Original sin is the only doctrine one can prove from the daily newspapers.

10. Why are the words of the Rite of Baptism for Children addressed not to the infants but to those present? Explain: The words of the rites of infant baptism are at least as much for the parents, godparents, and other witnesses as for the child.

Discuss

1. What kinds of initiation rituals have the members of your group gone through—confirmation, scouts, graduation? What were you like before and after?

2. Most of us were not aware of our baptism. But now we ought to be at least a bit more aware of it. Does it make any real difference in the way you consider yourself? It's okay to answer that honestly. If not, can you say why not?

3. Our society today is almost as irreligious as pagan Rome. Almost. What are the concrete signs that *The Lord of the Flies* is still not completely triumphant?

4. Reflect on your being a priest, monarch, and prophet. Those are pretty majestic terms. But the Gospel did not mean them in worldly terms; Jesus, who was all three, washed his disciples' feet. How do you scale these terms down—concretely, specifically—to everyday life? How can you serve, as Jesus did, with dignity, even in small things?

5. The group you are taking this course with is a microcosm of the Church. "Where two or three come together in my name, I am there with them" (Matthew 18:20). You were all baptized to serve. How—concretely, specifically—do you actually serve one another? On the other hand, what are the obstacles to this group's being a genuine community? List them. Then come up with several ways you could change that.

Activities

1. Interview a candidate who is taking part in your parish R.C.I.A. process. Have that person share with you the symbolism of (a) removing all clothing, (b) anointing with ordinary olive oil, (c) the triple immersion, (d) the anointing with perfumed oil, (e) donning a white garment, and (f) receiving the candle. What was the bishop doing in the second anointing with perfumed oil?

2. The early Church grew quickly because there was a clear difference in the freedom and joy with which converts led their lives. Identify the people you know who "get more out of life" than you do. In what do you see the difference? What's stopping you from getting more out of life?

3. Role-play one of the following. (a) You are faced with a business decision to close a plant that is the central source of income for a town. (b) A family has a loan with your bank that they simply cannot pay now without tragic effects on their lives.

Scripture Readings

Skim the passages. Pick one that appeals to you and (1) summarize its main point, (2) tell how it relates to the chapter, and (3) list one or two thoughts that entered your mind as you read it.

- Exodus 17:3–7   Water from the rock
- Ezekiel 47:1–9, 12   The water of salvation
- John 3:1–6   The meeting with Nicodemus
- John 7:37–39   Streams of living water
- Matthew 28:18–20   Go, teach, and baptize
- Galatians 3:26–28   You have put on Christ
- Ephesians 4:1–6   One Lord, one faith, one baptism
- 1 Corinthians 12:12–13 Baptized in one spirit

Journal

Prayerfully read this reflection.

> The baptized have become "living stones" to be "built into a spiritual house, to be a holy priesthood." By Baptism they share in the priesthood of Christ, in his prophetic and royal mission. They are "a chosen race, a royal priesthood, a holy nation, God's own people, that [they] may declare the wonderful deeds of him who called [them] out of darkness into his marvelous light."
>
> *Catechism of the Catholic Church,* 1268

Write about what this reflection tells you about who you are in the eyes of God. How do you feel about who you are and are called to become?

Chapter 5
Confirmation: Life in the Spirit

*Everywhere on earth they [disciples of Christ] must bear witness
to Christ and give an answer to those who seek an account
of that hope of eternal life which is in them.*   (cf 1 Peter 3:15)

CONFIRMATION OF BAPTISM

Survey

This survey is not an exercise for a grade, but a means to stir up interest and get an idea of varying opinions in your group. Some of the questions are matters of objective fact; others are merely subjective opinions. Circle the number on the rating scale that best reflects your current opinion about that statement.

> +2 = strongly agree,
> +1 = agree,
> 0 = cannot make up my mind,
> –1 = disagree,
> –2 = strongly disagree.

Then share the reasons for your opinion.

1. If an object is a watch, it ought to keep accurate time.

   +2   +1   0   –1   –2

2. People who are human beings ought to act like human beings.

   +2   +1   0   –1   –2

3. People who are physically adult Catholics ought to be becoming apostles.

   +2   +1   0   –1   –2

4. Confirmation is a rite of passage from passivity to activity in the kingdom of God.

   +2   +1   0   –1   –2

5. Understanding the shift from childhood to adolescence is more dramatic for girls than for boys.

   +2   +1   0   –1   –2

6. Originally, Baptism, Confirmation, and First Communion were a single sacrament of initiation.

   +2   +1   0   –1   –2

7. Growing up happens automatically; becoming adult takes effort.

   +2   +1   0   –1   –2

8. Psychologists agree the natural purpose of adolescence is to take responsibility for one's self.

   +2   +1   0   –1   –2

9. Baptism is related to Easter; Confirmation is related to Pentecost.

   +2   +1   0   –1   –2

10. One is capable of assuming full adult responsibility for one's self at about age twelve.

    +2   +1   0   –1   –2

A Puzzlement

Catechetical training is intended to make [human] faith become living, conscious, and active, through the light of instruction.

Vatican II, *Decree on the Bishops' Pastoral Office in the Church*

■ *What do the words "living, conscious, and active" really mean in regard to Christian faith?*

■ *What do these words have to do with Confirmation?*

Rite of Conversion

Baptism is a rite of initiation from the strictly secular world into the kingdom of God. Confirmation is a rite of initiation from passivity to activity within that kingdom. It is our enrollment and conversion into God's service forever.

Physical birth is the beginning of a lifetime process that at least ought to take a recognizable "shape," character, toward the end of adolescence, though it is a process that should never end but deepen until the end of life. Similarly, Baptism is the beginning of a lifetime process of growing spirituality that at least *could* reach a preliminary shape in late adolescence such that it would need a ritual like Confirmation to celebrate it. But Confirmation is only a one-way station on a lifelong journey of enriching the spirit.

SIGNED AND SEALED

Until recently, modern adolescents still had more than the puberty change to mystify them into realizing that the "whole world had changed." The sacrament of Confirmation is at least an opportunity to change that.

In Baptism, the first anointing is with the oil of catechumens, smeared on the chest, the medicine of strengthening.

We anoint you with the oil of salvation
in the name of Christ our Savior;
may he strengthen you
with his power,
who lives and reigns for ever and ever.
Amen.   *Rite of Baptism for Children*

The second anointing, which takes place after immersion into the waters of Baptism, is with perfumed chrism, the oil of thanksgiving that identifies the newly baptized with Christ, the Anointed One.

He [God the Father] now anoints you with the chrism of salvation. As Christ was anointed Priest, Prophet, and King, so may you live always as a member of his body, sharing everlasting life.

Rite of Baptism for Children

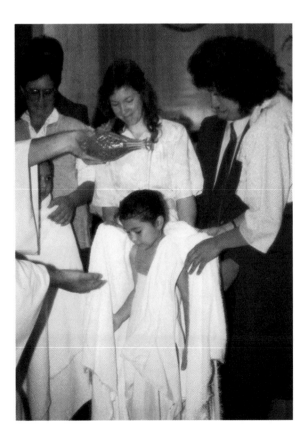

This chrism is the same blessed oil used in Confirmation. The celebrant traces the sign of the cross with chrism on the forehead and says,

> [Name], be sealed with the Gift of the Holy Spirit. *Rite of Confirmation*

As oil bonds the elements of bread, the prayers of Confirmation reflect the *bonding* of the baptized with Christ and his Mystical Body, and signify the gift of knowing not merely about Christ but knowing *Christ*. Confirmation is a sacrament both of inner growth and of external witness. Those confirmed are now "signed and sealed" with the sign of death and resurrection:

> By Confirmation Christians, that is, those who are anointed, share more completely in the mission of Jesus Christ and the fullness of the Holy Spirit with which he is filled, so that their lives may give off the "aroma of Christ" (2 Corinthians 2:15).

By this anointing the confirmand receives the "mark," the *seal* of the Holy Spirit.

A seal is a symbol of a person, a sign of personal authority, or ownership of an object. . . .

Christ himself declared that he was marked with his Father's seal. Christians are also marked with a seal: "It is God who establishes us with you in Christ and has commissioned us; he has put his seal on us and given us his Spirit in our hearts as a guarantee. This seal of the Holy Spirit marks our total belonging to Christ, our enrollment in his service for ever. *Catechism of the Catholic Church*, 1294–1296

MATURITY IN CHRIST

Originally, the name *confirmation* arose because the newly baptized had been led from paganism, through the flowing waters in a baptismal pool outside the church, into Christianity. They were then brought within the assembly where the bishop anointed them with chrism a second time and "confirmed" their baptism.

The baptism with its messianic anointing had been performed by priests and deacons out of the view of the assembly, since the candidates were naked; the bishop stayed with the assembly. The second anointing was a ritual in which the official Church through the bishop, ratified and accepted within the assembly the conversion of the faithful, the baptized people.

Now through an accident of history, we have the celebration of a "separated" sacrament that gives *baptized individuals* an opportunity to complete their full initiation into the Church—to ratify and accept the Church—which the Church in turn solemnizes and accepts. It is a celebration not only of "being confirmed" but also of "confirming." In Confirmation one willingly assumes an active participation in the Church's apostolate. The Church and individual are mutually confirming belief in one another.

For those baptized as infants, Confirmation can become a sacrament of Christian maturity, which is not the same as merely "growing up" physically or even in achieving human adulthood. Infants are "passive Christians."

Children receive First Communion when they are old enough to realize that "this food" is not ordinary but something special: Jesus. This realization comes with little "understanding" that their Baptism and this Eucharist associate them with the death-resurrection of Jesus, neither of which they in any way comprehend. Most are unaware death even exists.

But in adolescence young people at least *ought* to begin to be aware that they have souls and that the soul is the sum and substance of who *they* are. They at least ought to be aware of the bleakness and absurdity of a life without God, without the sinful or sacred, and thus the liberating function in human life of Jesus' defeat of death. Only then can Christianity have any felt meaning for them. Only then can they decide if they want to be Christian.

Confirmation affirms—both on the part of the Church and on the part of the individual confirmed—a level of maturity *in Christ,* a ratification of one's initiation into the Church. One is not to be merely passively baptized and attendant at Mass, but actively engaged in the apostolate.

The Descent of the Holy Spirit.
Titian (1477–1576).

Monika Hellwig, a contemporary theologian, summarizes it this way:

This goes back to a very old traditional theme which connects baptism with Easter and confirmation with Pentecost. At Easter the apostles experienced in a very vivid way the resurrection of Jesus from his terrible death. They knew then that Jesus had brought redemption into the world and that they had received that redemption, and they believed in him. It is only when we read the Pentecost story that we are told the other half of their response. In the power of the Spirit of God they then realize that they must organize themselves into a community of believers, the Church, so as to bring salvation to others.

Pentecost thus is the second foundation event to bring the Church into existence, and many call it "the birthday of the Church." Baptism is a reenactment, a recapturing, of Good Friday and Easter Sunday. Confirmation is a reenactment, a recapturing of Pentecost. Baptism is a resurrection gift; Confirmation is a Pentecost gift.

"From that time on [Pentecost] the apostles, in fulfillment of Christ's will, imparted to the newly baptized by the laying on of hands the gift of the Spirit that completes the grace of Baptism."

Catechism of the Catholic Church, 1288

Holy Spirit in Sacred Scripture

In Scripture, the presence of the Holy Spirit is always an occasion of the return of cosmos from chaos, freedom from slavery, rebirth from death.

FIRST COVENANT

The Holy Spirit appears at the very beginning of the Bible. In the first creation story the *breath* of God broods over the waters of chaos.

> *In the beginning, when God created the universe, the earth was formless and desolate. The raging ocean that covered everything was engulfed in total darkness, and the Spirit of God was moving over the water.*   Genesis 1:1–2

In the second creation story (Genesis 2:4–25), the writers make a special point concerning the creation of human beings as different from animals: God *breathes* the very *breath* of God into Adam.

> *Then God took some soil from the ground and formed a man out of it; he breathed life-giving breath into his nostrils and the man began to live.*
> From Genesis 2:7

In the story of the flood, God "caused a *wind* to blow, and the water started going down" (Genesis 8:1), and chaos once again yielded to cosmos. God speaks to Job from out of a whirl*wind*, giving Job the most difficult lesson of human life: God is not answerable to us.

> *Then out of the storm God spoke to Job. Who are you to question my wisdom?*
> From Job 38:1–2

God confronts the prophet Ezekiel with a valley of dry bones (like the people of Israel) and says:

> *"Mortal man, prophesy to the wind. Tell the wind that the Sovereign God commands it to come from every direction, to breathe into these dead bodies, and to bring them back to life."*
> From Ezekiel 37:9

NEW COVENANT

Luke's Gospel says that Jesus was conceived by the Spirit (the Breath) of God resting on Mary, his mother.

> *The angel answered, "The Holy Spirit will come on you, and God's power will rest upon you."*   Luke 1:35

Jordan River.

At Jesus' baptism by John in the Jordan, the soul of Jesus felt the Spirit come down and settle upon him "like a dove" (Luke 3:21). And then that same Spirit "hurled" Jesus into the desert to have the revelation of his Sonship tested by the Enemy (Luke 4:1–13). Empowered by that struggle, Jesus returned to the Nazareth synagogue and read from the words of Isaiah:

> *"The spirit of the Lord has been given to me, for he has anointed me."*
> Luke 4:18 *(The Jerusalem Bible)*

At the Last Supper (John 14–16), Jesus says to his disciples that he must die so that his Spirit, the breath of supernatural aliveness, may be born in them:

> *"I will ask the Father, and he will give you another Helper, who will stay with you forever. He is the Spirit, who reveals the truth about God.*   John 14:16–17

And that Spirit will teach them not only to remember all Jesus had said but finally to understand what he had done and taught them:

> *"The Helper, the Holy Spirit, whom the Father will send in my name, will teach you everything and make you remember all that I have told you."*   Luke 14:26

The Spirit will give them the courage to stand up and witness to him no matter how intimidating the audience:

> *"The Helper will come—the Spirit, who reveals the truth about God and who comes from the Father. I will send him to you from the Father, and he will speak about me. And you, too, will speak about me, because you have been with me from the very beginning."*   John 15:26–27

Jesus' death will be the climactic confrontation between God's offer of freedom and human clinging to self-absorption. If Jesus does not die, the spirit of prophecy will not take "possession" of them:

> *"It is better for you that I go away, because if I do not go, the Helper will not come to you. But if I do go away, then I will send him to you. And when he comes, he will prove to the people of the world that they are wrong about sin and about what is right and about God's judgment. The Spirit . . . will lead you into all the truth.*   John 16:7–8, 13

At his first appearance to the disciples, who were cowering in terror of reprisals in the upper room, the risen Jesus says:

"Peace be with you. As the Father sent me, so I send you." Then he breathed on them and said, "Receive the Holy Spirit."
John 20:21–22

In the Acts of the Apostles, it is clear that the life-giving Spirit of God is given to newcomers *through* Christ's new Body, the Church. At Pentecost, the Spirit took "possession" of them, with "a noise from the sky which sounded like a strong wind blowing" (Acts 2:2) and "what looked like tongues of fire which spread out and touched each person there" (Acts 2:3). Not just the apostles.

It was such a startling and transforming experience that Peter, who had lied three times about knowing Jesus on Good Friday morning, immediately went outside and started preaching! The eleven were so exhilarated that the crowd thought they were drunk, at nine in the morning! (Acts 2:15) Peter began quoting the prophet Joel:

" 'This is what I will do in the last days, God says: I will pour out my Spirit on everyone.' " Acts 2:17

And what follows (2:18–39) is about as good a summary of the gospel message as you are likely to find anywhere.

Reflection

This fullness of the Spirit was not to remain uniquely the Messiah's, but was to be communicated to *the whole messianic people.* *Catechism of the Catholic Church,* 1287.

■ *What does this saying tell you about yourself?*

■ *How do you give witness to that truth?*

TWO SEPARATE INITIATIONS?

Survey

This survey is not an exercise for a grade, but a means to stir up interest and get an idea of varying opinions in your group. Some of the statements are matters of objective fact; others are merely subjective opinions. On the rating scale under each statement circle the number that best reflects your current opinion about that statement.

+2 = strongly agree,
+1 = agree,
 0 = cannot make up my mind,
−1 = disagree,
−2 = strongly disagree.

Then share the reasons for your opinion.

1. The separation of Confirmation came about simply because there were too many Christians and too few bishops.

   +2 +1 0 −1 −2

2. Infant Baptism became most common because most adults in Europe were already baptized.

   +2 +1 0 −1 −2

3. In the new rite for the initiation of "adults" the celebration of Baptism and Confirmation are reunited once again—for adults.

   +2 +1 0 −1 −2

4. Human maturity automatically "clicks on" with the onset of physical puberty.

   +2 +1 0 −1 −2

5. I personally had a great deal of help understanding not only the physical but also the psychological changes puberty invites me to.

   +2 +1 0 −1 −2

6. Since the Holy Spirit is conferred in baptism, there is no real purpose to celebrate Confirmation.

   +2 +1 0 −1 −2

7. Children at age of twelve are psychologically capable of understanding what Confirmation involves.

   +2 +1 0 −1 −2

8. In our modern culture, living our Catholic faith is far more difficult than it was in all but a few times in history.

   +2 +1 0 −1 −2

9. You cannot make true converts of children.

   +2 +1 0 −1 −2

10. The Gospels are 180 degrees in the opposite direction from the present values our culture is trying to lead us.

    +2 +1 0 −1 −2

Separation of Baptism and Confirmation

The use of the *Rite of Christian Initiation of Adults* has caused Catholics in the United States to concern themselves with the question, At what age in the life of a baptized Christian is the sacrament of Confirmation best celebrated? Many responses to that question are offered. Some emphasize the psychological, emotional, spiritual development of the baptized person. Others emphasize the theology of initiation into the church community. Seeking a balance that harmonizes the two emphases is not easy.

In the United States today, there is a diversity of practices as to when a baptized person is to be called to be confirmed. But, perhaps, the sacrament is mostly celebrated by youth in their junior high through high schools years. But whenever the baptized celebrate their Confirmation, it is always done within the context of the relationship of the three Sacraments of Initiation:

Baptism incorporates us into Christ and forms us into God's people. This first sacrament pardons all our sins, rescues us from the power of darkness, and brings us to the dignity of adopted children, a new creation through water and the Holy Spirit. Hence we are called and are indeed the children of God.

By signing us with the gift of the Spirit, confirmation makes us more completely the image of the Lord and fills us with the Holy Spirit, so that we may bear witness to him before all the world and work to bring the Body of Christ to its fullness as soon as possible.

Finally, coming to the table of the eucharist, we eat the flesh and drink the blood of the Son of Man so that we may

have eternal life and show forth the unity of God's people. By offering ourselves with Christ, we share in the universal sacrifice, that is, the entire community of the redeemed offered to God by their High Priest, and we pray for a greater outpouring of the Holy Spirit, so that the whole human race may be brought into the unity of God's family.

Christian Initiation,
General Introduction

CONFIRMATION IN THE EARLY CHURCH

Establishing the actual practice of celebrating Baptism and Eucharist in the earliest Church is simple. But clearly establishing the underpinnings of the actual practice of Confirmation as a *separate* sacrament in the earliest days of the Church is not as simple.

There is a suggestion of Confirmation when Paul met with some who had been baptized by John the Baptist (Acts 19:1–6). Paul tells them:

> *"The baptism of John was for those who turned from their sins; and [John] told the people of Israel to believe in the one who was coming after him—that is, in Jesus."*
> *Paul placed his hands on them, and the Holy Spirit came on them.*   Acts 19:4, 6

In Acts we can read about a time when the apostles Peter and John "complete" the baptism of some Samaritans who were earlier converted and baptized "only in the name of Jesus":

> *The apostles in Jerusalem heard that the people of Samaria had received the word of God, so they sent Peter and John to them. When they arrived, they prayed for the believers that they might receive the Holy Spirit. For the Holy Spirit had not yet come down on any of them; they had only been baptized in the name of the Lord Jesus. Then Peter and John placed their hands on them, and they received the Holy Spirit.*   Acts 8:14–17

Other than these New Testament references, there is little more.

CONFIRMATION IN THE THIRD TO FIFTH CENTURIES

The reason why the celebration of Baptism and Confirmation became separated—quite widely separated in time—is easy to identify. The determining factor was the different roles that priests and bishops played in the complex rites of initiating catechumens into the church community.

The final rite of the "laying on of hands and anointing," which the Church has named confirmation, was "reserved" to the bishop. Thus Pope Innocent I (A.D. 401–417) distinguished the rite of "consignation" (confirmation anointing) from baptism and the baptismal anointing.

During the fourth century, after the conversion of Constantine in A.D. 313, there was a significant increase in the Christian population, a population that was spread all over the countryside.

It became more and more impossible to keep the sacramental celebration of initiation—Baptism, Confirmation, First Eucharist—intact at the vigil of the Easter Mass, with the bishop present to greet the newly baptized and confirm their baptism. Priests continued to baptize adults as well as those in danger of death, wishing to enter the Church.

Later infants born to Christian families also came to be baptized as soon as possible after their birth. But since only a bishop could confirm, those baptized were expected to have the bishop officially confirm the baptism as soon as possible by a separate laying on of hands and anointing with chrism. So the newly baptized either had to join a pilgrimage to the bishop's or central church or wait for one the bishop's infrequent visits to their church.

CONFIRMATION IN OUR DAY

At the moment, many years separate the celebration of Baptism and Confirmation for those baptized as infants. This conforms to the recent decision made by the the Catholic bishops of the United States that Confirmation may be celebrated between the age of discretion (usually seven) and the age of eighteen. This decision reflects the general law, or Canon Law, of the universal Church.

But this decision has not ended the discussion of identifying the most appropriate age for celebrating Confirmation. Each bishop is free to guide the people of his diocese in developing a pastoral plan that will meet the needs of the nonconfirmed baptized faithful. The celebration of Confirmation during the high school years (which conforms to the bishops decision) is a splendid opportunity for young people to experience a personal *conversion*.

How can we help high school youth enter into the "conversion" that this sacrament celebrates? How can we help them celebrate the "confirmation" of their baptism?

Reflection

Saint Thomas Aquinas wrote that what differentiated Confirmation from Baptism was that, while Baptism empowered one to receive the other sacraments, Confirmation provided a power to profess one's faith in words.

For many Catholics, even those who no longer practice their faith, the celebration of Confirmation was a memorable occasion (perhaps more for the dress-up and the fuss and the presents, the chance to see a bishop close up).

■ *If you have already celebrated your Confirmation, how much of an internal impact did it make on you at the time? Try to remember. Were you old enough that it made you feel more "grown-up," more responsible, a different kind of member of the Church?*

■ *If you have not celebrated your Confirmation, are you looking forward to your Confirmation or haven't you given it much thought? Why?*

We receive the Eucharist over and over again to keep the Spirit in us alive. But Baptism and Confirmation we receive once-for-all.

■ *How do those two dramatic events influence the life of your soul?*

■ *How do they keep your faith "living, conscious, and active"?*

RITE OF CONFIRMATION

[The baptized] continue on the path of Christian initiation through the sacrament of confirmation. In this sacrament they receive the Holy Spirit, who was sent upon the apostles by the Lord on Pentecost.

Confirmation is a festive and solemn liturgical celebration. The whole People of God, represented by family and friends of the candidates and by the members of the local community have an active part to play in this celebration in which all express their faith in the Holy Spirit.

INTRODUCTORY RITES OF THE MASS

LITURGY OF THE WORD OF THE MASS

CELEBRATION OF THE SACRAMENT

Presentation of the Candidates

Homily or Instruction

You have already been baptized into Christ and now you will receive the power of the Spirit and the sign of the cross on your forehead. You must be witnesses before all the world to his suffering, death, and resurrection; your way of life should at all times reflect the goodness of Christ. Christ gives varied gifts to his Church, and the Spirit distributes them among the members of Christ's body to build up the holy people of God in unity and love.

Renewal of Baptismal Promises

The Laying On of Hands

All-powerful God,
    Father of our Lord Jesus Christ,
by water and the Holy Spirit
you freed your sons and daughters from sin
and gave them new life.
Send your Holy Spirit upon them
to be their Helper and Guide.
Give them the spirit of wisdom and understanding,
the spirit of right judgment and courage,
the spirit of knowledge and reverence.
Fill them with the spirit of wonder and awe
    in your presence.

The Anointing with Chrism

The bishop dips his right thumb in the chrism and makes the sign of the cross on the forehead of the one to be confirmed, as he says:

[Name], be sealed with the Gift of the Holy Spirit.

General Intercessions

LITURGY OF THE EUCHARIST

After the general intercessions, the liturgy of the eucharist is celebrated according to the Order of Mass.

The Mass may conclude with this prayer over the people:

God our Father,
complete the work you have begun
and keep the gifts of your Holy Spirit
active in the hearts of your people.
Make them ready to live his Gospel
and eager to do his will.
May they never be ashamed
to proclaim to all the world Christ crucified
living and reigning for ever and ever.
Amen.

The bishop adds immediately:

And may the blessing of almighty God
the Father, and the Son, † and the Holy Spirit
come upon you and remain with you for ever.
Amen.

A RITE OF CONVERSION AT PUBERTY

How Baptism and Confirmation came to be separated is not the key issue. They are two sacraments, each celebrated by the church community with unique rites. For all our discussion on the nature and meaning of Confirmation and its most "fitting" place in the scheme of Christian initiation, we can allow the whole complex of problems involved in puberty to help us understand the *human* element that dramatic physical and psychological change could add to Confirmation.

Grace Builds on Nature

Puberty is a rite of passage that all adolescents experience and over which they have no physical control. But the whole purpose of adolescence in human development is to grow psychologically as well as physically (and spiritually) into personally apprehended and accepted *selves.*

Human maturity does not simply "kick on." The journey into human maturity is rather a gradual *process,* as slow and gradual as the process of an infant's learning muscle control. During puberty, everything is *changed.* For young people, it is a whole different world—or at least it is enormously different from what they thought it would be: How do I deal with it? Where is a compass to guide me through it?

Psychologists Carl Jung and Erik Erikson could offer us a great deal of insight in relating the issues of puberty—a universal life experience—to Confirmation.

Puberty is not merely a sexual or even a physical change. This former "child" now has:

- to begin taking on a newer, more demanding role,
- to prepare to enter a far larger community than the family or school,
- to begin making a living,
- to prepare for intimacy and partnership,
- to prepare for parenthood.

Puberty is a time when our bodies tell us we have been newly empowered in a very intimidating but fascinating way. That very physical change is one more *invitation* to adult responsibility.

Such a process could begin at the outset of puberty in a completely natural (not supernatural) way. It could be a time in which fully initiated men and women (much like sponsors do during the RCIA) could meet separately with the youth and encourage them to simply "let their hair down" about all the issues of adolescence: its problems, its challenges, its enrichment. Such an open ministry, act of service, would help young people drop the self-protective barriers of brashness or shyness, and to feel "at home," not only with their new selves but with the Church as "Mother."

Moreover, such a ministry would let young people "know" that the Church "understands" and would form a basis for a later probing of adulthood in the Church. It would give youth an *experience* of a real identification with a serving community if Confirmation and commitment to that community are to make any sense.

Grace builds on nature. You have to plow before you plant.

The Church would make itself more appealing and meaningful as a life-giving community *to the young person*. It would deal with the felt human problems everyone faces during adolescence (much as the RCIA deals with the life experiences of adult candidates and catechumens). It would integrate these "real" human problems into the young people's "spiritual puberty," before dealing with the transcendent: inadequacy, the meaninglessness of the lessons day after day, the fear of others' judgments, jealousy, sexuality, commitment. It would deal with the question young people so often ask, Why is fulfillment always in the *future*?

We would help our adolescents understand their parents and other adults as equally fragile, equally limited, equally needful of enlightenment. That would be a first step toward an apostolate. If young people cannot be vulnerable even to people whom they claim to love, little chance they will care for strangers. If they feel that the Church is a place that holds wisdom, savvy, a genial peace with the way ordinary human life is, their desire to live the Gospel might be nourished. And we might purchase "credibility" for the Gospel.

Although Confirmation is sometimes called the "sacrament of Christian maturity," we must not confuse adult faith with the adult age of natural growth.

Catechism of the Catholic Church, 1308

Conversion in a Secularized Society

What was once a single integrated process for adults desiring to be fully initiated into the Church is now celebrated by most young people as three sacramental moments widely separated in one's lifetime. This separation has now been removed for adult catechumens and candidates by the *Rite of Christian Initiation of Adults*.

This reintegration of Baptism-Confirmation-Eucharist can help our high school confirmation candidates focus on the conversion they too are celebrating. Unfortunately, many young people who have been baptized as infants have never had a true conversion experience. These same young people who are living in our almost totally secularized culture are also dramatically less able than youth brought up in a culture suffused with religion to recognize and respond to such a conversion.

Beyond faith in God, the Gospel demands a complete reversal, a turning around, of the "values" that young people today have been led to believe are simply givens and beyond question. If religious education focuses on conversion—rather than merely ingesting data and passing tests, its first and greatest task is to try to *de-paganize* our youth. Till then, the Gospel, the Church, and every one of the sacraments have no chance whatever to take root in their lives.

It is far easier to be Christian when the entire society around you is at least nominally Christian, professes the same values, worships fairly frequently and in a similar manner.

In the past history of Western Christianity, there were interpersonal and interfaith raw points, but all Western lives were governed, for the most part, by the same values.

Things were not as serene as a Norman Rockwell painting, but in general all adhered to a common, altruistic ethos— uprightness, honesty, thrift, fairness, neighborliness. In the last half century, however, that ethos has gone topsy-turvy.

If youngsters from that past era could somehow be transported to today, they would be flabbergasted, and not just at the new-fangled gadgets but at the complete overturning of values that even they respected.

But today's media in every way— programs to commercials to MTV—have transformed greed and lust from objection-able vices to admirable virtues. The basic goal of life is not substance but appearance. "Success" no longer means living a life to be proud of but getting as much as one can as soon as one can: money, fame, sex, and power. Even the Bowery Boys and the Dead-End Kids would be shocked. So-called "values" and behavior even they would have shunned, we now take as not only acceptable but common-place.

To ask for "confirmation" of one's Baptism takes a great deal of conversion, since the Gospel that Baptism testifies to is a 180-degree turnabout from the values that permeate our society and saturate young people's personal value systems. Youth undergoing such a conversion have to learn to perceive, think, and evaluate in a way radically different from that to which they have become accustomed.

While the central symbols of the baptismal rite—water, oil, and touching— are symbols found in other religions, they are also culturally conditioned by a 2000-year Christian tradition. Today, even as *natural* symbols they are foreign to many young people. Often their only contact with water is in pipes and pools; their only experience of oil is for salads and suntans; and touching is an intrusion.

The Connection between Initiation and Conversion

Why not wait for Confirmation—just as for the three sacraments celebrated by adults at the end of RCIA—until the individual youth *wants* to be confirmed because he or she has in fact experienced a conversion? Why not find ways to induce that conversion?

Why not? Such a practice builds on nature—grace builds on nature—and would take advantage of a golden opportunity to evoke "conversion" at a more suitable age. Young people who have not celebrated "Confirmation" are still baptized and can still live an exemplary life. But if Confirmation followed a genuine personal conversion, we would have more lifelong active apostles.

The 1983 Code of Canon Law states: "The sacrament of confirmation is to be conferred on the faithful at about the age of discretion unless the conference of bishops determines another age" (891). The National Council of Catholic Bishops, as we have seen, has determined that the age range for celebrating Confirmation in the United States to be seven through eighteen.

Some catechists and liturgists would insist that waiting until eighteen causes the loss of Confirmation's "initiation character." For whom? Surely not for "born Catholics" who have no felt awareness of death and therefore not of resurrection, and therefore no ability to understand what being initiated by baptism "into Christ's death and resurrection" involves. One is tempted to believe most lifelong Catholics have little understanding of that massive truth:

- partly because Confirmation could have received far more intense preparation,

- partly because that preparation carefully avoided any connection with puberty and therefore a totally different role in the church community,

- and most importantly because that preparation had far more to do with ingestion and testing of theological data and far less to do with conversion of heart and a complete turnabout of priorities.

What about Confirmation's significance to the *recipient?* No candidate for Confirmation ever expressed a feeling that Confirmation somehow "lessened" the meaning of Baptism and first Eucharist. Rather, for many, it was the first time in their lives they ever really questioned what Baptism and first Eucharist had meant in the first place!

If a parish begins with adults helping young people reflect together on the problems and joys of their adolescence, their puberty, there would already be a basis for the young people's trust that the Church was "home," a place to find some meaning for the fragments of their lives. The confirmation candidate's baptismal godparents could be the young person's guide and sponsor through the process of preparation for Confirmation, and in the process could revivify their own faith, deepen their own conversion.

The process of preparation for Confirmation could mirror the stages and intervening rites of the RCIA:

■ **Inquiry and Evangelization:** The first would be a stage of inquiry during which the young people and their sponsors sit and talk, one-on-one, about the fact that the young people just might be missing out on a very important dimension of human life: the transcendent.

They could mull over together the readings for each Sunday's Mass, puzzling over how these insights could enrich the life of young people today, living in a secularized culture. Then, as with the RCIA, sponsors and candidates would come forward during Mass for a Rite of Acceptance, in which the sponsors testify to the candidates' worthiness and write their names in the registry of those accepted for more intense preparation.

■ **Catechumenate:** The second stage would parallel the catechumenate, a time of formation with other candidates and sponsors and the parish team. This would involve reading, discussing, probing together the heart (not just the mind) of the Gospel, and including a period of active service.

On Trinity Sunday, as with the rite for adult candidates on the First Sunday of Lent, those requesting Confirmation and their sponsors could take part in a celebration in a rite of election or enrollment of names and the celebrant welcome them to the group to be confirmed on Pentecost.

■ **Purification and Enlightenment:** They would be helped to understand that the seven gifts of the Holy Spirit given in Confirmation—wisdom, understanding, counsel, fortitude, knowledge, piety, and awe (fear) of God—are not gifts in the worldly sense. Rather, like all gifts of love, undeserved, they are invitations to activate those powers in one's life.

The final weekend, paralleling the Easter Triduum, there could be a three-day retreat for candidates and sponsors, concluding with the celebration of Confirmation during Mass. As the initiation of adults takes place at the Easter Vigil, let Confirmation take place on Pentecost. This could take place even without a bishop, since priests can now be delegated to confirm. Moreover, it is the Church that ratifies this choice, and the Church is in the pews, and let the assembly witness their approval with applause. And at the celebration of the sacrament itself, let the music be the candidates' music, perhaps written by themselves during the formation period.

■ **Mystagogy:** As with the initiation of adults, there should be a postconfirmation catechesis. The celebration of Confirmation ought to reflect the conversion that it celebrates. Like adults who have been initiated, the newly confirmed need a growing and deepening awareness that the gospel revelation about the dimensions of human life is *true* and *internalized*.

In the confirmation of their Baptism, the newly confirmed, who have been fully initiated into the Church, ought to experience a genuine sense of belonging. They ought to *feel* freer. (Can I see your freedom? Can I feel your joy?) The sacraments are surely not magic, but they ought to *feel* magical! And the whole church community should realize throughout the whole process, what has happened is not just the preparing of candidates to *be* confirmed but fulfilling its own responsibility to *"confirm."*

Such a process would change the whole emphasis of catechesis from merely imparting information, usually forgotten before the last test is finished, to genuine evangelization, conversion, and initiation into the mystery of Jesus Christ. Confirmation would truly celebrate the Spirit's invitation to personal conversion, a journey between extremes, darkness and light, slavery and freedom, falsehood and truth, death and life.

To be genuine, Confirmation cannot be a treadmill onto which one is "expected" to climb at a certain age because all of the other youth of the same age are "doing it." Celebrating one's Confirmation is a response to the invitation, the call, of the Spirit. This has to be a reasoned, free choice. In adolescence young people can be invited to the world of fuller responsibilities and commitments. But they cannot become "adult" unless they are truly free to make their own commitments, free to enter the journey of conversion. Love is not love unless it is freely given.

Reflection

Imagine that friends of yours have just had a new baby and have asked you to be the child's godparent.

■ *After reading the chapter, what goes through your mind before you respond to that invitation?*

Understanding Confirmation

Review

1. In Baptism, one is incorporated (embodied) in the Church and ordained an apostle, guaranteed the power of the Holy Spirit when one asks for it. What does Confirmation "add" to Baptism? It might help first to answer the question, What did Pentecost "add" to the disciples' experience of Easter? Which was the greater and more definitive conversion?

2. The ancient languages used the same word for "spirit" (soul) and for "breath" (wind). Recall the scriptural passages used in the text in which breath or wind is a symbol of empowering.

3. The two visible symbols used in the sacrament of Confirmation are anointing with perfumed oil (chrism) and laying on of hands. What does oil do to the ingredients of bread? How is that symbol appropriate for a sacrament in which the Church commits itself to the individual and the individual commits himself or herself to the Church?

4. Touch is important to the life of the soul: the mother caressing a child who wakes from a nightmare, a pat on the back, holding a weeping friend, shaking hands. What does the symbol of the bishop leaving the business of the diocese aside awhile to lay his hands on each separate candidate for Confirmation "say" about what Confirmation does?

5. What are the practical reasons Confirmation became a sacrament separate from baptism?

6. What are some of the arguments for conferring Confirmation as close as possible to Baptism? What are some of the arguments for delaying it until the individual is capable of making a reasoned personal commitment?

Discuss

1. Nearly every school nowadays has a service project, some completely voluntary, some as a requirement for graduation. More than a few students are reluctant to participate, partly out of fear, partly out of inertia, but quite often also out of a feeling that one person is not going to make that much difference. Those who have taken part in a service project, pool your experiences. Many say, "I went there to do something for them, but I found that they did as much for me." What effect does unselfish service have on the human soul?

2. Have any members of the group been on Outward Bound or some other wilderness experience? What was it like? What effect did it have on the soul? Anyone been on a retreat? What effect did it have on the soul? If there were a wilderness experience in which men tried to help boys understand about being an adult male and women helped girls understand about being an adult female, would you be interested in going along? Why or why not?

3. Most of the readers of this book will have already received Confirmation. Personally, are you satisfied that you celebrated Confirmation at the age you did? Or would you personally rather have waited? Explain.

4. The word *pagan* identifies a person who either worships many gods or who is irreligious altogether (no connection to God) and hedonistic (devoted to pleasure as a way of life). In what ways is our culture pagan? In what ways do you find people your own age pagan—even though they might not assent to the word.

Activities

1. The coming-of-age rituals of primitive societies were (and are) terrifyingly dramatic. Like an early-Church catechumen's experience of baptism, children of those cultures know—undeniably—that they now have a quite different relationship to the community than before. Research the "coming of age" ritual of one primitive society. In small groups brainstorm what important truths about adolescence—and about life—a young person's soul would miss without such a definitive experience.

2. Puberty is not instant adulthood. Rather it is only the very beginning of a long process which—again—is an invitation that can be refused or ignored. List the ways eighteen-year-olds are different from twelve-year-olds. Then list the ways eighteen-year-olds might give witness to the fact that they have been confirmed. Then list the ways twelve-year-olds, who have been confirmed, might give witness. What are the real differences?

3. It was difficult—even deadly—being a young Christian in pagan Rome, during the French Revolution, and other times of persecution. But now the Church is not being persecuted by our culture. Interview people who are in their 50s, 40s, 30s, and 20s. Have each describe what are the three things that make it difficult for them to witness to their Catholic faith. Report your findings to your group. Then as a group identify the difficulties that you and the interviewees have in common.

4. Work together in small groups to identify an issue in your community that challenges you to give witness to your faith. Then plan a group response and implement it. List the ways your giving witness to your commitment to Christ can make a difference.

Scripture Readings

Skim the passages. Pick one that appeals to you and (1) summarize its main point, (2) tell how it relates to the chapter, and (3) list one or two thoughts that entered your mind as you read it.

• Isaiah 42:1–3	I have endowed my servant with my Spirit
• Ezekiel 36:24–28	I will place a new Spirit in your midst
• Matthew 25:14–30	Come to the joy of your master
• Luke 8:4–15	Some seed fell into rich soil
• John 14:15–17	The Spirit of truth will be with you
• Acts 1:3–8	You will receive the Spirit
• Romans 8:14–17	You will receive the Spirit
• Galatians 5:16–17, 22–25	Let us be directed by the Spirit

✎ Journal

Through the sacrament of Confirmation you become fully initiated "into Christ's death and resurrection." What does such an "initiation" invite you to do? How *can* you respond daily to the invitation? How *do* you respond?

Chapter 6

Eucharist:
The Central Sacrament

*"Think of it, Wat! God, in a bit of bread, come to bring
morning into the darkness of our bellies! Hosannah!"*
H. F. M. Prescott, *The Man on a Donkey*

DEATHS AND REBIRTHS

Survey

This survey is not an exercise for a grade, but a means to stir up interest and get an idea of varying opinions in your group. Some of the statements are matters of objective fact; others are merely subjective opinions. On the rating scale under each statement circle the number that best reflects your current opinion about that statement.

> +2 = strongly agree,
> +1 = agree,
> 0 = cannot make up my mind,
> −1 = disagree,
> −2 = strongly disagree.

Then share the reasons for your opinion.

1. A God who could bring a universe out of nothing, feeling out of inanimate matter, rational thought out of apes would find no problem in changing bread and wine into the Body and Blood of Christ.

   +2   +1   0   −1   −2

2. We undervalue food and water simply because we have so much of them.

   +2   +1   0   −1   −2

3. The laity have no right to tell priests that the Mass as celebrated does little to feed their souls.

   +2   +1   0   −1   −2

4. The solitary Christian is a contradiction.

   +2   +1   0   −1   −2

5. Life is designed purposely as an evolution through a series of deaths and rebirths.

   +2   +1   0   −1   −2

6. According to statistics, one third of the people in this room will not reach age seventy.

   +2   +1   0   −1   −2

7. The only thing you can take through the doorway of death is what you have made of your soul.

   +2   +1   0   −1   −2

8. What makes a meal different from mere feeding time is conversation, the sharing of probing ideas.

   +2   +1   0   −1   −2

9. At the Last Supper, the main focus of Jesus' long speech was Judas's betrayal.

   +2   +1   0   −1   −2

10. If the media had their way, we would all be self-absorbed adolescents all our lives.

    +2   +1   0   −1   −2

A Puzzlement

On the night he was betrayed, Jesus took bread, gave thanks to God, and gave it to his friends, saying, "Take and eat it. This is my body."

Then he took a cup, gave thanks to God, and gave it to his friends. "Drink it, all of you; this is my blood, which seals God's covenant, my blood poured out for many for the forgiveness of sins" (from Matthew 26:26–28).

Reflection

Think of a time when you felt, "I'm absolutely famished! I could eat a horse!" Those times in your life have probably been relatively rare. But there have been (and are) times in human history when many people were (and are) that hungry.

- *Why is it that you have never been that hungry?*

- *What effect has that lack of hunger had on your ability to value the Eucharist?*

- *A wise man once said, "Too much is as least as dehumanizing as too little." What does that mean?*

Think about bread. It is so commonplace that we hardly ever think of it. We pick a loaf off the shelf, toss it into the cart, carry it home, store it, and go for it when we're ready. But trace the history of that loaf of bread back, even before planting the seed: harrowing the ground, clearing the rocks, breaking the clods of earth.

- *Trace the "history" of the last piece of bread you ate back to its very beginning. How many people did how many things before the bread got to your table?*

- *"Through your goodness we have this bread to offer, which earth has given and human hands have made." Do those words mean anything different to you after that reflection than they did before? If not, why not?*

Think about wine. Like wheat-to-bread, grape-to-wine is a process, even longer than wheat-to-bread. The seed takes far longer to grow; the roots dig down; the vines slowly begin to spread out along the wires, sucking water from the earth and life from the sun. Pruning, weeding, waiting. And waiting.

The wine is the blood of the grapes. The grapes must be crushed—that is, die. The blood on the doorposts of Egypt was the beginning of the Hebrews' freedom. And the blood sprinkled on them in the desert was the sign of their covenant with Yahweh, God. And Jesus uses wine as the embodiment of his own blood to mark our freedom and our new covenant with God.

- *Does any of this discussion have any felt meaning for you? Why or why not?*

- *Is it possible that, without your knowing it till now, you have been missing out on a great deal that is important about the possibilities of human life?*

Taking Part in Mass

The very first question to face about taking part in Mass is the very bold one: Why bother? Whatever books explain about the celebration of Eucharist, its celebration is always embedded concretely in a ceremony that is, quite frankly, too often experienced as deadly dull. "Why should I go if I get nothing out of it?" "Why can't I just pray out in the woods?"

Very reasonable questions! A response to the second question, however, might be: "When was the last time you actually did go out and pray in the woods? Praying out in the woods during the week is a terrific idea, and if you did it, taking part in the celebration of the Mass would be less boring—guaranteed."

The truth of the matter is that the meaningfulness of our taking part in the celebration of Mass is in direct proportion to our personal commitment to Christ. If our commitment to Christ is halfhearted, taking part in Mass will surely be halfhearted. Any relationship—a friendship, a job, a marriage—gives back only what we put into it. If we "allow" God to exist only when we are sick or are facing a test for which we have not studied or are working at a job that is in jeopardy, taking part in the celebration of Mass will be no more than dropping into a dreary soup kitchen where you occasionally go for a handout.

A pivotal question about the Eucharist is whether in the one go-round you have with life you are missing out on something—something very important—without taking part in it.

LIFE-DEATH-REBIRTH

If you have the time and inclination to stand back and look at your life, you will come to realize that life is—over and over—a series of invitations to "deaths" and better "rebirths."

Birth itself is, paradoxically, a "little death." For nine months, we float serenely in the womb. We are warm, fed, without a worry in the world. Then suddenly, through no fault of our own, we are forcibly ejected out into the cold and noise. By that very fact of being born, we are ultimately condemned eventually to die.

Weaning and potty training are "little deaths" for us when we are infants and toddlers. They are moments we begin to lose that carefree life where everything is done for us—but without that loss we would never possess any independence. In the play years our parents send us out to play with the other children—but without that loss of always being in their presence we would never learn to solve our own disputes.

Preschool and kindergarten are sometimes a heartbreaking loss. We feel stranded among strangers. But without that "little death" we would never begin to learn the skills to cope with life on our own. In adolescence, the child "dies" so that the adult can emerge like a butterfly from a cocoon. Marriage is a death to self, to "unlimited" freedom, but it is also a sacrifice one is willing to make for the joy of never again being alone.

Parenthood is just such a sacrifice: "death" and "rebirth" as a person far richer than before. A couple could live their lives serenely together. Instead they commit themselves to other lives, to twenty-plus years of apprehension, unpayable bills, broken arms, outgrown clothes, mediocre grades—but also the joy, the pride, the sense of having contributed life to life. Old age comes as a "little death" too, but it is the opportunity to savor, to sit back and see life as a coherent story, to find wisdom.

Death and rebirth, you see, are the law of human life.

CONVERGENCE AND CONVERSION

The entire Old Testament is also the testimony that the will of God is death and rebirth, over and over. When the episode in the Garden of Eden had failed, Yahweh gave the first humans a second chance. In the story of the Flood, Yahweh invited Noah and his family to start over. Yahweh called Abraham and Sarah from Ur of the Chaldees to head south and start yet again.

When the Hebrews were languishing in slavery in Egypt, Yahweh sent Moses to challenge the Pharaoh and lead the people through the desert to Canaan to begin again. When the people had been led off again in slavery to Babylon, Yahweh finally led them back to Jerusalem to start over.

In the Incarnation, the Son of God, Jesus, went through stages of "death" and "rebirth." In fact, his first "death" was the Incarnation itself, surrendering the privileges of divinity in order to learn as we do, step by step, with no assurances. Although Jesus never shared the agonies and joys of parenthood, he did have twelve rather taxing "sons." And he surely knew the death that awaits us all.

Saint Augustine says that he believed Jesus went to his death as eagerly as a bridegroom goes to his bride, because he trusted what lay beyond. In the twelfth century, Peter Abelard (1079–1142) wrote that Jesus did not die as a ransom for sinful humanity or as a penalty to "buy off" a vengeful God. Rather, the atonement achieved by Jesus was an at-one-ment, a fusion of all humankind with God.

For centuries humanity had been yearning for God and God had been yearning for humanity. At last the two intersected in Jesus on the cross. Convergence and conversion. That is what the Eucharist celebrates. The Gospel proclaimed by Jesus is not about death; it is about life, rebirth.

"I have come in order that you might have life—life in all its fullness." John 10:10

But the only way to new life is through surrender of the old life. Conversion is such a surrender. It is not just a coat you put on to go to church. Conversion means to lose the old self, as Jesus did both at the Incarnation and at the Crucifixion.

"I am telling you the truth: a grain of wheat remains no more than a single grain unless it is dropped into the ground and dies."   John 12:24

Like all the changes life inflicts on us, the call to conversion is one more invitation we can refuse, the invitation to more abundant life, to life in all its fullness.

We write to you

about the Word of life,

which has existed from

the very beginning.

We have heard it,

and we have seen it

with our eyes;

yes, we have seen it,

and our hands

have touched it. . . .

What we have seen and

heard we announce

to you also,

so that you will join

with us in the fellowship

that we have

with the Father

and with his Son

Jesus Christ.

·We write this in order that

our joy may be complete.

1 John 1:1, 3–4

Reflection

Focus on the reality that the Eucharist celebrates: death and rebirth.

■ *Does that pattern—death and rebirth—seem to make more sense out of life than just enduring it: this, and then that, and then the other and then dying?*

Perhaps there is need for a prior meditation on death itself. Unless death is real to you, the entire meaning of the Gospel and the Eucharist will remain empty. It might seem morbid to "wrap your mind around" your own inevitable death, but actually embracing death is quite liberating.

■ *What—and more importantly whom—would you miss?*

"Owning" your death—and the death of people close to you—makes all those people more precious, doesn't it? It is more difficult after that to take them for granted.

■ *What are the grudges that seem so important to you?*

■ *Are they worth keeping, or would you be more free if you made peace?*

What can you take with you through the doorway of death? Surely none of the realities the media have been selling to you as important since your diaper days. Surely not the bodies so many work on so diligently. Only your self. Your soul. The invisible you no one sees—and we can only guess about.

■ *What will you have to take with you when you go?*

The Last Supper
Leonardo da Vinci (1452–1514)

Meals

There is a real difference between ingesting food and sharing a meal. When infants are hungry, they are very much interested in food, but they are not much interested in sharing a meal. Conversation makes the difference between "eating" and "sharing" a meal. And the conversation part makes children fidget and want to "be excused." But for adults, somehow the conversation and the food improve each other.

Even school children know that peanut butter and jelly become less boring when they eat with their friends in the cafeteria. There is probably nothing lonelier than going to a nice restaurant, ordering an out-of-the-ordinary meal, and eating it alone, hearing other families and friends all over the room laughing and talking.

We do not ordinarily consider dining with complete strangers, say at a formal banquet, a meal. Rather taking part in such formal celebrations is often a chore, an obligation.

Perhaps that is one reason why taking part in the Mass—sharing the eucharistic meal—is so often a chore: we don't know—or perhaps even care about—the other people in the "room."

The conversation at the Last Supper was not much different from that at an ordinary Sunday Mass today. In the longest description of the Last Supper (John 13–17), the conversation is more nearly a monologue in which, with a few interventions from the disciples, Jesus speaks of:

- his "going to the Father" and its necessity for their sake,
- the relationship Jesus and his followers must have with "the world,"
- the role of the Holy Spirit in their future,
- the glorification that awaits him,
- the commandment to love.

All of which the disciples, despite three years of intensive training, found completely befuddling, as their few interventions prove. They were just like ourselves, their innermost selves and values concentrated on getting ahead.

For Jesus, his approaching death is central to the Last Supper. Yet the disciples seem to have no sense of his—and their—imminent doom. Later—even after they had gone through the trauma of the Crucifixion, and the overwhelming experience of Jesus reborn from death, their very last question to Jesus before his Ascension was:

> *"Lord, will you at this time give the*
> *Kingdom back to Israel?"*   Acts 1:6

The disciples were still hankering to sit on those thrones, to find who would be "greatest in the Kingdom" (Matthew 18:1). It wasn't until the Spirit came upon them at Pentecost that they finally understood. And that understanding not only made the celebration of the Lord's Supper a memorial alive with meaning but it made their martyrs' deaths alive with meaning too.

Until you can feel within yourself that experience of the reality of death and the reality of rebirth, you will never feel the reality of the Lord's Supper—even when it is celebrated well.

> *"At the Last Supper,*
> *on the night he was betrayed,*
> *our Savior instituted the*
> *Eucharistic sacrifice*
> *of his Body and Blood."*
> *Catechism of the Catholic Church, 1323*

PASSOVER

At the Passover celebration, Jews recall the days of Israel's enslavement, which they can never forget—just as they can never now forget the Holocaust.

Jews have celebrated Passover year after year since hundreds of years before the birth of Jesus. As they set the Passover table with unleavened bread, a shank of lamb, wine, bitter herbs, an egg, they put themselves into a multidimensional meditation on who they are as a people. It is called the Passover because the vengeance of Yahweh passed over their ancestors' blood-spattered doorposts while the Egyptian firstborn were slain. It is also called the Feast of Unleavened Bread, "the bread of affliction." But most important of all, it is called "the day of our freedom."

Before the Passover celebration begins, the entire family hunts through the house to be sure no leavened foods—bread or cake or beer—are there. If they are to set out free and fresh, they must have no contamination from the past. Like their ancestors, they will begin the year over again with the "bread made in haste," without waiting for it to rise. For Jews, "the day of our freedom" is not just the once-for-all freedom of those ancestral slaves from Egypt. It is the freedom of all those around this table at this time. Its celebration marks a commitment to start the year fresh, clean, free. It is a memorial of a "then" that becomes a "now."

Each new generation of Jews must "enter into" the bitter experience of slavery. The members of each new generation must try to relive that slavery experienced by their ancestors as if they themselves had just endured it. They must let it seep into their very bones, anguishing over the deep alienation and rejection, feeling there is no escape from the vicious circles of violence.

Without that deep sense of enslavement, they have no way to appreciate what the liberation of Exodus meant—and means. Just as resurrection means nothing to a Christian until he or she has a *felt* realization of death, so freedom means nothing to a Christian or a Jew without a *felt* realization of slavery.

Each year Jews reexperience not only the cruelty of enslavement but the paralyzing effect of the *slave mentality*. They reexperience the bleak conviction that nobody can do anything about anything, the helpless belief that everything is "out of our hands." They come to realize that without God, the only thing we have in common is our inescapable powerlessness. But in reenacting the Passover seder, Jews for the last twenty-five hundred years have found hope (because God has set them free before, again and again) and the courage to start fresh.

THE LAST SUPPER

Jesus celebrated Passover many times in his life. But his final Passover seder was crucial to him. At that meal Jesus took the unleavened bread out of which the new life of freedom comes, prayed, and then said:

> "This is my body which will be given up [broken] for you." Then he took the final cup, prayed, and said, "This is the cup of my blood, the blood of the new and everlasting covenant. It will be shed for you and for all so that sins may be forgiven. Do this in memory of me."
> Eucharistic Prayer II

Just as Jesus' physical body made him present to his disciples at that moment, so will this eucharistic bread and wine be the extension of his self, his real presence with us, for the rest of time.

Contemporary celebration of Passover Seder.

But it is not just Jesus' real presence the Eucharist embodies. It is also a *relationship:* his body is "given up *for you*" and his blood "shed *for you*" for the purpose of setting you free from your sins, from the anchors that keep you from growing.

Jesus concluded his final seder by asking his disciples to gather and celebrate this ritual as a memorial of him. (But a case could be made that he also was asking us to forgive sins in his memory as well. "As we forgive those who trespass against us.")

Like the Jews of Egypt—and all time since—Christians, too, are "a pilgrim people on earth." Our lives are a journey, and the Eucharist is our compass and our manna. Each celebration of Mass is a memorial of a "then" that becomes a "now."

> Each time we celebrate
> we try to reach out to [Christ]
> as he reaches out to us.
> We try to enter into
> the experience of his death
> and its meaning to him and to us,
> trying to broaden our vision
> to the dimensions of his vision,
> to raise our goals in life
> to the height of his goals,
> and to overcome
> the alienation and unfreedom
> and confusion of our lives
> by bringing them
> into confrontation with
> the utter freedom
> and simplicity of his engagement
> with the Father.
>
> Monika Hellwig

THE EARLY CHRISTIAN MASS

In the earliest Christian communities, long before the conversion of Constantine (A.D. 280?–337) removed the danger of being Christian, Sunday was the Lord's Day; but it was also a working day. Christians had to get up before dawn and make their way through the streets to the home of a Christian family. Each carried a small biscuit, hidden in their clothes, because their religion was outlawed; and to be caught with the biscuit could mean their lives. They slipped in where a deacon looked them over to see if they were known and trusted; spies were commonplace.

They moved on to a large room where people milled about, talking. Many of those who had gathered knew one another, since they met one or two evenings during the week to pray together, hear instructions, and reflect on the letters of the apostles. There were no soldiers present, even in civilian clothes. Christians were rigid pacifists, and a soldier's oath entailed offering incense to the emperor.

At one end of the room sat the bishop of the city, dressed like every other man in working clothes. Seated around him were several others, the "elders" or "presbyters (priests)" or "deacons." The bishop stood and greeted the assembly, and all replied. Then they turned and embraced one another, moving freely about because there were no pews. There was a genuine sense of fellowship; all present were risking death to be there.

On a table in front of the bishop there was a plate and cup, and on either side of the table stood a deacon, one holding a plate and the other a cup. Someone from every family filed up and put the biscuit they had brought onto the plate and poured a bit of wine into the cup.

Then the bishop and elders stood with their hands outstretched over the plate and cup. Silently, they focused attention on the bread and wine, which symbolized their unity as the body of Christ. Then the bishop invited all present to lift up their hearts as their offering and to give thanks to the Lord. He then chanted a short prayer to thank God for creation, for caring for them, and for their re-creation as a new people in Christ.

Then the bishop broke a piece from one biscuit and ate it, and took three sips of wine while the deacons broke the rest of the breads. One by one the people filed up to the bishop, who said, "The bread of heaven in Christ Jesus," and each answered, "Amen," taking a piece of bread, then going to the cupholder.

The cupholder said, "In God the Father almighty," and the person responded, "Amen," and took a first sip. As the person took a second and third sip, the cupholder said, "In the Lord Jesus Christ" and "In the Holy Spirit in the holy church."

There was no rush. This, after all, was the whole purpose in their coming together. At the end, the bishop gave a blessing. Then some came forward for fragments of the bread to carry home for those who had been unable to be present because of illness or work.

There are elements in the ancient eucharistic ritual that might make the celebration of our own eucharistic liturgies more meaningful—especially the custom of milling about beforehand, renewing or making acquaintances, and offering the sign of peace at the beginning of the celebration.

There are many today, however, both old and young, who find that whole element of "hospitality" distasteful. That distaste is worth reflection. It is very real and at times strongly felt. But what does it say about the person who experiences it, about the very heart of what the Mass means? Does the Gospel give us the option of being shy or, worse, anonymous? That repulsion at greeting strangers sounds very little like Jesus or his Gospel. Perhaps a key there.

> At the heart of the Eucharistic celebration are the bread and wine that, by the words of Christ and the invocation of the Holy Spirit, become Christ's Body and Blood. Faithful to the Lord's command the Church continues to do, in his memory, and until his glorious return, what he did on the eve of his Passion.
>
> Catechism of the Catholic Church, 1333

Reflection

We might not realize the ways in which we ourselves are unfree and contribute to the unfreedom of others. We might be just too busy to notice. For instance, on any given night, you are free to do many things: watch TV, go out with friends, read a book, paint a picture, play Monopoly with the family, do homework, take a walk.

■ *How can you be free if you do not assess your options?*

■ *How can you be free with only one genuine option—which isn't really a choice at all?*

Ironically, to be free costs. It costs the time to assess one's options, without fear; to settle on a line of action, without fear; and to make a commitment to follow it, without fear. That commitment, of course, closes out all the other options. Freedom is like money in your pocket.

It is nice to know you have it, but of absolutely no value whatever until you expend it on something you want more than you want to hold on to the money, more than you want "keeping your options open."

■ *Is it possible that—without realizing it— you do in fact have "the slave mentality," the conviction that "they"—society, the government, the media, your own moods—are in charge?*

■ *Is it possible that "nobody can do anything about anything," especially not me?*

The questions to ask yourself are:

■ *Do you genuinely want to be free?*

■ *And are you willing to take the unavoidable steps to lay hold of that freedom?*

■ *Do you really want to surrender habit, "the great deadener," in order to live life more abundantly, to suffer a "little death" in order to be reborn?*

CELEBRATION OF THE BODY OF CHRIST

Survey

This survey is not an exercise for a grade, but a means to stir up interest and get an idea of varying opinions in your group. Some of the statements are matters of objective fact; others are merely subjective opinions. On the rating scale under each statement circle the number that best reflects your current opinion about that statement.

+2 = strongly agree,
+1 = agree,
 0 = cannot make up my mind,
−1 = disagree,
−2 = strongly disagree.

Then share the reasons for your opinion.

1. The Eucharist means nothing for those who are not truly grateful to be alive.

   +2   +1   0   −1   −2

2. Like parenthood, life is a risk with no guarantees.

   +2   +1   0   −1   −2

3. Without a regular time to reflect, we tend to forget how gifted we are.

   +2   +1   0   −1   −2

4. None of us was able (since we didn't exist) to do anything to *deserve* to exist.

   +2   +1   0   −1   −2

5. The focal person at the celebration of Mass is the priest.

   +2   +1   0   −1   −2

6. The Eucharist is "given" by the priest and "received" by the people.

   +2   +1   0   −1   −2

7. The Eucharist does not merely remind us of the Last Supper, it re-creates it.

   +2   +1   0   −1   −2

8. At its most basic, the Eucharist is an act of gratitude, no matter how poorly celebrated.

   +2   +1   0   −1   −2

9. The consecrated bread and wine are less important than the people the bread and wine unite and enliven.

   +2   +1   0   −1   −2

10. The Mass is only incidentally about death. More than anything, it is about life.

    +2   +1   0   −1   −2

Giving Thanks

The word *eucharist* comes from the Greek *eucharistia*, "giving thanks." The celebration of the Eucharist is motivated by beliefs similar to those that underlie the American feast of Thanksgiving: a realization that the harvest was not entirely the pilgrims' doing, gratitude for the good that had come out of their sufferings.

But as we have seen, without a felt realization of death, the people and things we do honestly love gradually become taken for granted. We act as if we would always have them and—more importantly—as if we had done something to *deserve* them.

Without a regular time to reflect on life, we tend to forget how *gifted* we have been. And gratitude—giving thanks, eucharist—depends on remembering.

THE WORK OF THE WHOLE CHURCH

The Church itself, the body of Christ, is a sacrament. The celebration of the Eucharist is an act of the Church *as* the body of Christ. Vatican II completely reversed the idea that began in the Middle Ages and almost completely "priestified" the Eucharist, making the priest the only active agent in the Mass. Today we appreciate more that it is *Christ* who offers the liturgy through the priest *and* the assembly, the body that is the Church. That renewal of perspective is made clearest when we compare what the priest used to say in preparation of the gifts and what the priest says now.

Before the revision of the rites of the Mass, the priest said:

> Accept . . . this spotless host which I, your unworthy servant, offer you. . . .

Now, he says:

> Blessed are you, Lord, God of all creation. Through your goodness we have. . . .

Saint Paul draws his understanding of the Eucharist from the Old Testament: remembrance of the Passover and the liberation of the Exodus. But now Jesus Christ is our paschal lamb, our Passover lamb. John the Evangelist underlines that truth in his Gospel when he shows that Jesus was killed at the same time the Passover lambs were slain (John 19:31).

Vatican II gives the meaning of this act of the Church:

> At the Last Supper, on the night when He was betrayed, our Savior instituted the Eucharistic Sacrifice of His Body and Blood.

He did this in order to perpetuate the sacrifice of the Cross through the centuries until He should come again, and so to entrust to His beloved spouse, the Church, a memorial of His death and resurrection: a sacrament of love, a sign of unity, a bond of charity, a paschal banquet in which Christ is consumed, the mind is filled with grace, and a pledge of future glory is given to us.

Constitution on the Sacred Liturgy

The Mass, then, is not about death—much less about sin. It is about the rebirth that can come about through death.

KEY DIMENSIONS OF THE EUCHARIST

There are four key concepts in the heart of the Eucharist that are emphasized by Vatican II:

◼ The Eucharist is a sacrament;

◼ it is a remembrance;

◼ it is an act of worship;

◼ it is a communion or fellowship.

Sacrament

Eucharist is no longer seen as a holy *thing* that is "given" by the priest and "received" by the people. The Eucharist is a sacred *action*, celebrated *by* a sanctified people gathered as the body of Christ.

Remembrance

The Liturgy of the Word reminds us of our story: our roots in Judaism and in the life of Christ and the early Church. In the Liturgy of the Eucharist the wine reminds us that the blood sprinkled on the Hebrews at Mount Sinai was a sign of their covenant. The wine consumed at Mass is "a cup of my blood, the blood of the new and everlasting covenant."

But the Eucharist does not merely remind us of a single event: the Last Supper or the Crucifixion. Rather as Passover reminds Jews not only of the night they awaited liberation but also of their trek through the desert and the blood covenant at Sinai, the Eucharist reminds us of the Paschal Mystery—Holy Thursday, Good Friday, Easter, and the infusion of the Spirit into the Body of Christ on Pentecost—as a single liberating event.

Worship

Eucharist is an act of reverence and honor in gratitude to God. Its celebration helps us remember clearly who God is and who we are. It is both an act of humility and an act of exaltation. In contrast to God, we are shadows in the Light; but because of the death-resurrection-exaltation of the God-Man, Jesus Christ, we too have been "lifted up." Because of Christ, each of us is "Cinderella."

Communion

All religion is a "connection," a transcendent reaching into the reality of God and an immanent reaching outward to our sisters and brothers.

We unite ourselves to the story that gives our lives meaning (the Liturgy of the Word). We offer our innermost selves with the ordinary bits of bread and cup of wine ("We lift up our hearts"); we share ourselves outward to those around us (the sign of peace) and then commune with God (the communion). To celebrate the Eucharist—our thanksgiving—is to celebrate the reconciliation of God and humankind and of human beings with one another—and within ourselves.

Because there is the one loaf of bread, all of us, though many, are one body, for we all share the same loaf.

1 Corinthians 10:17

A bonding takes place, nurtured by the Host, who in this case is also the servant and the food. Eucharist is a communion among people not only divided from one another but conflicted even within themselves. It extends reconciliation to sisters and brothers: "Do this in memory of me."

Our weekly giving-thanks is to make contact with people where they are, to enable them to see better, hear better, make more visible the reality of their faith and trust in Christ.

Reflection

List the names of all the people you truly love and who you know truly love you. Do not rush. There may be many more people than at first you think. When those names run out, think of the people you really enjoy being with, whether you would feel at ease putting the word *love* on the relationship or not. Again, do not move on too quickly. Daydream awhile. When you have finally "run out of steam," pause and ponder the truth that one day you will inevitably lose them. Think about that a long while.

Now list all the things in your life that you really like: music, books, running, quiet evenings by a river, ice water after a workout, movies. Just keep going until the list peters out. Then mull some more. Then pause and ponder the truth that you might never have known those joys. Think about that a long while.

- *If the Giver of all those gifts—which we did nothing to "deserve"—asks, "Do this in memory of me," what would be the only response any person of honor would give?*
- *What kind of person would refuse?*

The eucharist points to the possibility of bonding in the middle of rubble; . . . and in the middle of this century's persistent hunger for meaning, it offers signs of connectedness that link people to other people and to all the living things in the universe.
Doris Donnelly

PRAISING AND THANKING GOD AT MASS

All other liturgical rites and all the works of the Christian life are linked with the eucharistic celebration, flow from it, and have it as their end. "General Instruction of the Roman Missal"

INTRODUCTORY RITES

The purpose of these rites is that the faithful coming together take on the form of a community and prepare themselves to listen to God's word and celebrate the eucharist properly.

Greeting

Rite of Blessing and Sprinkling Holy Water

> Dear Friends,
> this water will be used
> to remind us of our baptism.
> Let us ask God to bless it,
> and to keep us faithful
> to the Spirit he has given us.

Opening Prayer

LITURGY OF THE WORD

Christ is present to the faithful through his own word.

After First and Second Readings

Reader: The word of the Lord

All: Thanks be to God.

Responsorial Psalm

Alleluia or Gospel Proclamation

Gospel

The people, who by their acclamations acknowledge and confess Christ present and speaking to them, stand as they listen to [the Gospel proclaimed].

Homily

Profession of Faith

General Intercessions

LITURGY OF THE EUCHARIST

At the last supper Christ instituted the sacrifice and paschal meal that make the sacrifice of the cross to be continuously present in the Church.

Preparation of the Altar and the Gifts

Eucharistic Prayer

Now the center and summit of the entire celebration begins.

Presider: Let us give thanks to the Lord our God.

Assembly: It is right to give him thanks and praise.

Presider: Take this, all of you, and eat it:
           this is my body which will be given up for you.

           Take this, all of you, and drink from it:
           this is the cup of my blood,
           the blood of the new and everlasting covenant.
           It will be shed for you and for all
           so that sins may be forgiven.
           Do this in memory of me.

Assembly: Dying you destroyed our death,
           rising you restored our life.
           Lord Jesus, come in glory.

Communion Rite

Through the breaking of the bread the unity of the faithful is expressed and through communion they receive the Lord's body and blood in the same way the apostles received them from Christ's own hands.

CONCLUDING RITE

Prayer Over the People

Presider: Lord,
           come, live in your people
           and strengthen them by your grace.
           Help them to remain close to you in prayer
           and give them a true love for one another.

Dismissal:

Presider: Go in peace to love and serve the Lord.

Assembly: Thanks be to God.

Whether the words written in the gospel versions are the actual words used by Jesus or whether they are faith formulas the early Christian communities used at their own re-creation of the Last Supper is not the real issue. It was clearly the *faith choice* of early communities to use the words, *"This is my body"* (Matthew 26:26). *"This is my blood"* (Matthew 26:27).

They did not say, *"Let this be a reminder."*

Their faith chose the word *is*.

The emphasis in the gospel accounts is not on the *objects* on the communion table. It is on the *relationship* those objects focus: the crucified-resurrected-exalted Jesus Christ and the body of believers that the Spirit still energizes.

The emphasis is on *breaking* the bread and *sharing* the cup. We too are to "break ourselves up" and "share" the pieces. The interest of the gospel writers and the early Christians was not in what happened to the bread and wine, but what happened to the *people*. Saint John Chrysostom (345?–407) wrote:

> Through the food the Lord has given us, we become members of his flesh and of his bones. We are "mixed into" that flesh, and he has kneaded his body with ours.

The Holy Roman Emperor Charles V (1500–1558) gathered representatives of Rome and each of the Protestant factions, begging them all to agree that at least *somehow* Jesus was *more* intensely present in the Eucharist than anywhere else on earth. The God we believe in *somehow* created a universe out of nothing and somehow *became human, one of us*. Such a God would surely have found no difficulty in becoming present to us as bread and wine. But, stubbornly, the different factions refused, each nursing a pet theory. How foolish.

The Presence of Christrst

Probably no doctrine—other than the question of how Jesus could be both divine and human—has divided dedicated Christians more than *how* Jesus manages to be present in the Eucharist.

Christians have argued whether the bread and wine were "only" symbols (that is, merely suggested the presence of Christ) or the consecrated bread and wine "really" were the Body and Blood of Christ (as really present as Jesus was at the Last Supper). That debate puts the *things* involved in the Eucharist (the bread and wine) as more important than the *relationship* between Christ and us.

Vatican II: A Renewed Understanding

For hundreds of years, the question of Christ's presence "at" the Eucharist was focused almost exclusively on his presence "in" the Eucharist: within the consecrated bread and wine. Vatican II broadened the scope of our understanding to center first on the eucharistic action and then, within that *action*, on four distinct ways in which Christ is present:

- Christ is present in the assembled people;

- Christ is present in God's word;

- Christ is present in the priest; and, above all,

- Christ is present in the bread and wine.
Constitution on the Sacred Liturgy

Further, Vatican II said that Christ is not present among us to be simply adored or ministered to. Christ is there for us, an active presence to be used as the channel between us and God and between God and us. There is only one Christ present in each Eucharist, but he appears in different roles of the one action.

- The risen Lord is present in the *assembly* and that presence unites them as his Body.

- The risen Lord is present in *God's word*. "It is Christ himself who speaks when holy scriptures are read" (Saint Augustine).

- The risen Lord is present in the *priest* as the primary agent in action of the people's sacrament—to make a perhaps crude analogy, the priest-presider is the lens through whom the power of the Spirit in the people focuses on the action. "When [anybody] baptizes it is really Christ Himself who baptizes."

- And the risen Lord is present in the *eucharistic species,* the food we share, to do and be what food has always done: nourish and unite.

Each of the four ways of being present does what all symbols do: act as channels for grace. The Eucharist is a rite of conversion whereby the eternal enters the everyday, the sacred energizes the secular and empowers us to go on striving. It makes a difference to believe that the presence of the risen Lord actually is not only in the assembly and God's word and the priest but *in* the bread and wine.

Reflection

Consider again moments when you experienced the numinous in nature. That presence was the *anima mundi,* the power of the Artist radiating from what God created. In the light of those experiences, consider the moment at which the priest, in the name of the body of Christ, says the words of consecration, when the Timeless focuses from beyond time into the bread and wine—and, through them, into us.

- *No matter how "boring" the celebration of Mass is to the shallow-souled, no matter how routine it seems, is that problem perhaps more a problem of sensitivity in those who criticize it? Explain.*

If preachers concentrated more on our savior's message and less on the means by which he arrived and departed this world, we would all be a lot better off.

Will Rogers

Understanding the Eucharist

Review

1. Why is a felt understanding of one's own death crucial to judging the value of the sacraments—or in fact the value of anything?

2. Explain: Life is a series of invitations to death and rebirth. How is that principle echoed throughout the Old Testament? The Incarnation? The life of Jesus?

3. Why is the solitary Christian a contradiction? What is such a person missing?

4. How does the Eucharist mirror the Jewish experience of Passover and liberation from the slavery? Why is death and resurrection essential to a Christian's understanding of the Last Supper and the celebration of the Eucharist today?

5. Explain: Each Mass is a memorial at which a "then" becomes a "now."

6. What is the root meaning of the word *eucharist?*

7. Explain: Too much is at least as dehumanizing as too little. What relation does that have to evaluating the celebration of Eucharist? Why are bread and wine good natural symbols of what the Mass "says"?

8. Explain: Eucharist can "happen" only as an act of the Church *as* the body of Christ. Since Vatican II, how has the Mass been "de-priestified"?

9. How does the Eucharist remind us of who we really are as a people and as individual members of that people? Why should that realization enrich our souls?

10. In what ways is Christ truly present at the Eucharist as Christ is present nowhere else?

Discuss

1. There are those—even exemplary Christians—who say the Eucharist is nothing more than a symbolic remembrance, not a presence of Christ as real as Jesus was at the Last Supper. How would you respond to them?

2. One of the most consistent objections about taking part in the celebration of Mass is "I don't get anything out of it." Why is that a not-quite-legitimate objection?

3. For a moment play the scientists' favorite game: What if? What if what happens at Mass really *is* the infinite God focusing into the bread and wine "to bring morning into the darkness of our bellies"? What would that mean to what we think is really important?

4. Because you did nothing to deserve to exist, then life—and everything in it—is a gift, love undeserved, grace. Why do we take life for granted?

5. Where do you go when you want to think things over? Do you do it on a regular basis or just when you are down in the dumps? What effect would it have on your soul— your self—if you sought out solitude regularly?

6. Why are many of us uptight during the sign of peace at Mass? We claim that we participate in Mass for "communion"—with God and one another, yet we are reluctant to let down our guard. How does that contradict the Gospel?

7. How is the Eucharist a multileveled "reconciliation"? Explain: "The eucharist points to the possibility of bonding in the midst of rubble."

Activities

1. Think back to the reflections about bread and wine on page 127. When the priest says at Mass "which human hands have made," how many hands is that? Who has formed what we prepare to offer at Mass?

2. If your taking part in the celebration of Mass is "boring," what are the reasons? Do not lay all the blame on someone else.

3. To what extent do we all have "the slave mentality"?

Scripture Readings

Skim the passages. Pick one that appeals to you and (1) summarize its main point, (2) tell how it relates to the chapter, and (3) list one or two thoughts that entered your mind as you read it.

- Exodus 12:1–8, 11–14 — The law for the Passover meal
- Exodus 24:3–8 — The blood marking the covenant
- Deuteronomy 8:2–3, 14–16 — Food finer than you have ever known
- Luke 9:11–17 — All ate and were satisfied
- Luke 24:13–15 — The road to Emmaus
- Acts 2:42–47 — Fellowship in the breaking of bread
- Hebrews 9:11–15 — The blood of Christ purifies us from sin
- Revelation 1:5–8 — A royal notion of priests

✎ Journal

Reflect on the ways you have "died" in your life—a lost parent or sibling, a near-death experience. How has that experience changed your soul?

Daily conversion and penance find their source and nourishment in the Eucharist, for in it is made present the sacrifice of Christ which has reconciled us with God. Through the Eucharist those who live from the life of Christ are fed and strengthened.

Catechism of the Catholic Church, 1436

Sacraments
of
Healing

Chapter 7

Penance and Reconciliation: The Sacrament of Forgiveness

For by our interior qualities, each of us outstrips the whole sum of mere things. We find re-enforcement in this profound insight whenever we enter into our own hearts. God, who probes the heart, awaits us there. There we discern our proper destiny beneath the eyes of God.
From *Pastoral Constitution on the Church in the Modern World*

WHAT IS SIN?

Survey

This survey is not an exercise for a grade, but a means to stir up interest and get an idea of varying opinions in your group. Some of the statements are matters of objective fact; others are merely subjective opinions. On the rating scale under each statement circle the number that best reflects your current opinion about that statement.

+2 = strongly agree,
+1 = agree,
 0 = cannot make up my mind,
−1 = disagree,
−2 = strongly disagree.

Then share the reasons for your opinion.

1. You cannot value the sacrament of Reconciliation without a felt sense of sin.

   +2 +1 0 −1 −2

2. Even when one has done something objectively wrong, guilt trips are psychologically damaging.

   +2 +1 0 −1 −2

3. The healthy soul turns guilt into responsibility.

   +2 +1 0 −1 −2

4. What you get without guilt is concentration camps, pushers, and toxic waste dumps.

   +2 +1 0 −1 −2

5. Being moral has nothing to do with one's religion. Even decent atheists want to be moral.

   +2 +1 0 −1 −2

6. Sin and moral evil are also an offense against oneself.

   +2 +1 0 −1 −2

7. Having a "rubbery" conscience is something like a chemical addiction.

   +2 +1 0 −1 −2

8. Consistent honesty with oneself is not always the best policy.

   +2 +1 0 −1 −2

9. Consistent honesty with others is almost never the best policy.

   +2 +1 0 −1 −2

10. Like it or not, we live in a real web of moral relationships with everyone on earth.

   +2 +1 0 −1 −2

A Puzzlement

In *The Great Divorce*, C. S. Lewis's fantasy about heaven, travelers from purgatory to the fields outside heaven are invited to come in. Only one thing they cannot bring with them: their self-absorption. For many, that is too precious to surrender, so they get back on the bus and return to the dull gray town that is purgatory and now, for them, hell: "Better to reign in hell than serve in heaven."

One boy has a lizard on his shoulder, whispering, whispering. The boy cringes at what he hears, yet he is fascinated by it. One of the heavenly creatures asks if the boy wants him to kill it, but the boy shrugs and says, "Oh, no. See. He's quite quiet now." A second time the heavenly personage asks, and the boy curses at him: "Why can't you just creep up and kill it without my knowing!" Finally, the wretched boy screams, "Yes! Yes, *kill* it!" The shining person grasps the lizard and crushes it, throwing it down and breaking its back.

But the body begins to shimmer and grow, and the lizard transforms into a great white stallion! And the boy leaps on the stallion's back and rides whooping through the fields into heaven.

- *What is the lizard?*
- *What is the stallion?*

Moral Ecology

Just as we can never appreciate resurrection without a felt awareness of death, just as we can never appreciate freedom without a felt awareness of slavery, we can never appreciate the liberation of the sacrament of Reconciliation without a felt awareness of alienation, fragmentation, sin. Sin is a sense that things are out of kilter, that I'm not really okay as a person, that I am no longer "at home."

MORAL EVIL

Today, it is commonplace to close our minds to anything that might turn into a "guilt trip." Yet that sense of guilt (when the cause is undeniably real) is a very healthy human feeling, like hunger in our bellies that keeps us alive. It is a hunger in the mistreated soul that urges us to make things right again. The healthy soul turns guilt into responsibility,

■ first by acknowledging it,

■ then by admitting it openly,

■ and then by doing something to change our deadening habits.

What you have in a world without the sinful or sacred—without guilt—is Auschwitz, gang rapes, pushers, saturation bombing, toxic waste dumps, terrorists. It is undeniable that our society desperately needs to stop suppressing legitimate guilt and turn it into responsibility.

We can never appreciate the liberation of Reconciliation without a felt awareness of alienation, fragmentation, sin.

Although we frequently use the two terms interchangeably, there is a significant difference between *moral evil* and *sin*. Even good atheists, who have no belief in "sin," are well aware of the prevalence of moral (human) evil. Leaving God for the moment out of the background against which we measure ourselves, we can see that there still is an objective web of relationships between each of us and the whole physical planet we share: the physical ecology. If any one of us violates that web—by shooting poison into the atmosphere, spewing chemicals into rivers, defacing walls with graffiti, or even throwing a single hamburger box out a car window—we are all eventually going to pay, even the perpetrators: an ugly, deadened, deadly world.

Just so, there is also an objective web of relationships between each of us and all the *human* inhabitants with whom we share the planet: a moral (human) ecology. If any one of us violates that web—by holding human beings in slavery, allowing them to starve in agony, raping or murdering or assaulting them, insulting them with noise, or even by lying to them—we are all eventually going to pay: a world in which no one can trust anyone else.

SIN

If morality (without any reference to religion) means simply what we have to do to consider ourselves decent human beings, any child is capable of moral evil, which violates the "horizontal" web of relationships that we have with all human beings. But strictly speaking, it may not be a "sin," because sin further violates the "vertical" relationship we have to the One who created us. If that personal relationship with God doesn't exist, one may not (strictly speaking) have knowingly committed sin. But one is still guilty of moral evil.

Sin is also an offense against ourselves, in which we curtail our own freedom and gradually weigh ourselves down with the anchors of habit. Sinning changes our personalities—and by that very fact affects the people who care for us. Every sin is a failure to become what we might have been, and gradually it corrodes our ability to be that fullest self. Our self-absorption becomes almost literal: we devour ourselves till there is no self left.

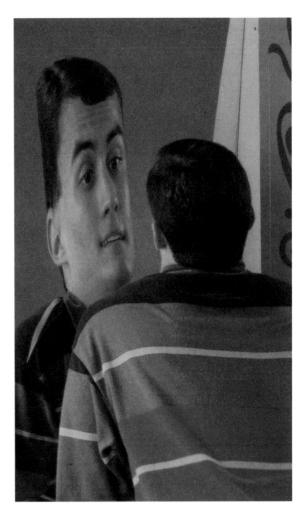

Oscar Wilde portrays this dramatically in his story *The Picture of Dorian Gray*, in which a handsome and gifted young man gives himself over to a life of self-indulgence, degrading women, exploiting others' weaknesses, defrauding his friends. But one day the young man notices that his portrait over the fireplace looks a bit different. And as the weeks go by it becomes so obviously shriveled and deformed that he has to hide it in the attic, where it continues to mirror his true corrupted soul.

Sin is one of the most basic terms in the Christian vocabulary, as common as *grace* or *God,* because sin really means "being *out of* a relationship with God, being disconnected." The Church not only preaches penitence but promises forgiveness for that disconnectedness.

There is unarguably a "dark side" to human nature. On the one hand, being scrupulously aware of that dark side can lead to despair; on the other, being defensively unaware of it can lead to a life of triviality and illusion.

The Greek word for sin is *harmatia*, an archery term for "missing the mark." Not just making an error in judgment in a particular case, but missing the whole point of human life; not just a violation of a law but an insult to a friendship with the One to whom we owe existence—and all the gifts that follow from that first one; not just a servant's failure to carry out a master's orders, but the ingratitude of a child to his or her parent.

THE STATE OF SIN AND
THE STATE OF GRACE

The *state* of sin is a state of an enslaved consciousness, a surrender of freedom, and one can get real insight into its nature from comparing it to chemical addiction. Like habituation to drugs, habituation to sin causes hardening of the heart so that, as Carson McCullers said, the heart grows pitted and tough like the seed of a peach. Like taking drugs, sinning becomes an unshakable habit, so that every next time makes sinning easier. And the indifferent sinner "dies" as a human being, just as addicts do, because one's best self never has a chance to be born.

The continued *state* of either "sin" or "grace" is a matter of one's whole *basic disposition* to God. It is rooted at the depth of the self—the soul—and determines the overall pattern and choices of one's life. Hitler and mob hitmen clearly have a "basic disposition to God" quite different from that of Thomas More and Mother Teresa. None of us believes he or she is as wicked as Hitler or as holy as Thomas More. The crucial question is: Which direction are you running?

It is worth noting, too, that the position most deadly to the good person is not evil; the most lethal position is utter indifference. As God says in the Book of Revelation:

"I know that you are neither cold nor hot. How I wish you were either one or the other! But because you are lukewarm, neither hot nor cold, I am going to spit you out of my mouth!"
Revelation 3:15–16

"The third chapter of Genesis," as Sean Fagin says, "tells us nothing about what happened at the beginning of time, but . . . it is a story to explain what is happening *all* of the time." It is a skeletal sketch that every sin since has duplicated: human self-absorption; the arrogance that believes *I* can get along without God, *I* can determine what is right and wrong, despite the quite explicit purposes written by God right into the natures of rocks, vegetables, animals, and human beings.

We become blinded by self-interest, and in those rare honest moments when we do open our eyes, we realize we are "naked" and helpless. Not only have we turned away from God; we no longer feel "at home" even with ourselves or with our neighbors. Even then, like Adam, we resort to excuses:

"The woman you put here with me gave me the fruit, and I ate it." Genesis 3:12

How often has each of us resorted to the same kind of scapegoating? While the Genesis event never actually happened as told by the writer of Genesis, it happens uncountable times every day. It may be a mythical story, but it tells the whole psychology of sin.

"The sacrament of penance," writes George McCauley, S.J., "is . . . a conversation between Christians about sin." Something very salutary in us wants to converse, to talk, about the way we have used and misused our freedom. But sitting or kneeling to confess doesn't wipe out the scapegoating. We grow afraid; we hedge.

"We quickly become expert," McCauley continues, "at hiding our true selves behind words. We dissemble with them; we throw up verbal roadblocks which delay entrance into the private citadel of our thoughts. With words we put people off and we lead them on. We pick and choose from among our meager treasure of words to find those which best ornament our pale souls."

That is what the sacrament of Reconciliation is for: complete honesty with ourselves, to *submit* to the truth, to be humbled into freedom. Through that honesty, we can begin to transform the power of our vices into the grace of God's aliveness, like the lizard becoming the stallion, to carry us—not into heaven—but into a life that makes sense again, where we are okay, "at home."

When we approach Reconciliation, the sacrament of forgiveness, we take one liberating step away from self-deception. We become not just the observers of our weakness but its accusers. We move beyond admission of guilt, beyond even recognition of a need for forgiveness. We now desire to be *whole* again.

> Sin is before all else an offense against God, a rupture of communion with him. At the same time it damages communion with the Church. For this reason conversion entails both God's forgiveness and reconciliation with the Church, which are expressed and accomplished liturgically by the sacrament of Penance and Reconciliation.
>
> *Catechism of the Catholic Church,* 1440

Reflection

- When you have a bad tooth, it's often "tolerable"; it causes distress only every once in a while; leave it alone and maybe it will take care of itself. What's the only sensible thing to do?

- When you watch television and keep channel-surfing from one dull program to another and another, do you settle for the least dull, sure that the next program is "bound" to be better, or do you get up and do something completely different?

- When you suffer the "blahs," the feeling that life has become little better than one-dull-thing-after-another, what do you do? Take charge of your mood and start taking control of your life out of its hands, or merely wait for "something to show up"?

- Very honestly, what is your basic disposition toward life? For ever-fuller life, or for death-in-life?

JESUS AND PERSONAL CONFESSION

Survey

This survey is not an exercise for a grade, but a means to stir up interest and get an idea of varying opinions in your group. Some of the statements are matters of objective fact; others are merely subjective opinions. On the rating scale under each statement circle the number that best reflects your current opinion about that statement.

+2 = strongly agree,
+1 = agree,
 0 = cannot make up my mind,
−1 = disagree,
−2 = strongly disagree.

Then share the reasons for your opinion.

1. The sins Jesus took most seriously were sexual sins.

   +2 +1 0 −1 −2

2. To deny one's real sins is hypocrisy.

   +2 +1 0 −1 −2

3. Our sins are forgiven even if we do not bother to ask for forgiveness.

   +2 +1 0 −1 −2

4. The first step toward peace of soul is complete honesty with oneself.

   +2 +1 0 −1 −2

5. When Jesus dealt one-on-one with sinners, he demanded a full catalog of each and every sin.

   +2 +1 0 −1 −2

6. Jesus always gave a penance to "make up" for what the person had done wrong.

   +2 +1 0 −1 −2

7. The father of the prodigal son embraced and kissed the boy even before the boy apologized.

   +2 +1 0 −1 −2

8. A good deal of what Jesus spoke about in his many sermons was punishment for sins.

   +2 +1 0 −1 −2

9. According to Jesus we will have to account for each of our sins at the Last Judgment.

   +2 +1 0 −1 −2

10. Although Jesus was very sympathetic to weakness, he was no pushover.

    +2 +1 0 −1 −2

Jesus and "Sinners"

Jesus never became indignant over prostitution and adultery. Nor was Jesus irate at Judas's impending treachery; in fact he washed Judas's feet (John 13:12), and in the moment before his arrest Jesus said to Judas:

"Be quick about it, friend!"   Matthew 26:50

Likewise, the risen Jesus didn't revile Peter for his triple cowardice; he merely asked—three times:

"Simon son of John, do you love me?"
John 21:15–17

Jesus did not consider wealth a sin. He loved the rich young man, even though the youth was unable to sell all; Lazarus and his family seemed comfortable. Jesus made no complaint that Zacchaeus gave away "only" half his ill-gotten goods; a penniless Samaritan would have been no help for the victim in the ditch; and if Joseph of Arimathea had not been wealthy, Jesus would have gone unburied.

Jesus seemed none too cautious for the niceties of Sabbath observance (Mark 2:27) or about enjoying food and wine; in fact, his enemies accused him of being "a glutton and wine drinker" (Luke 7:34). Even "heretics" had gentler treatment from Jesus than they could expect from the later Church; according to the parable of the weeds (Matthew 13:24–30), they should be left as they are until the harvest.

In fact, the only sinners who upset Jesus—strongly—were the clergy and Temple minions! He reacted fiercely to the hypocrisy and grandstanding of the Pharisees, resorting to some rather insulting (not to mention imprudent) terms: "frauds," "blind fools," "hypocrites," "blind guides," "vipers' nests" (Matthew 23). And one can almost hear Jesus grind his teeth confronting the thickheaded materialism of his own twelve "seminarians."

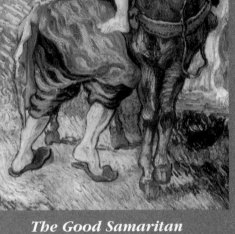

The Good Samaritan
Vincent van Gogh (1853–1890)

What is common to these offenses is the sinners' consistent refusal to see anything wrong with their suppositions, no sense of a need for repentance, since the rectitude of their convictions was unquestionable to them.

Oh, Jesus mentions sins aplenty: fornication, theft, murder, adultery, greed, maliciousness, deceit, sensuality, envy, blasphemy, arrogance, an obtuse spirit. He was not as blasé about sin as many nominal Christians like to believe he was. But perhaps the root sin is the last in his list: "an obtuse spirit," the self-absorption that refuses to admit one did wrong and the inertia that finds it too much effort and embarrassment to go back to the first wrong turn and start over.

> *God gives us the strength to begin anew. It is in discovering the greatness of God's love that our heart is shaken by the horror and weight of sin.*
>
> Catechism of the Catholic Church, 1432

Unconditional Love and Forgiveness

But Jesus also offered forgiveness aplenty. When Peter asked how many times we must forgive, Jesus told him "seventy times seven" times (Matthew 18:22), and if God expects as much of us, we can expect at least as much of God. Though sinless himself, Jesus had a remarkable empathy for weakness. Quoting Isaiah, he said:

> *"He will not break off a bent reed, nor put out a flickering lamp."*   Matthew 12:20

To the teachers of the Law in his hometown Jesus said:

> *"I assure you that people can be forgiven all their sins and all the evil things they may say. But whoever says evil things against the Holy Spirit will never be forgiven, because [that person] has committed an eternal sin."*   Mark 3:28–29

Perhaps that puzzling, sole unforgivable sin is despair, but a case could also be made for its being "an obtuse spirit," impregnable even to the Spirit's movement, suggesting something is amiss and needs forgiving.

Unconditional love and forgiveness of debts are difficult for us to comprehend. Even catechesis (still) opts for the economic metaphor: a God so ego-bruised by Adam and Eve there could be no love from God till every last shekel of ransom was paid in the blood of Jesus. Which is, however well-intentioned, blasphemous. God loves us as helplessly as a mother loves her child on death row. Our sins do nothing to God; their effects are in *us*, even though we refuse to see them as self-servingly as Dorian Gray.

The key—as so many gospel parables show—is opening our eyes, submitting to the cure of our blindness. Jesus did not come to hawk guilt, but to offer freedom.

Wailing Wall, Jerusalem, Israel.

As he said in his inauguration "platform" in the Nazareth synagogue, he was sent to declare the Year of God (Luke 4:16–19): unconditional amnesty for those willing to *avail* themselves of it.

As the four episodes we will consider here prove conclusively, in no single case was there need to crawl, to vacuum the soul of every peccadillo, to submit to a retaliatory penance—much less "the temporal punishment due to sin" even after an all-merciful God has forgiven. Unconditional amnesty. The only requisite—in the moral practice of Jesus— was admitting one's *need* of forgiveness.

THE WOMAN KNOWN AS A SINNER (LUKE 7:36–50)

Simon the Pharisee had invited Jesus to dinner, though Simon forgot or forbore the courtesy of offering his guest a greeting kiss, water to wash his feet, and oil to anoint his brow. As they dined, a woman known in the town to be a sinner entered, stood behind Jesus by his feet, weeping. She wiped the tears from Jesus' feet with her hair, kissing them and anointing them with oil.

Simon fumed; if Jesus were a prophet, he would know what kind of woman this was. His rectitude was at stake, not her

shame. But Jesus pointed to the woman: she, a known sinner, had done for him everything the upright Pharisee had failed to do. Jesus spoke up and said to him:

> *"I tell you, then, the great love she has shown proves that her many sins have been forgiven. But whoever has been forgiven little shows only a little love."*   Luke 7:47

The woman said nothing. No careful catalog of sins; no pleading. She merely came to Jesus and humbled herself. And all her unspoken sins were forgiven. Jesus said nothing about restitution or atonement. "Your sins are forgiven." Period.

THE ADULTEROUS WOMAN (JOHN 8:1–11)

As Jesus was teaching in the Temple, Pharisees brought a woman who had been caught in adultery. (Nothing said of her consort.) According to the Law of Moses, she should be stoned; what did *he* say? Jesus merely bent and began tracing in the dirt. When they persisted, he said:

> *"Whichever one of you has committed no sin may throw the first stone at her."*
>
> John 8:7

And he bent back to his puzzling tracery. Gradually, the accusers drifted away, leaving only Jesus and the woman. He finally looked up and said, "Where are they? Is there no one left to condemn you?"

She replied, "No one, sir."

And Jesus said, "Well, then, I do not condemn you either. Go, but do not sin again."

Again, no questions like the ones priests were once taught to ask routinely: "What caused this? Are there problems in your marriage? Are there any other sins? And the sins of your past life?" No homilies, and surely no anger—only quiet acceptance and the admonition to avoid doing it again.

THE SAMARITAN WOMAN (JOHN 4:4–40)

On a journey through Samaria, Jesus stopped at the Well of Shechem and sent his disciples to the village for provisions. A Samaritan woman came to draw water and expressed surprise that he, a Jew, would ask water of a Samaritan. Jesus said:

> *"If you only knew what God gives and who it is that is asking you for a drink, you would ask him, and he would give you life-giving water."*   John 4:10

Again, a matter of seeing, not only through mindless prejudice but through the invitation to a freer, richer life.

There was an easy, teasing banter between them, playing on the idea of the water in her well and water that gives eternal life. When Jesus asked her to call her husband, she answered forthrightly, "I don't have a husband." And he replied (surely with a grin):

> *"You are right when you say you don't have a husband. You have been married to five men, and the man you live with now is not really your husband. You have told me the truth."*   John 4:18

But Jesus did not pursue her multiple sexual unions. Instead, he spoke about something more important, a time when, soon, authentic worshipers will worship the Father in Spirit and truth. At that the woman ran to gather the villagers. And when the disciples returned and begged Jesus to eat, he replied:

> *"I have food to eat that you know nothing about."*   John 4:32

Any confessor who has set a penitent free knows that repletion.

Christ and the Samaritan Woman at the Well
Annibale Carracci (1560-1609)

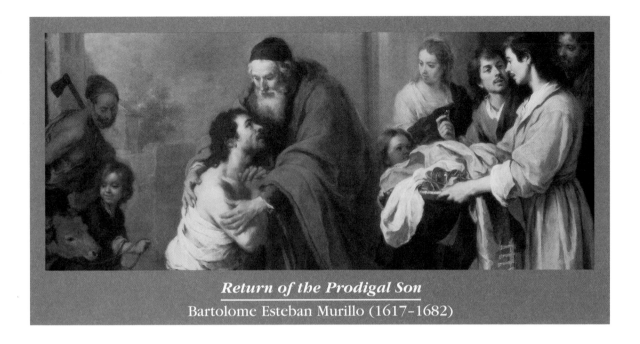

Return of the Prodigal Son
Bartolome Esteban Murillo (1617–1682)

THE PRODIGAL FATHER (LUKE 15:11–32)

The clearest insight into Jesus' (and God's—and therefore our) treatment of sinners is this story. The only character in both parts of the story is the father, the one the Storyteller wanted his audience to identify with. Note the details.

When the younger son demanded "his share" of the estate, the father did not say, "*What?* It's *my* estate that I've worked a lifetime for!" Instead, he gave it, as unhesitatingly as God gives us life, without strings, unconditionally, to do with what we choose, even against the divine will.

When the boy had frittered his inheritance away, reduced to feeding swine, he saw his mistake and headed for home, making up a memorized confession. But the father saw him a long way off . . . his heart filled with pity. Which implies the father was out there every day, hoping. And the father ran to the boy, not the other way round, threw his arms around him and kissed him—*before* the boy could apologize!

The boy got only the first sentence of his speech out before his father hushed him, and calling to his servants said:

> *"Hurry! Bring the best robe and put it on him. Put a ring on his finger and shoes on his feet. Then go and get the prize calf and kill it, and let us celebrate with a feast! For this son of mine was dead, but now he is alive; he was lost, but now he has been found."*   Luke 15:22–24

The father did not say, "I want an account of every shekel before you get back into this house!" Nothing of the shame the boy had caused him, because at the moment the boy's shame was more important than his own. Not a penance but a *party!* Because the lost sheep had found his way home. The whole Gospel.

But there was another son, just as blind and perhaps farther from "home" than the profligate had ever been. He found the cause of the merriment and slumped into a sulk. But notice again the father came out *to* the son because the son refused to come in and celebrate his brother's rebirth.

The key—as so many gospel parables show—is opening our eyes, submitting to the cure of our blindness. Jesus did not come to hawk guilt, but to offer freedom.

A Matter of Emphasis

Jesus does talk of punishment. The God he pictured and embodied is not a Cosmic Patsy who forgives anything, even when we have no inclination to apologize. The key to Jesus' moral practice—in every case, without exception—does involve the humility to admit one has wandered, and to come home.

But of the nearly four thousand verses in the Gospels, Jesus speaks of hell in Mark only once, in Luke three times, in Matthew six times, in John not at all. He speaks of judgment in Mark only once, in Luke twice, in Matthew and John six times each. In his lengthiest consideration of judgment (Matthew 25:31–46), the crucial question pivots on none of the sins Jesus mentioned (fornication, theft, murder, adultery, and so on) but on the sole issue of one's sensitivity or obtuseness to the suffering of Jesus in the hungry, the thirsty, the imprisoned.

Contrast the relative rareness of Jesus speaking about hell or judgment with the profusion of times in the Gospels when he both spoke and acted as one come to heal and to forgive. You come away with a picture of Christian moral practice that is far different from what many Christians have come to expect.

The older boy could think only of what he had done for his father, forgetting that, without his father, he would never have existed. Like so many, he had tried to merit the love his father had already felt for him nine months before he had ever seen the boy's face. His self-absorption and self-righteousness had blinded him to the whole point.

There is no doubt we sin. There is no doubt we too often blithely slither off the hook and become amnesiac about our faults. But there is also no doubt that, according to Jesus, being forgiven ought to be a great deal easier than we fear.

We cannot emphasize too strongly that our sins do no harm to God, only to our own souls. God is God simply because God *can't* be offended! If the notion makes any sense at all, it is that we *try* to offend God, and it just won't work and we end up offending ourselves. In the Gospel, God does not uproot the weeds, but allows them to stay till the harvest. God gives us freedom—which is something we find terribly difficult to give to one another.

Once again, we have to beware becoming prisoners of our metaphors. Pictures of the Last Judgment are very much colored by references to the Old Testament Day of Yahweh, a day of wrath. But we forget that Jesus came precisely to set us free of that image of God: God is *Abba*, "Papa." On the other hand, we can't over-emphasize that metaphor either, making God no more judgmental than a doting Grandpa.

In the judgment that Jesus envisions, the sole question (Matthew 25) will be about how compassionate—how forgiving and merciful—we were ourselves. In a very real sense, it will not be God judging us, but our finally seeing ourselves against the background of God and judging ourselves:

> *For God did not send his Son into the world to be its judge, but to be its savior.*
> *Those who believe in the Son are not judged; but those who do not believe have already been judged, because they have not believed in God's only Son. This is how the judgment works: the light has come into the world, but people love the darkness rather than the light.* John 3:17–19

> *Jesus calls to conversion. This call is an essential part of the proclamation of the kingdom: "The time is fulfilled, and the kingdom of God is at hand; repent, and believe in the gospel." In the Church's preaching this call is addressed first to those who do not yet know Christ and his Gospel. Also, Baptism is the principal place for the first and fundamental conversion.*
>
> Catechism of the Catholic Church, 1427

Reflection

A National Opinion Research Center study in 1964 showed that 38 percent of American Catholics confessed monthly; in 1974, that had declined to 17 percent. And yet in that same period, weekly communion increased from 20 percent to more than 80 percent.

- *What factors would you suspect contributed to that?*

- *What is your own personal attitude toward sin: your own comfort/discomfort with it?*

- *When you've done something undeniably belittling, how do you react?*

- *What is your response to the invitation to sit down with a fellow sinner and "have a conversation about sin"?*

- *Is your attitude toward God the same as Adam and Eve's: We can get along without you very well? Explain.*

PENANCE, CONFESSION, RECONCILIATION

Survey

This survey is not an exercise for a grade, but a means to stir up interest and get an idea of varying opinions in your group. Some of the statements are matters of objective fact; others are merely subjective opinions. On the rating scale under each statement circle the number that best reflects your current opinion about that statement.

+2 = strongly agree,
+1 = agree,
 0 = cannot make up my mind,
−1 = disagree,
−2 = strongly disagree.

Then share the reasons for your opinion.

1. Baptism is the Church's commitment to a person and it cannot be taken away.

   +2 +1 0 −1 −2

2. Sin puts the sinner in spiritual "debt" to God, which cannot be wiped out except by penance.

   +2 +1 0 −1 −2

3. Acts of penance—fasting, self-denial, pilgrimages—are an investment that binds God.

   +2 +1 0 −1 −2

4. The purpose of confession is—at least for the moment—to be completely honest with oneself.

   +2 +1 0 −1 −2

5. In Reconciliation, the priest sits as a judge over the sinner.

   +2 +1 0 −1 −2

6. If a penitent fails to mention even one serious sin, none of the other sins is forgiven.

   +2 +1 0 −1 −2

7. Since Vatican II, it is possible to celebrate Reconciliation without individual confession of sins to a priest.

   +2 +1 0 −1 −2

8. Like all sacraments, Reconciliation is about death and rebirth.

   +2 +1 0 −1 −2

9. Therapy can help patients cope, but it cannot "reconnect" them to God.

   +2 +1 0 −1 −2

10. The only thing required for reconciliation with God and others is the genuine desire to come "home."

   +2 +1 0 −1 −2

World Youth Day, Denver, Colorado, 1993.

Penance in Church History

I t is clear that Jesus did forgive sinners one-on-one, just as we do today in Reconciliation. But in the early Church, Baptism was the principal means of redemption from sin, and the Eucharist was the weekly means to sustain conversion. In the earliest days of the Church there does not seem to be any evidence at all of a ritual by which individuals could periodically be honest with themselves, the Church, and God and receive absolution.

FIRST TO SIXTH CENTURIES A.D.

During the second century of the Church's existence, a question arose whether baptized Christians whose notorious public sins had excluded them from the Church could be rebaptized. The main such sins were idolatry, apostasy, murder, abortion, and publicly flaunted adultery. But Baptism was the Church's commitment to sinners and, like the fidelity of God, couldn't be taken away, even though they had cut themselves off from communion, from the faithful.

Instead, the Church gave such sinners a public penance (wearing burlap, kneeling outside the church door during the Eucharist), so that they could demonstrate not only to everybody else but to *themselves* that they had changed. And then they had a ritual ceremony in which the bishop welcomed the prodigal "home."

This gradually became an "order of penitents," similar to the "order of catechumens," the major difference being that the penitents had already been baptized once-for-all. The only evidence of "private" penance for those who had fallen away was for the dying. But by the sixth century, few sinners entered the order of penitents voluntarily, and those who did found it an expression of commitment very like the one made by vowed religious today. But in some places, many people became ceremonial penitents for the season of Lent, which corresponded to the catechumen's final preparation for Baptism at Easter. By the tenth century, all Christians were expected to be penitents for Lent.

MIDDLE CENTURIES

From the sixth to the ninth centuries, public penance was gradually replaced by the "tariff" penitential form made popular by Irish monks reevangelizing Europe after the invasions. The monks preached the unfortunate metaphor that sin left a contaminating "stain" on the soul and the sinner in deep "debt." This was the beginning of a withdrawal from the celebration of confession with a "church," or communal, dimension to one focused almost entirely on the individual "debtor, paying a debt to God."

Each wickedness was listed in a book for priests with a proportionate penance for each (like obligatory sentencing). That insidious economic metaphor, which ultimately degraded into the literal sale-for-money of indulgences to remit the guilt of past sins, led to the Church being split in half against itself yet again in the Reformation.

While the earliest years had emphasized a second conversion as the price of reentry into the Church, the Middle Ages saw "satisfaction" and "making amends" as the cause of divine forgiveness. The metaphor was not "familial" but "economic."

Throughout the middle centuries, theologians disputed back and forth what was required for genuine redemption in the sacrament of Penance. Some (Peter Abelard, 1079–1142; Peter Lombard, 1100?–1164?) argued that:

- confession and absolution were the outward physical signs of an inward conversion of soul,

- sinners are forgiven even before they confess, and

- the function of the priest is to declare definitively that they are demonstrably forgiven.

Others (John Duns Scotus, 1265?–1308) believed the confessed sins were not the causes of forgiveness but the conditions for the absolution to be effective. And by the Council of Trent in the sixteenth century (which was unaware of the historical development of the sacrament), penance was even more tightly constricted to a "judicial forum." The priest-confessor was judge, in which the penitent had to bring forward every single sin and tell how many times he or she had committed each—not the penitential practice of Jesus.

VATICAN II

The focus of Vatican II is clearly on the gratuitous mercy of God, on love undeserved but always at the ready, and on the fulfillment of the human soul.

> Jesus, however, not only exhorted [people] to repentance so that they should abandon their sins and turn wholeheartedly to the Lord, but he also *welcomed sinners* and reconciled them with the Father.
>
> *Rite of Penance*, "Introduction"

Vatican Council II approved three rites for the celebration of the sacrament of Penance:

- first, there is the rite we are all familiar with, one-on-one, penitent and priest;

- second, a public, or communal, rite for many penitents celebrating together, including individual confession and absolution;

- third, a public rite, permitted under very special circumstances, for many penitents confessing their sinfulness and receiving absolution together without individual confessing of sins to the priest at that moment.

The theme of reconciliation runs through all the sacraments, primarily because the truth that undergirds all Christianity is death and rebirth, disruption and starting over again, conversion. Individuals want a richer life than paganism can offer, and those on the Ship of Peter reach out into the chaotic waters and "pull them in."

The prime gospel model for the sacrament of forgiveness is the story of the prodigal son. God, like the father in the story, is always forgiving, but the boy had to come home in order for the forgiveness to take effect. The problem in the story is the elder son who, to the end, is still unwilling: better to sulk in hell than serve in heaven.

God always forgives; the problem is with the self-righteous—and even more, the indifferent—who feel they have no need of it: Dr. Monika Hellwig makes it very clear:

> What this means is that the repentance and the forgiveness are two different ways of describing the same event. It is not really that the repentance comes first and after that God forgives. It would be closer to the truth to say the forgiveness comes first and that is what makes the repentance possible in the first place.

COMMUNAL RITE OF PENANCE

The whole Church, as a priestly people, acts in different ways in the work of reconciliation which has been entrusted to it by the Lord. . . . Furthermore, the Church becomes the instrument of conversion . . . through the ministry entrusted by Christ to the apostles and their successors. . . . Communal celebration [of this sacrament] shows more clearly the ecclesial nature of penance. The faithful listen together to the word of God, which proclaims his mercy and invites them to conversion.

INTRODUCTORY RITES

Song
Greeting
Opening Prayer

CELEBRATION OF THE WORD OF GOD

If there are several readings, a psalm or other appropriate song or even a period of silence should intervene between them, so that everyone may understand the word of God more deeply and give it . . . heartfelt assent. If there is only one reading, it is preferable that it be from the gospel.

Reading(s)
Homily
Examination of Conscience

Love of God
- How am I faithful or unfaithful to God's commandments?
- Have I been careful to grow in my understanding of the faith, to hear God's word?
- How am I including God in my future?

Love of Neighbor
- How am I serving others to build up the kingdom of God and a better future for the world?
- Do I use my friends and others for my own ends?
- How do I show my love and respect for the people who have authority and responsibility to care for me?

Love of Self
- How am I developing my potential as a human, a child of God?
- What use have I made of time, of health, of the gifts God has given me?
- Where is my life going?

RITE OF RECONCILIATION

General Confession of Sins

The deacon or another minister invites all to kneel or bow, and to join in saying a general formula for confession. Then they stand and say a litany or sing an appropriate song. The Lord's Prayer is always added at the end.

Individual Confession and Absolution

Members of the assembly who wish may now confess their sins privately to a priest. Each person who does so receives a penance and is absolved from sin, with the words:

> God, the Father of mercies,
> through the death and resurrection of his Son
> has reconciled the world to himself
> and sent the Holy Spirit among us
> for the forgiveness of sins;
> through the ministry of the Church
> may God give you pardon and peace,
> and I absolve you from your sins
> in the name of the Father, and of the Son, †
> and of the Holy Spirit.

The penitent answers: Amen.

Proclamation of Praise for God's Mercy
Concluding Prayer of Thanksgiving

CONCLUDING RITE

Priest: May the Lord guide your hearts in the way of his love and fill you with Christ-like presence.
All: Amen.
Priest: May he give you strength to walk in newness of life and to please him in all things.
All: Amen.
Priest: May almighty God bless you, the Father, and the Son, † and the Holy Spirit.
All: Amen.
Deacon: The Lord has freed you from your sins. Go in peace.
All: Thanks be to God.

Reconciliation / Spiritual Direction / Therapy

The model for all three—sacramental reconciliation, spiritual direction, and therapy—is the same: a one-on-one encounter in which each person places confidence in the other. All three encounters are attempts, with wisdom, compassion, and tough love, to heal alienation—from others, from the world, from oneself.

Penance, given the constraints of time, ought to be a relatively brief encounter; the purpose is forgiveness. But the confessor should be wise enough to realize when the person's problem really needs more time and perhaps continuous discussion. Then the confessor can recommend that the penitent find someone—a friend, a relative, a religious, a priest—with whom he or she can work out the problem of healing on a longer-term basis. But the confessor ought also to be wise—and humble—enough to discern when the penitent has a problem so deep-seated that it can never be healed even by the wisest and best-intentioned nonprofessional.

INDIVIDUAL RITE FOR RECONCILIATION

Priest and penitent should first prepare themselves by prayer to celebrate the sacrament. The priest should call upon the Holy Spirit so that he may receive enlightenment and charity. The penitent should compare his [or her] life with the example and commandments of Christ and then pray to God for the forgiveness of his [or her] sins.

WELCOMING THE PENITENT

Penitent: In the name of the Father, and of the Son, and of the Holy Spirit. Amen.

Priest: May God, who has enlightened every heart, help you to know your sins and trust in his mercy.

Penitent: Amen.

CELEBRATION OF THE WORD OF GOD

The priest may read or say from memory a text of Scripture which proclaims God's mercy and calls [us] to conversion.

CONFESSION OF SINS AND ACCEPTANCE OF SATISFACTION

The penitent may say a general prayer for confession before he [or she] confesses his [or her] sins.

> I confess to almighty God,
> and to you, my brothers and sisters,
> that I have sinned through my own fault
> in my thoughts and in my words,
> in what I have done,
> and in what I have failed to do;
> and I ask blessed Mary, ever virgin,
> all the angels and saints,
> and you, my brothers and sisters,
> to pray for me to the Lord our God.

[The priest] urges [the penitent] to be sorry for his [or her] faults, reminding [the penitent] that through the sacrament of penance the Christian dies and rises with Christ.

The penitent confesses his [or her] sins. The priest encourages the penitent to have sincere sorrow and offers suitable counsel to help the penitent begin a new life.

Then the priest imposes an act of penance or satisfaction on the penitent. . . . This act of penance may suitably take the form of prayer, self-denial, and especially service of one's neighbor and works of mercy. These will underline the fact that sin and its forgiveness have a social aspect.

PRAYER OF THE PENITENT AND ABSOLUTION

The penitent says an act of contrition. For example:

> My God,
> I am sorry for my sins with all my heart.
> In choosing to do wrong
> and failing to do good,
> I have sinned against you
> whom I should love above all things.
> I firmly intend, with your help,
> to do penance,
> to sin no more,
> and to avoid whatever leads me to sin.
> Our Savior Jesus Christ
> suffered and died for us.
> In his name, my God, have mercy.

The priest extends his hands . . . over the head of the penitent and pronounces the formula of absolution.

- The form of absolution indicates that the reconciliation of the penitent comes from the mercy of the Father;

- it shows the connection between the reconciliation of the sinner and the paschal mystery of Christ;

- it stresses the role of the Holy Spirit in the forgiveness of sins;

- finally, it underlines the ecclesial aspect of the sacrament because reconciliation with God is asked for and given through the ministry of the Church.

PROCLAMATION OF PRAISE AND DISMISSAL

Priest: Give thanks to the Lord, for he is good.

Penitent: His mercy endures for ever.

Priest: The Lord has freed you from your sins. Go in peace.

Then the confessor can recommend that the penitent consult a good psychiatrist, psychologist, marriage counselor.

But the functions of penance and spiritual direction on the one hand are quite different from the functions of psychotherapy on the other. Therapists would never intrude their religious beliefs (or disbelief) on the interchange, nor would they be swayed by the client's religious beliefs (unless those beliefs were part of the problem). The therapist is trying to help clients understand what events and relationships in the past have left them unable to cope with the present. The therapist wants to lead patients to an understanding, acceptance, and peace with the *causes* of an unsatisfactory relationship with self and others.

On the contrary, the good confessor very much wants to share his vision of human weakness and dignity with penitents; the confessor is after all a forgiven sinner himself. Like the psychiatrist, the confessor wants to begin healing rifts in that "horizontal" moral web of human relationships, but unlike the psychiatrist, the confessor wants to begin healing the "vertical" relationship with God as well. The confessor wants to help penitents understand, accept, and be at peace with the fact that—no matter what the causes—there is a *reason* to feel completely free of the burdens that those actions have put on their souls, to *accept being accepted* by God, no matter what they have done. They are "at home." At least for a while, cosmos has replaced chaos once again.

Spiritual direction might be too manipulative and regulatory a term. Rather, those concerned with healing or enriching the life of the soul—precisely what separates us from animals and robots—is greatly helped by seeking out someone they know who is *wise* and with whom they can periodically discuss what is going on in their lives, good and bad, with complete frankness.

If people drink too much, swear too much, lose patience too much, there is no reason to cover it up, especially from themselves. The purpose is to see things—and themselves—*as they are* and to discern together realistic ways of growing more profoundly human and more deeply Christian.

Ambassadors of Christ

The word *mercy* is not really a good translation for the Hebrew *hesed*. *Hesed* has more the sense of Yahweh's *faithfulness* to Israel despite her constant betrayals.

> *"The mountains and hills may crumble, but my love for you will never end; I will keep forever my promise of peace."*
>
> Isaiah 54:10

Nor is God's forgiveness merely a gift simply given and received. It is an empowerment to forgive, as well.

The capacity for forgiveness usually arises out of the experience of being forgiven—love undeserved. Jesus invites us to the same:

> *"Be merciful just as your Father is merciful."*   Luke 6:36

Jesus healed people despite the restrictions of the Sabbath and despite people being foreigners.

In the Lord's Prayer we acknowledge that we will be forgiven only insofar as we forgive. Forgiveness is, in fact, the sole reason Jesus came: to declare the amnesty of God (Luke 4:19). Jesus proclaimed:

"This is my blood, which seals God's covenant, my blood poured out for many for the forgiveness of sins."
                                    Matthew 26:28

Saint Paul continues:

All this is done by God, who through Christ changed us from enemies into God's friends and gave us the task of making others God's friends also. Our message is that God was making all human beings God's friends through Christ. . . .
      Here we are, then, speaking for Christ, as though God were appealing through us.
                    From 2 Corinthians 5:18–20

At Mass we remember and celebrate Jesus, "It will be shed for you and for all so that sins may be forgiven. Do this in memory of me" (Roman Missal). Not just share the cup but also forgive sins. As learning to cope with the pain makes most of us more compassionate, so periodic confession makes people less judgmental, more merciful, clear-eyed enough to acknowledge the sin but aware of the weaknesses in their own lives.

The whole power of the sacrament of Penance consists in restoring us to God's grace and joinign us with him in our intimate friendship.

Catechism of the Catholic Church, 1468

Parents, for instance, whose unmarried daughter shocks them with the news she is pregnant have several options. They can rant and rave; shake a finger and say, "Now this is what you're going to do, young lady!"; collapse into self-pity and wonder what they had done wrong; or put their arms around her and share her sorrow. That last choice is not an act of in-charge parents; it is an act of love. At least for the moment, the girl's shame is more important than their own.

The worst human beings can do to Christ is not to spit in his face, mock him, scourge him, boot him through the streets, crucify him. The worst they can do is ignore him.

Reflection

Think of a time when, contrary to all your expectations, someone forgave you, a time when you felt graced; loved undeservedly.

■ *What had you done, and how did the person you hurt respond?*

Think of a time when, with a great deal of fear and embarrassment, you spilled out something shaming in confession, and the priest welcomed you back and made you feel completely free of guilt.

■ *How did you feel?*
■ *Was the relief when it was over worth the cost of bringing it out into the open? Why?*

Think of someone you have had a longtime grudge against.

■ *Would it be worth the undeniable discomfort and embarrassment to set both of you free of that burden? Why or why not?*

It is *called the* sacrament of conversion
because it makes sacramentally present
Jesus' call to conversion. . . .
It is *called the* sacrament of Penance,
since it consecrates the Christian sinner's
personal and ecclesial steps
of conversion, penance, and satisfaction.
It is *called the* sacrament of confession,
since the disclosure or confession of sins
to a priest is an essential element of this sacrament.
In a profound sense it is also a "confession"—
acknowledgment and praise—
of the holiness of God and of his mercy. . . .
It is *called the* sacrament of forgiveness,
since by the priest's sacramental absolution
God grants the penitent "pardon and peace."
It is *called the* sacrament of Reconciliation,
because it imparts to the sinner the love of God
who reconciles: "Be reconciled to God."
He who lives by God's merciful love
is ready to respond to the Lord's call:
"Go; first be reconciled to your brother."

Catechism of the Catholic Church, 1423–1424

Understanding Penance and Reconciliation

Review

1. What is the difference between moral evil and sin?

2. Explain: "The sacrament of penance is a conversation between Christians about sin. This human need is attested to by groups as diverse as bartenders and psychiatrists."

3. What does *The Picture of Dorian Gray* say about the effect of unacknowledged sins on our inner selves—our souls?

4. What are the only sins Jesus got angry about?

5. How does the text explain the one unforgivable sin: "Whoever says evil things against the Holy Spirit"? Why is that sin unforgivable? What is the relationship between forgiveness and feeling the need to ask for forgiveness?

6. In the four scriptural episodes in which Jesus "heard confessions," what elements of confession are conspicuously *absent* from what we have been led to believe confession is all about?

7. The Samaritan woman at the well had had five "husbands." How does Jesus deal with that?

8. How are reconciliation, spiritual direction, and psychotherapy alike? How are they radically different?

9. The text uses the (admittedly inadequate) linear, spatial metaphor "horizontal" to describe our relationships with one another and "vertical" to describe our relationship with God (inadequate because it makes God seem "up there"). How are the two identical—and yet different?

10. Baptism and Confirmation are gifts only insofar as they are judgments that one is worthy of the challenge to be an apostle. Similarly, forgiveness is also a challenge. To what? What metaphor did Saint Paul use to describe that mission?

Discuss

1. A student once wrote, "In confession I skip over the things I'm really ashamed of and then, just before the priest gives me absolution, I interrupt and say that I also lied." Comment.

2. You were supposed to be home by midnight, but you were having fun and didn't get home till two. If your parents ask the next day, and you're perfectly honest with them—no matter the penalty, what effect would that have the next time, when you actually are innocent but seem guilty? What effect does consistent honesty have not only on your soul but on your reputation?

3. Like an overawareness of death, over-awareness of sin can become morbid. Nowadays, however, most people at least seem armored against any awareness at all either of death or sin. How are their souls impoverished by that lack of awareness?

4. When you think of Nazi concentration camps, *The Exorcist,* or *The Lord of the Flies*, evil is obvious. Why isn't it obvious when we read the first half of the newspaper? Or do we even bother to read that part?

5. Psychologists have shown that small children cannot tell the difference between the real deaths they see on the TV news and the faked deaths they see on cop shows. What effect does that have on their souls?

6. We all want freedom—or we say we do. Yet all of us balk at confessing as we balk at going to the dentist. Why? Why are a few moments of embarrassment weighted more heavily than a sense of freedom? What does it feel like *after* you're finished with the dentist? What does it feel like after you've had reconciliation?

7. The older brother of the prodigal son had never done anything really "wrong." But what was his relationship with his father? Remind you of anyone?

8. If Jesus is the model of all Christians, what does his way of handling sinners—even Judas who betrayed him and Peter who lied about knowing him—suggest about our handling of those who offend us? Each time we say the Our Father, unthinkingly, we ask God to forgive us only insofar "as we forgive those who trespass against us." Is there anyone who's hurt you whom you haven't forgiven? What would a Christian do about that?

9. Is there any value at all in "doing penance," as many do in Lent, not to atone to God but for other reasons? Before you answer too quickly: aren't lifting weights and doing windsprints inflicting pain on yourself? If they have a purpose, what is it? How is that purpose similar to doing penance?

10. Any priest you encounter would be more than happy to hear your confession at any time convenient for the two of you. He would also be more than willing, say, once a month, to sit down with you and talk over the state of your soul. That's what he was ordained for, to serve the Church. Would you ever think to ask a priest if you could "kick things around" once in a while? What would be the obstacles? Are they very weighty?

Activities

1. The media has a penchant for portraying events that reveal the many forces of evil at work in our society. Identify three to five "stories about evil" that have made the headlines. In small groups share your findings. Come to a group consensus on (1) how each event has harmed the web of relationships that build up a society, and (2) how the perpetrators of the evil should be dealt with.

2. Debate this statement: The media's focus on the evil in our society serves no positive or constructive purpose.

3. Research one other "creation story" and report on how it tells of the origin of evil in the world.

4. In the four thousand verses of the Gospels, how much space does Jesus give to hell, punishment, and judgment? Does that mean there is no hell, punishment, or judgment?

Scripture Readings

Skim the passages. Pick one that appeals to you and (1) summarize its main point, (2) tell how it relates to the chapter, and (3) list one or two thoughts that entered your mind as you read it.

- Genesis 3:1–19   The fruit of the tree
- Deuteronomy 30:15–20   Life and prosperity, death and evil
- Isaiah 5:1–7   Wild grapes
- Zechariah 1:1–6   Return to me
- Luke 19:1–10   The Son of Man seeks those who are lost
- John 15:9–14   Do what I command you
- Romans 3:22–26   Redemption in Christ Jesus
- Ephesians 6: 10–18   Stand firm against evil
- Revelation 2:1–5   Do penance

✎ Journal

The writers of the Scriptures portray God as one who forgives unconditionally. What kind of "forgiver" are you? Why is that? Think about an incident in which someone "offended" you. How did you deal with that incident? How are you now dealing with the person who offended you? Are you an "unconditional" forgiver? Why is that?

Chapter 8

Anointing of the Sick: Sickness and Death

"Happy are those who mourn;
God will comfort them!"
Matthew 5:4

DOORWAY TO TRANSCENDENCE

Survey

This survey is not an exercise for a grade, but a means to stir up interest and get an idea of varying opinions in your group. Some of the statements are matters of objective fact; others are merely subjective opinions. On the rating scale under each statement circle the number that best reflects your current opinion about that statement.

+2 = strongly agree,
+1 = agree,
 0 = cannot make up my mind,
−1 = disagree,
−2 = strongly disagree.

Then share the reasons for your opinion.

1. If you want a fulfilled life, put up your guard and never let it down.

    +2 +1 0 −1 −2

2. When Jesus asks us to "carry a cross," the cross is the burden of being human, not animal.

    +2 +1 0 −1 −2

3. The reason suffering and death came into being is that a man and woman once ate a piece of fruit.

    +2 +1 0 −1 −2

4. Like birth, weaning, and adolescence, suffering is an opportunity.

    +2 +1 0 −1 −2

5. In the Gospels, Jesus never asked anyone to "offer up" suffering in atonement for sin.

    +2 +1 0 −1 −2

6. Health is not merely the absence of pain but involves the whole person: body, mind, and soul.

    +2 +1 0 −1 −2

7. Self-possessed people can face suffering better than people who never have taken possession of their souls.

    +2 +1 0 −1 −2

8. A nurse's smile and touch are as important as her medical skills.

    +2 +1 0 −1 −2

9. Those who deny themselves the experience of the ill and frail impoverish their own lives.

    +2 +1 0 −1 −2

10. Medical personnel can often let health care devolve into no more than a mere job.

    +2 +1 0 −1 −2

A Puzzlement

He had an improbable name: Bill Fold. A merchant seaman without family, in a terminal cancer ward. His larynx had been removed, and he could communicate only in writing. More debilitating, he had also contracted tuberculosis, so he was in complete isolation; all visitors entering his room had to be gowned and masked.

One day the priest chaplain who visited him every week asked if there was anything he could do for him, and Bill quickly wrote on his pad, "I'd like to have the last rites." The priest was puzzled. Doctors said Bill could last another year.

At the time, anointing was restricted to those in imminent danger of dying. But the large dark eyes were so pleading that the priest threw caution and church law to the winds. He heard Bill's confession, anointed him, and gave him communion.

When it was over, his eyes puddled with tears, Bill wrote on his pad, "I'm so grateful. Is there anything I can do for you?"

The priest thought a moment and then said, "When you get there, Bill, mention my name."

And Bill wrote, "I shall."

As he was leaving, the priest said, "Bill, it must get very lonely."

And Bill wrote, "Yes. But isn't it wonderful that God has given me the strength and trust to deal with my suffering?"

And that night Bill Fold died.

■ *What did Bill mean by "God trusts me enough"?*

Suffering

Since the rise of the omnipresent electronic media and their total domination of a great part of our lives, we have become thick-skinned to the assaults of others' sufferings on our souls. The anguished eyes of starving children, raped and battered women, mothers grieving for children shot by strangers are too much to bear. Seeing a drunk or an addict sprawled senseless on the sidewalk makes us avert our eyes as we would from an animal smashed on the road. When students see seniors degrading ninth graders, they turn away like the priest and the Levite in the gospel story of the Good Samaritan. But by being so protective of our sensibilities—and our children's—we impoverish our souls.

World Trade Center bombing victim, 1993.

FUNDAMENTAL QUESTION

Philosophers from Gautama Buddha (563?–483 B.C.) to Karl Marx (1818–1883) began their observations with the question of human suffering. If you haven't started there, you haven't started. Religion asks that same question in many ways:

- Does life have some focal meaning *despite* this suffering I endure?

- Is there some cosmos in the midst of this disorienting chaos?

- If God is *both* all-powerful *and* all-loving, then *why* am I visited with this evil?

It is the Job question: "Why let people go on living in misery?" (Job 3:20). So too with Christianity; the meaning of suffering is at its very heart.

> *"But before the end comes, the gospel must be preached to all peoples. And when you are arrested and taken to court, do not worry ahead of time about what you are going to say; when the time comes, say whatever is then given to you.*

> *For the words you speak will not be yours; they will come from the Holy Spirit. People will hand over their own brothers and sisters to be put to death, and parents will do the same to their children. Children will turn against their parents and have them put to death. Everyone will hate you because of me. But whoever holds out to the end will be saved."*   From Mark 13:10–13

Whoever wants to follow Jesus to fulfillment is asked to carry a cross:

> *"If any of you want to come with me, you must forget yourself, carry your cross, and follow me."*   Matthew 16:24

What is the cross? Being asked to live a human rather than an animal life. Facing suffering not with helpless groans but with dignity. The suffering of Jesus—as with the suffering of Job—is the suffering of the innocent. Why would a good God create a world in which the innocent could suffer and all must die?

Los Angeles Earthquake, 1994.

MEANING OF SUFFERING

Tertullian (160?–230 A.D.), Saint Augustine (354–430 A.D.), and other theologians of the past said that suffering is God's retribution for sin, just as today some very un-Christian Christians say AIDS is God's punishment for sexual promiscuity. Suffering, these theologians said, can be offered up for others.

Pope John Paul II in his 1989 letter on *The Christian Meaning of Suffering* said that through suffering people are destined to *go beyond* themselves. Suffering is the doorway to transcendence. The answer to the question of human suffering is right there in Jesus, the Christ.

In the Gospels, Jesus never asks any suffering person to "offer up" that suffering to God, in atonement for his or her sins or for someone else's. The God Jesus serves does not "require" suffering, but offers suffering as an "opportunity." For what?

Just as guilt becomes meaningful when we turn it into responsibility, suffering becomes meaningful only when—like any other natural crisis in life—we open our minds and hearts to wider horizons. Sister Thea Bowman (1937–1990), who struggled and suffered with and died from cancer, saw her suffering this way:

Perhaps it's an incentive for struggling human beings to reach out to one another, to help one another, to love one another, to be blessed and strengthened and humanized in the process. Perhaps it's an incentive to see Christ in our world and to view the work of Christ and feel the suffering of Christ.

Sister Thea Bowman, (1937–1990).
(Artist: Marshall Bouldin, 1988)

Illness and suffering have always been among the gravest problems confronted in human life. . . . Every illness can make us glimpse death.

Catechism of the Catholic Church, 1500

SICKNESS AND THE WHOLE SELF

The preamble to the charter of the World Health Organization presents us with a holistic view of health:

> Health is a state of complete physical, mental, and social well-being and not merely the absence of disease or infirmity.

The root meaning of the word *health* is "completeness," "wholeness." Health involves the *whole* person: body, mind, and soul. Each of us is not—or was not meant to be—just an uneasy composite of antagonistic functions. We are meant to be a *self*, known, accepted—a person we are more or less "at home" being.

Sickness does not attack just the body. It attacks a total human being. Illness forces us to confront the limitations that bodiliness imposes on our souls: on our hopes, our dreams, our desire to be meaningful. Illness is a crisis of faith, hope, and love.

It is a crisis of faith insofar as it challenges not only our trust in God (the problem of Job) but also our faith in life itself. The future, which seemed since childhood to stretch indefinitely forward, has now contracted, often to a predictable number of months. "I am no longer independent. I have to yield myself to others."

It is a crisis of hope because it defers our plans or perhaps even makes them totally unrealizable. "I can't even control my own life. I'm not in charge, even of my own destiny."

It is a crisis of love, disrupting relationships with friends and family. "How can I be such a burden to them? How can I strain their tolerance like this?"

When one's life is threatened, it inevitably lessens one's concerns to the self: my pain, my needs, my heartbreak. It is difficult to love when one becomes self-absorbed, devouring the self.

Sickness is the hardest challenge to the soul, the inner self. Nurses, doctors, and aides in hospitals and nursing homes can tell within a day the patients who are self-possessed, optimistic, confident, "at home" within themselves, and those who are self-absorbed, alienated, bitter, "lost."

If illness affects the whole person—not just the body but also the soul as well—then the approach to healing must be holistic as well, caring for the *whole* person. A nurse's smile and touch are as important as her medical knowledge and skills. Sister Jennifer Glenn, Congregation of the Sisters of Charity of the Incarnate Word, gives us this vision of Christian healing:

> True healing consists less in cure than in conversion. . . . The Christian work of healing invokes the power of God made available in Jesus Christ to enable the sick and all who participate in their sickness to resolve whatever aspects of the crisis of hope, faith and love stand in the way of their wholehearted commitment to the life of the reign of God.

It is not only the patient who is involved in this illness but family and friends too—and also the doctors, nurses, aides, and the workers who mop the floors. All need healing, need compassion, need reminding not only of their own mortality but of the web of human relationships that bind them to one another and to each of their patients. Just as health-care workers can tell the patients who have a hold on their own souls and those who are fragmented, patients can tell the health givers who are truly that, and those who treat patients as biological problems.

> *Illness can lead to anguish, self-absorption, sometimes even despair and revolt against God. It can also make a person more mature. . . . Very often illness provokes a search for God and a return to him.*
>
> Catechism of the Catholic Church, 1501

Sickness and Sacrament

A sacrament is an external symbolic action that physicalizes an internal reality, like faith, hope, love. The sacramental activities of the Church that are concerned with the needs of the sick and the dying are not restricted to "the last rites," to be performed at the final moments of one's life. Suffering is a process that may go on for years. And the people who are suffering sickness can be a "sacrament" to those around them, and those around those who are sick can be "sacraments" to them.

THE SICK AS MINISTERS

Picture yourself as a sick person bedridden in a hospital room, having visitors. Seeing them come into the room, you force a smile. You are cheered because you are no longer alone, yet you are praying your visitors will not stay too long, suffering their kindness, telling the symptoms yet again and again.

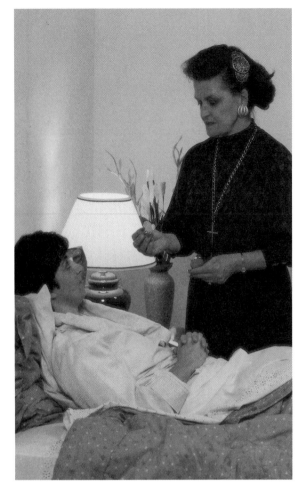

We who live in a culture that glorifies youth, health, and attractiveness, and that tries to deny human weakness and dependency, *need* the reminder that the physically impaired offer us. Experiencing their illness with them helps us discern the hollow falsity of the "conventional wisdom" about what is truly important. People suffering with sickness remind us of the precariousness of life, and, therefore, how precious each of our days is. Those who deny themselves the experience of the ill, the elderly, the impaired, because of the discomfort, awkwardness, intrusion on their time, impoverish themselves.

MINISTRY WITH THE SICK

In today's culture the emphasis has shifted almost totally to the technical, medical aspects of the problem of illness, which often are not only painful but humiliating. In such a culture, the sick person's need for the support of the community is even more essential.

All the baptized are called to be sacraments to the sick—and the elderly. The whole ministry with people who are sick is not to be placed solely on the shoulders of the ordained ministers of the Church. The fact that the priest or deacon does visit the ill and elderly is praiseworthy, but there are far more lay people in a parish who need to share in that ministry. Lay ministers can visit people in need of buoying up. Neighbors can visit friends who have "taken leave" of the Church and would never tolerate the presence of a priest, and "soften them up"—plow before planting. Family and friends can be a great comfort and support, a reminder that—even in the hospital—one is still "at home." The sick person does not have to face fear and uncertainty alone.

But as a believer you feel what all sacraments are meant to make us feel: you are not alone. You are "at home." As one who is sick you are in a very true sense a "minister for others."

People who suffer from sickness are living pleas to other Christians for compassion; they are Christ suffering:

> *"I tell you, whenever you did this for one of the least important of these followers of mine, you did it for me!"*
>
> Matthew 25:40

They witness by their honest faith, their struggle against illness, their willingness to accept the challenge of weakness with dignity and hope.

Medical personnel are also obviously ministers to the sick, not only ministering to the body but to the soul as well. Their kindness and compassion are as important as their knowledge and medicines.

Even nonbelievers can be ministers in that sense, just as nonbelieving teachers who enable young people to reason make students more able to respond to the challenge of humanity and Christianity.

The parish is a segment of the body of Christ with which the sick person has been identified. As Saint Paul said:

> *If one part of the body suffers, all the other parts suffer with it.*
> 1 Corinthians 12:26

Not only should the parish assembled at Mass each Sunday join in praying for suffering fellow members when their names are mentioned, but they should also make the effort to go and visit with them. We can minister to the sick and elderly of our parish in many ways: we can babysit the children while the mother or father stays with her or his spouse in the hospital, drop off food, run errands.

From the very earliest days of the Church, after the Sunday celebration of the Eucharist, family members took bits of the consecrated bread home for relatives who were too ill to attend. Today, ministers of the sick do the same. They come to the priest–presider at the end of the communion rite to be publicly sent forth from the assembly to those who cannot be there.

The Rite for the Visitation and Communion of the Sick itself is a kind of small rendering of the Mass:

- Greeting
- Penitential Rite, a prayer for forgiveness
- Reading from Scriptures, silent reflection, or a sharing of insights into the passage
- The Lord's Prayer
- Communion
- Concluding Rite, prayer of thanksgiving
- Blessing

Reflection

Gold and silver are precious because they are rare. Earth, air, water seem to be unimportant—until they are threatened by drought or pollution. Then at least those who are not totally self-absorbed begin to understand their true value.

- *List—in no particular order—the things you would miss most painfully if they or you were threatened.*
- *Now painstakingly put them in order of priority.*

Christ's compassion toward the sick and his many healings of every kind of infirmity are a resplendent sign that "God has visited his people" and that the Kingdom of God is close at hand. . . . [Christ's] preferential love for the sick has not ceased through the centuries to draw the very special attention of Christians toward all those who suffer in body and soul. It is the source of tireless efforts to comfort them.

Catechism of the Catholic Church, 1503

SACRAMENT OF THE SICK

Survey

This survey is not an exercise for a grade, but a means to stir up interest and get an idea of varying opinions in your group. Some of the statements are matters of objective fact; others are merely subjective opinions. On the rating scale under each statement circle the number that best reflects your current opinion about that statement.

+2 = strongly agree,
+1 = agree,
 0 = cannot make up my mind,
−1 = disagree,
−2 = strongly disagree.

Then share the reasons for your opinion.

1. The norm for receiving the sacrament of the Anointing of the Sick is "danger of death."

   +2 +1 0 −1 −2

2. Celebrating the Anointing of the Sick places an obligation on God to heal those who are anointed.

   +2 +1 0 −1 −2

3. The celebration of the sacrament of the Anointing of the Sick heals not the body but the soul.

   +2 +1 0 −1 −2

4. Ministers of the sick are empowered to administer the sacrament of the sick.

   +2 +1 0 −1 −2

5. Like Baptism, Anointing of the Sick is also a healing for those who care for the sufferer.

   +2 +1 0 −1 −2

6. The anointing of the dying symbolizes sending "one of our own" on a mission.

   +2 +1 0 −1 −2

7. The noblest response to losing a loved one is to suppress grief.

   +2 +1 0 −1 −2

8. Holding a wake service with a coffin present is a morbid and useless exercise.

   +2 +1 0 −1 −2

9. By the time children are ten or so, they ought to begin coping with the reality of death.

   +2 +1 0 −1 −2

10. The most crucial question of human life is, Is that all there is?

    +2 +1 0 −1 −2

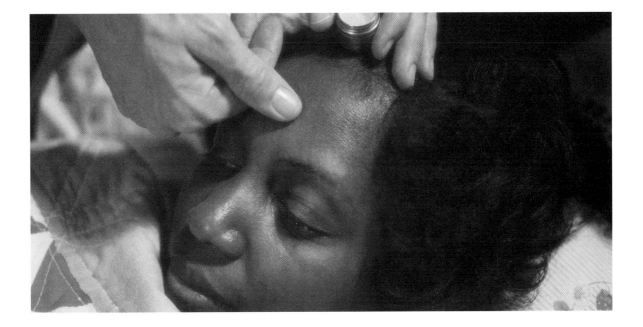

Anointing the Sick

In the New Testament, we read that Jesus sent out the Twelve and they anointed sick people and healed them.

They went out and preached that people should turn away from their sins. They drove out many demons, and rubbed olive oil on many sick people and healed them.   Mark 6:12–13

But the classic New Testament text regarding this sacrament and the Church's anointing of those who are sick is found in the Letter from James:

Are any among you sick? They should send for the church elders, who will pray for them and rub olive oil on them in the name of the Lord. This prayer made in faith will heal the sick; the Lord will restore them to health, and the sins they have committed will be forgiven. So then, confess your sins to one another and pray for one another, so that you will be healed. The prayer of a good person has a powerful effect.   James 5:14–16

SUBJECT OF THE SACRAMENT

Before the changes instituted by Vatican Council II, the norm used to decide whether a person could receive this sacrament—which used to be called Extreme Unction—was that a person be in the "danger of death." Now the norm is that one be "seriously impaired by illness or old age." On the one hand, someone cannot be anointed merely because he or she is mildly "indisposed." On the other, anointing after death is forbidden—the soul is gone; the rite can benefit no one.

But what if a person is still alive but in a coma or deranged?

Anointing may be conferred upon sick people who, although they have lost consciousness or the use of reason, would, as Christian believers, probably have asked for it were they in control of their faculties.

Rite of Anointing and Pastoral Care of the Sick, "Introduction"

The sacrament of the Anointing of the Sick has a twofold purpose:

- first, to bring all the support and encouragement of the Church to those who are suffering, and
- second, to help them put this challenge into the perspective of the death and resurrection of Christ.

It promises no miracles. Rather it is a healing of the soul, healing the bitterness, the fear, the loneliness. The celebrating of this sacramental ritual puts this agonizing event into the context where it does have meaning: eternity.

Suffering and illness are not in themselves redemptive. In fact the experience of pain tends to erode faith rather than build it up.

But experiencing pain can become meaningful, even empowering, if the sufferer realizes that it was up the painful path to Calvary that Jesus found rebirth.

Anointing the forehead of the sick person, the priest prays:

> Through this holy anointing
> may the Lord in his love and mercy
>   help you
> with the grace of the Holy Spirit.

Then anointing the sick person's hands he prays:

> May the Lord who frees you from sin
> save you and raise you up.

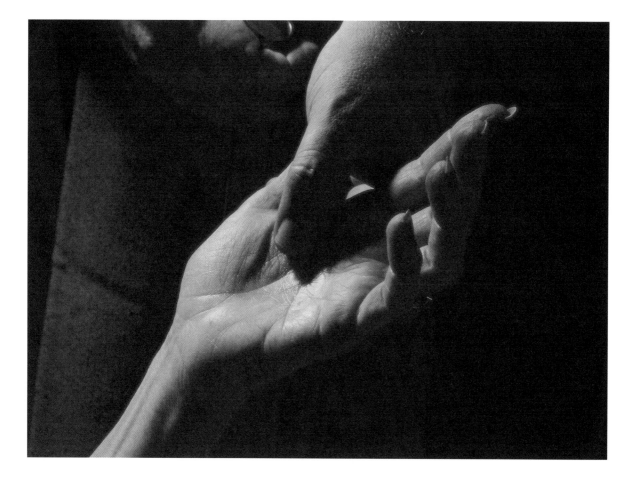

MINISTER OF THE SACRAMENT

At present, the only one empowered to administer this sacrament is a priest or a bishop. Some theologians argue for a return to the practice of the earlier Church in which lay persons brought oil blessed by the bishop to anoint the ill and dying. And there is much to be said for that.

- Priests are becoming fewer.

- Deacons are quite often given charge of the ministries for the sick in a parish.

- There are far more lay people, and they already do bring communion to the sick and elderly.

However, perhaps the presence of the priest himself is more meaningful *to the sick person* than are his actions, prayers, or oils, at least in the case of the final anointing when death is imminent. For the person's entire lifetime, the Roman collar has somehow "said" that God must have a purpose. The presence of the priest "says" that we know Jesus went through all this too. This reminder not only shows us that death is inevitable even for the Best of Us but also shows us how to do it well.

The first grace
of this sacrament is one
of strengthening,
peace and courage
to overcome the difficulties
that go with the condition
of serious illness
or the frailty of old age.
This grace is a gift
of the Holy Spirit, who renews
trust and faith in God
and strengthens against the
temptations of the evil one,
the temptation to
discouragement and anguish
in the face of death.

Catechism of the Catholic Church, 1520

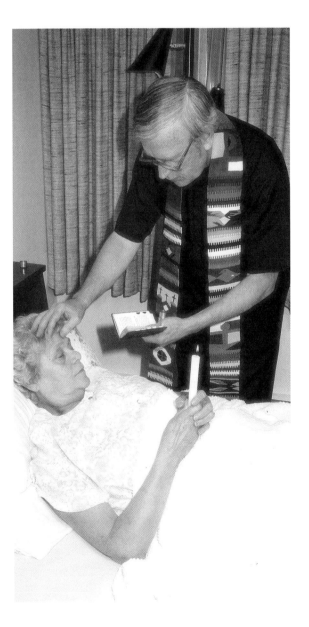

RITE OF ANOINTING OF THE SICK

The sacrament of anointing prolongs the concern which the Lord himself showed for the bodily and spiritual welfare of the sick, as the gospels testify, and which he asked his followers to show also. . . . Christ, therefore, strengthens the faithful who are afflicted by illness with the sacrament of anointing, providing them with the strongest means of support.

PREPARATION FOR THE CELEBRATION

The sick person who is not confined to bed may receive the sacrament of anointing in the church or some other appropriate place.

INTRODUCTORY RITES

The priest may sprinkle the sick person and those present with holy water.

Greeting

Sprinkling with Holy Water

> Let this water call to mind our baptism into Christ,
> who by his death and resurrection
> has redeemed us.

Instruction

> My dear friends, we are gathered here in the name
> of our Lord Jesus Christ who is present among us.
> As the gospels relate, the sick came to him for healing;
> moreover, he loves us so much that he died for our
> sake. Through the apostle James, he has commanded
> us: "Are there any who are sick among you? Let them
> send for the priests of the Church, and let the priests
> pray over them, anointing them with oil in the name
> of the Lord; and the prayer of faith will save the
> sick persons, and the Lord will raise them up; and if
> they have committed any sins, their sins will be
> forgiven them."

Penitential Rite

LITURGY OF THE WORD

Reading
Response

LITURGY OF ANOINTING

Litany
Laying On of Hands

Prayer over the Oil

> Make this oil a remedy for all who are anointed with it;
> heal them in body, in soul, and in spirit,
> and deliver them from every affliction.

Anointing

First the priest anoints the forehead, saying:

> Through this holy anointing
> may the Lord in his love and mercy help you
> with the grace of the Holy Spirit.

Then he anoints the hands, saying:

> May the Lord who frees you from sin
> save you and raise you up.

Prayer after Anointing

The priest may pray this prayer after anointing a young person:

> God our healer,
> in this time of sickness you have come
> to bless [Name] with your grace.
> Restore him/her to health and strength,
> make him/her joyful in spirit,
> and ready to embrace your will.

The Lord's Prayer

LITURGY OF HOLY COMMUNION

Communion

The priest shows the eucharistic bread to those present, saying:

> This is the Lamb of God
> who takes away the sins of the world.
> Come to me, all you that labor and are burdened,
> and I will refresh you.

Silent Prayer
Prayer after Communion

CONCLUDING RITE

Blessing

The priest blesses the sick person and the others present.

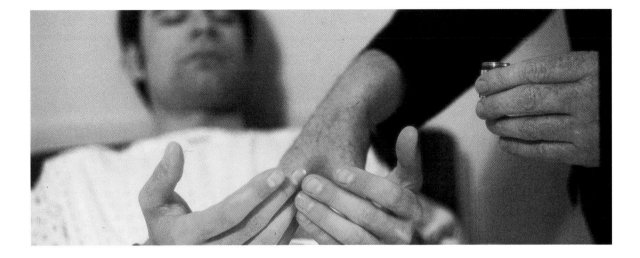

RITE OF ANOINTING

Oil is a *seal*, as in "signed and sealed."
Anointing with oil says, "This is one of
ours!" And often, as with anointing of kings
and prophets, it is a sign of mission: "We
are sending you on to give witness to us
there," as Bill Fold promised he would for
the priest who anointed him. But until then,
we are missioning you to be witnesses to
us, about what faith, hope, and love really
mean. But most importantly the anointing of
a sick person unites the sufferer with Christ,
the Messiah, the Anointed One.

Touching is also a very important
symbolic action in Jesus' mission. A woman
suffering from bleeding for many years
believed that if she could only *touch* the
hem of Jesus' garment, she would be cured,
and so she was:

> *A woman who had suffered from severe
> bleeding for twelve years came up
> behind Jesus and touched the edge of his
> cloak. She said to herself, "If only I touch
> his cloak, I will get well."*
>
> *Jesus turned around and saw her,
> and said, "Courage, my daughter! Your
> faith has made you well." At that very
> moment the woman became well.*
> Matthew 9:20–22

A man with a skin disease came to Jesus
and said:

> *"Sir, if you want to, you can make me
> clean."*
>
> *Jesus reached out and touched him.
> "I do want to," he answered. "Be clean!"
> At once the man was healed of his
> disease.*   Matthew 8:2–3

Another time, two blind men followed
Jesus, shouting:

> *"Have mercy on us, Son of David!"*
>
> *When Jesus had gone indoors, the
> two blind men came to him, and he
> asked them, "Do you believe that I can
> heal you?"*
>
> *"Yes, sir!" they answered.*
>
> *Then Jesus touched their eyes and
> said, "Let it happen, then, just as you
> believe!"—and their sight was
> restored.*   Matthew 9:27–30

As Jesus was traveling to Sidon,
some people brought to him a man who
was deaf and could hardly speak. They
begged Jesus to place his hands on him
and heal him.

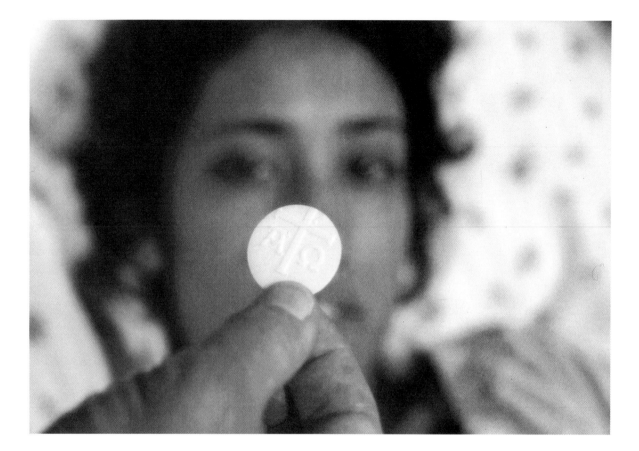

So Jesus took him off alone, away from the crowd, put his fingers in the man's ears, spat, and touched the man's tongue. Then Jesus looked up to heaven, gave a deep groan, and said to the man, "Ephphatha," which means "Open up!"

At once the man was able to hear, his speech impediment was removed, and he began to talk without any trouble.   Mark 7:33–35

The touch was important, but in each case its effectiveness was in *response* to the victim's faith, just as the effectiveness of forgiveness depends on the sinner's felt need to be forgiven.

During the celebration of this sacrament, the priest lays his hands on, or touches, the head of the sick person in silence. Laying on of hands on the recipient of a sacrament—

in Baptism, Confirmation, Reconciliation, Holy Orders, Anointing of the Sick—is a direct connection between two human beings. The human body both defines us as particular selves and separates our inward selves from others' inward selves. Touch bridges that gap. The laying on of hands at the anointing reenacts all those saving contacts the person has felt with the body of Christ through touch.

Unfortunately in our society we are very wary of touch. Rather than being a way to bridge the gap between our separated selves, touching seems a threat, an intrusion within our defenses, almost a violation of some unwritten law. One only has to see how restrained we are at sharing the sign of peace, which is part of our celebration of the Eucharist.

Death

Like all the sacraments the Anointing of the Sick is a liturgical and communal celebration, whether it takes place in the family home, a hospital or church, for a single sick person or a whole group of sick persons.

Catechism of the Catholic Church, 1517

eath seems the ultimate insult. Strive and strive and strive for this, like Sisyphus, a legendary king of Corinth condemned eternally to rolling a heavy rock up a hill in Hades only to have it roll down again as it nears the top. Saint Thomas Aquinas (1225?–1274), with stark forthrightness, called the last anointing, *sacramentum exeuntium*, "the sacrament of those on their way out." But death was the ultimate insult for Jesus too. THE most crucial question of human life is, Is that all there is?

Tomb of the Unknown Soldier. Arlington National Cemetery.

The Greek word *paschein,* from which we get the word *paschal* (as in the Paschal Mystery of Jesus), means "to suffer," in the sense of "bearing" or "enduring" something one cannot avoid. Suffering means "being acted *upon,*" not in the sense of being totally "passive," but in being "receptive," as one ought to be in prayer.

There is a vast difference between death undergone angrily and helplessly like an animal suffers death and death understood and accepted, as Jesus' death was:

> *Jesus cried out in a loud voice, "Father!*
> *In your hands I place my spirit!"*
> Luke 23:46

In a genuinely Christian death, the dying person is not just a "victim" or a passive spectator; he or she is an active agent in willingly surrendering this life in the hope of another, death to rebirth.

FINAL ANOINTING AND VIATICUM

Viaticum means, literally, "food for the journey." In the Greek and Latin cultures, *viaticum* meant a coin placed in the mouth of the dead person to pay Charon, the ferryman, for the journey across the River Styx into the underworld.

In the Christian sacrament, the Host is that "coin." Christians send off their dying with the gift of Life Himself. The gift is not to "pay" for safe passage; it is a provision for the trip. Viaticum is described as:

> The celebration of the eucharist as viaticum, food for the passage through death to eternal life is the sacrament proper to the dying Christian. It is the completion and crown of the Christian life on this earth, signifying that the Christian follows the Lord to eternal glory and the banquet of the heavenly kingdom.
> *The Rite of Anointing and the*
> *Pastoral Care of the Sick*

FUNERAL RITES

The ritual of a Christian funeral and burial is part of the whole process of preparing a Christian for death that begins with the first anointing, continues through the supportive community during the person's illness, and concludes with the final anointing and viaticum and the death itself.

As with Baptism, these final rites are celebrated at least as much for the grieving friends and relatives, who are also in need of healing, as they are for the deceased Christian.

We genuinely begin to grieve when we openly acknowledge that we have suffered a loss. Sometimes it is simply too huge a loss to encompass. But until we yield to the truth, we live an illusion. We simply have to express our feelings, or they corrode within us.

> Because many of us have learned to fear great emotion, because we fret we will be out of control, because we have been taught not to "offend" others with emotional expressions, we lean toward damming the emotion that is straining to be released. However, the healthy and meaningful expression of our emotions facilitates our passage through the grief process.
> Joan Guntzelman

We must *choose* to let go. A widow or widower, for instance, might refuse to give away a dead spouse's clothes, in a form of denial. But, however painful, this must be done. Life has to go on, no matter how unexpectedly different. The rites for Christian death are the church community's attempt to help the bereaved cope with that grief.

The Crucifixion
El Greco (1541–1614)

Without a felt sense of death, we live a life deceiving ourselves into believing that we have an endless number of days, and not valuing each day as precious.

Far more important, however, is the need of those left behind for compassion and consolation. A wake is no time to provide the distraught family and friends with "all the answers." Their sense of loss is not intellectual. Rather, it is a mixture of "feelings" of confusion, anger, emptiness, sometimes even a guilty sense of relief that their loved one's suffering is over—as well as their own agony helplessly watching it.

The physical *presence* of friends and neighbors is sacramental. It is an embodiment of grace, love unexpected and undeserved. And if it is not too embarrassing or inappropriate, putting your arms around the bereaved and communicating solely by touch says "You are not alone."

On the evening before the funeral, those present in the home of the deceased person or in the funeral home gather for a rite that in a very real way helps take the sting out of bereavement by sharing the loss. The ritual pattern of the service follows the pattern of a celebration of God's word:

- Greeting
- Prayers
- Scripture reading
- Homily
- General Intercessions
- Lord's Prayer

The presider concludes the rite, praying:

> Blessed are those who have died in the Lord; let them rest from their labors, for their good deeds go with them.

The Wake

Like all times when we are surprised into a contemplation of the limits that death places on human life, the custom of having a wake—or "watch"—with the dead body present, either with t he coffin open or closed, seems a morbid practice to many people. But surely it is a humanizing experience for adults.

Then the presider signs the body's forehead with a cross, recalling the signing that first greeted the deceased at Baptism and at Confirmation, praying:

> May the love of God
> and the peace of the Lord Jesus Christ
> bless and console us
> and gently wipe every tear from our eyes:
>   in the name of the Father,
> and of the Son,
> and of the Holy Spirit.

All respond, "Amen."

The Funeral Liturgy

The whole progression of the rites for a Christian death is a celebration of death leading to rebirth. All the rites celebrating Christian death and burial emphasize hope and consolation by immersing the faithful back into the symbols of Good Friday and Easter Sunday.

At the door of the church, the priest-presider welcomes the bereaved family in the name of the assembly, saying:

> Praised be God, the Father of our Lord Jesus Christ, the Father of mercies, and the God of all consolation! He comforts us in all our afflictions and thus enables us to comfort those who are in trouble, with the same consolation we have received from him.

The priest then blesses the coffin with holy water, which recalls the deceased person's baptism into Christ's death and resurrection. The pallbearers or others then cover the coffin with a white cloth, which symbolizes the white baptismal garment, while the priest says:

> On the day of his (her) baptism, [Name] put on Christ. In the day of Christ's coming, may he (she) be clothed with glory.

The procession passes up the main aisle and the pallbearers place the coffin at the foot of the Easter candle, which symbolizes the Easter event—the totem rooted in the earth and pointing toward heaven, burning with life.

After the introductory rites, the Liturgy of the Word is celebrated. Although the homily may be partly a tribute to the deceased, its primary purpose is to help those assembled make sense of death. Without the hope of rebirth, death makes no sense at all—nor does suffering, or in fact human living.

At preparation of the gifts and the altar, the priest or deacon, after incensing the gifts and the altar, incenses the coffin. The rising smoke physicalizes our prayers for the deceased, rising heavenward.

Finally, after communion, when some family member or friend may have given a more personal eulogy of the life and character of the deceased, the priest in the name of the whole assembly and the whole Church commends the deceased on his or her final journey.

> Father,
> into your hands we commend our brother (sister).
> We are confident that with all who have died in Christ
> he (she) will be raised to life on the last day and live with Christ for ever.

Burial

The actual burial is the most difficult element of the rites of Christian burial for those who cared for the one who has died. The burial is a final physical separation, and the prayers emphasize our continued hope that one day we will all be reunited forever. The spirit of the moment is captured in these Scripture verses:

> *All I want is to know Christ and to experience the power of his resurrection, to share in his sufferings and become like him in his death, in the hope that I myself will be raised from death to life.*
> Philippians 3:10–11

The minister prays with and for those gathered around the grave, asking for comfort, consolation, strength, trust in God for them, and eternal rest for the dead.

Then the priest, announcing that life is a journey through the doorway of death to life everlasting, says to both the living and the dead, "Go in the peace of Christ."

Christian life is the road of conversion, the road of death to life. Death is our final conversion, our final radical change, our final connection to the peace of Christ.

In Baptism we first become one with the church community, living and dead, and with the risen Christ and the communion of saints. Our celebration of the Anointing of the Sick, viaticum, and the Church's funeral rites is our final celebration of this mystery of our faith.

Penance, the Anointing of the Sick and the Eucharist as viaticum constitute at the end of Christian life "the sacraments that prepare for our heavenly homeland" or the sacraments that complete the earthly pilgrimage.

Catechism of the Catholic Church, 1525

Reflection

There is no denying that all the Christian rituals that surround death are sad and painful.

■ *Imagine someone you truly loved had died. Try to describe how you would feel without that person as you take part in the wake. In the funeral liturgy. In the group of family and friends gathered to support one another at the graveside.*

If it helps to prod your imagination, read the opening of Albert Camus's *The Stranger,* in which a young man who believes in no transcendent dimension to human life describes the death of his mother.

Understanding Anointing of the Sick

Review

1. With what reality does every philosopher have to begin? Explain: "Carrying a cross" is the burden of acting like a human rather than like an animal.

2. Explain: Sick people can be sacraments to those around them. Those around sick people can be sacraments to the sick. It is easy to see how medical people and friends can be ministers of hope, but how can the sick person minister?

3. How does suffering bring reality into our lives? Not only when we suffer, but when those we love suffer.

4. In what ways does suffering pose a crisis of faith, hope, and love—again not only when we suffer but when those we love suffer?

5. Why would an all-loving God allow the innocent to suffer?

6. Why is the sacrament of the sick not "magic"? What are its two purposes?

7. Again, what is the symbolism of oil? What is the symbolism of touching?

8. What is the root meaning of the word *pascal* as in "pascal candle"? What is "the Pascal Mystery"? What does the Easter weekend experience have to do with our own "private" suffering?

9. Explain: There is a vast difference between death undergone angrily and helplessly like an animal and death understood and accepted.

10. Why is it essential for the bereaved to express grief? The funeral is also sacramental. For whom?

Discuss

1. Dilemma: One of your parents has become bedridden, at times unable to recognize members of the family, needs bathing and feeding. Which is better—not easier but more reasonable: to put him or her in a nursing home or have the entire family pitch in and care for him or her at home?

3. Anyone in the group ever been in the hospital for something serious? Can you share what it was like? How did the nurses and aides differ from one another? Were some doctors solicitous and others business-like? How did you feel about visitors, when you were in pain, when you were eager to get out of there?

4. How does one face suffering and death without a belief in God and in a life more "fair" than this one?

5. How do medical personnel keep from letting health care, on the one hand, "burn them out" from overinvolvement with patients or, on the other, harden them so that caring for others is less personally involving than tending sheep?

6. At least some in the group must have lost a parent or sibling or good friend. Try if you can to share the process from the time you knew of the death, through the wake, funeral and burial, and afterward. How did you feel about God, human life, your own future?

7. Is it okay to get angry at God—to bawl God out for a fare-thee-well, and then forgive God, for all the good times? What happens to the soul if one doesn't?

8. Touching is, at least in a small way, healing to anyone suffering—whether physically or psychologically. It says, "I'm helpless, but I'm here. You're not alone." Do you find it difficult to touch others, even in such a situation? Can you say why? How does that reluctance impoverish both you and the other person?

Activities

1. Pool your experiences of service projects, especially those dealing with the elderly, physically and mentally impaired children, hospitals, the sick poor. How does serving their needs enrich your soul?

2. All suffering is not physical. There are people walking the corridors of your school who suffer intolerance, mockery, perhaps even physical abuse. In small groups list the ways students cause other students to suffer. Then develop a plan to work against the causes of the suffering. Implement the plan.

3. Interview someone other than a priest who ministers to the sick in your parish. Ask the person to describe (1) his or her ministry and (2) the reasons for his or her involvement in that work of the parish. Report your findings to the group.

4. Several tragedies have recently caused great suffering to the people of our country, for example, the bombing of the World Trade Center, and the bombing of the Federal Building in Oklahoma City. Brainstorm the reasons people might inflict such suffering on others.

5. Debate: Evil is more powerful than God. Otherwise there would not be such great suffering in the world.

*[Suffering is] an incentive
for struggling human beings
to reach out to one another,
to help one another, to love one another,
to be blessed and strengthened
and humanized in the process.*

Sister Thea Bowman

Scripture Readings

Skim the passages. Pick one that appeals to you and (1) summarize its main point, (2) tell how it relates to the chapter, and (3) list one or two thoughts that entered your mind as you read it.

- Job 7:12–21 — Destined for life with God
- Isaiah 52:13–53:12 — He bore our sufferings
- Matthew 9:28–30 — Healing of two blind men
- Matthew 11:25–30 — Come to me
- Mark 4:35–41 — Why are you fearful?
- Mark 7:32–35 — Healing of a deaf-mute
- Luke 6:19 — Jesus teaches and heals
- 1 Corinthians 12:12–27 — If one suffers, all suffer
- Romans 8:14–17 — Glorified with him
- Revelation 21:1–7 — No more death

Journal

Christ invites his disciples to follow him by taking up their cross in their turn. By following him they acquire a new outlook on illness and the sick. Jesus associates them with his own life of poverty and service. He makes them share in his ministry of compassion and healing.
Catechism of the Catholic Church, 1506

Think of a time when you suffered from personal illness or the illness a loved one was experiencing. How did that illness affect you? What was your outlook on that suffering? Did you look upon that illness as an "opportunity"? Explain.

The Sacraments
at the Service
of Communion

Chapter 9

Holy Orders: The Sacrament of Apostolic Ministry

*They cannot be ministers of Christ unless they are witnesses and dispensers
of a life other than this earthly one. But they cannot be of service to [human beings]
if they remain strangers to the life and conditions of [human beings].*
Decree on Ministry and Life of Priests

IN ORDER TO SERVE

Survey

This survey is not an exercise for a grade, but a means to stir up interest and get an idea of varying opinions in your group. Some of the statements are matters of objective fact; others are merely subjective opinions. On the rating scale under each statement circle the number that best reflects your current opinion about that statement.

> +2 = strongly agree,
> +1 = agree,
>   0 = cannot make up my mind,
> −1 = disagree,
> −2 = strongly disagree.

Then share the reasons for your opinion.

1. Priests should not concern themselves with matters outside the strictly spiritual.

   +2   +1   0   −1   −2

2. Like all the sacraments, Holy Orders is a gift that is a challenge.

   +2   +1   0   −1   −2

3. The sacrament of Holy Orders makes up for a priest's personal faults.

   +2   +1   0   −1   −2

4. Until Vatican II, the Church was very much "clericalized" and "priestified."

   +2   +1   0   −1   −2

5. It is the human priest who transforms the bread and wine at Mass.

   +2   +1   0   −1   −2

6. Celibacy makes priests holier than ordinary Christians.

   +2   +1   0   −1   −2

7. Just before the ordination of a priest, the bishop asks approval from the Church, the people present.

   +2   +1   0   −1   −2

8. In the earliest churches there were both men and women deacons.

   +2   +1   0   −1   −2

9. From the time they are ordained, deacons must remain celibate, even if they are married.

   +2   +1   0   −1   −2

10. Everyone—lay people as well as priests—is ordained a minister in Baptism.

    +2   +1   0   −1   −2

A Puzzlement

In the middle '70s, when Barbara Walters still hosted the *Today* show, a priest was invited to talk about the recent film *The Exorcist*, in which he had appeared. During a commercial, Ms. Walters leaned over and whispered, "You're obviously an intelligent man. *How* can you be a priest?"

■ *Why would Barbara Walters ask the guest, "You're obviously an intelligent man. How can you be a priest?"*

■ *Why do you think people choose to become priests?*

Orders

In classical Latin, the word *ordo* was used to designate certain groups in society, such as the senatorial order, the order of scribes, the order of matrons. In the Church too there were the orders—the order of catechumens, of penitents, of bishops, of priests, and of deacons. And although priesthood, as marriage, is primarily a sacrament of mission and service, both sacraments are also "rites of conversion" into a whole new way of life. They are both *honor* and *munus*, both "tribute" and "burden."

EARLY RITES OF ORDINATION

In the New Testament the gesture of the laying on of hands symbolizes the designation or appointment of one to an "order" within the church community. But the New Testament mentions laying on of hands in only four places. And in some of these references the gesture may not identify a sacramental rite but merely a human gesture signifying that the Church community entrusted individuals with a particular task.

In the Acts of the Apostles we read that the disciples in Jerusalem had chosen seven helpers (Stephen, Philip, Prochorus, Nicanor, Timon, Parmenas, and Nicholaus) to free them of the burden of dispersing funds to the needy. They prayed and laid hands on them:

> *The group presented them to the apostles, who prayed and placed their hands on them.*   Acts 6:6

In another situation, the elders laid hands on Paul and Barnabas, sending them on a mission. Neither act seems permanently empowering.

> *While they were serving the Lord and fasting, the Holy Spirit said to them, "Set apart for me Barnabas and Saul, to do the work to which I have called them."*
> *They fasted and prayed, placed their hands on them, and sent them off.*
> Acts 13:1–3

Detail of Paul from *Peter and Paul*
El Greco (1541–1614)

In Paul's two letters to Timothy, which were written even earlier than the Acts of the Apostles, we find reference back to what had quite likely been a rite of ordination known to the church community at that time (A.D. 100). Paul's First Letter to Timothy is primarily about church life and practice. In this letter, Paul describes Timothy as a model church leader, a good servant of Christ Jesus, and refers to Timothy's ordination:

> *Until I come, give your time and effort to the public reading of the Scriptures and to preaching and teaching. Do not neglect the spiritual gift that is in you, which was given to you when the prophets spoke and the elders laid their hands on you.*
> 1 Timothy 4:13–14

The Second Letter to Timothy is a more personal letter. It encourages Timothy within the context of his ordination, to endure the burden of dealing with souls in his care:

> *I remind you to keep alive the gift that God gave you when I laid my hands on you. For the Spirit that God has given us does not make us timid; instead, his Spirit fills us with power, love, and self-control.* 2 Timothy 1:6–7

Notice "the spiritual gift" was not given by the elders or by Paul but by God *through* the laying on of their hands. We can assume that these are pastoral letters to a "bishop," both from the reference in each letter to the laying on of hands on Timothy and from the fact that the last two chapters of 1 Timothy list a broad range of responsibilities in overseeing the apostolate and the community.

Note also that "gifts" from the Holy Spirit are not empowerments in the sense of immediately infusing some virtue, like plugging into an electric current or putting gas in a car. Paul's words are a reminder to the recipients that, whatever they are called upon to do for the kingdom, they are not alone.

However there is one power that is in fact "infused." By the sacrament of Holy Orders, the candidate is empowered to *sanctify*. Anointing the hands of the newly ordained priest, the bishop says:

> The Father anointed our Lord Jesus Christ through the power of the Holy Spirit.
> May Jesus preserve you to sanctify the Christian people
> and to offer sacrifice to God.
> *Ordination of a Priest*

MINISTER / OFFICIAL

Two somewhat conflicting functions in the ministerial priesthood began to emerge. First and most important is a spiritual power:

- to call the risen Christ into bread and wine,
- to forgive sins,
- to preach the word of God,
- to heal,
- to witness vows.

From what we can gather about the earliest churches, that was the service the ordained provided the community of believers.

But as the body of Christ grew from isolated church communities dotted around the Mediterranean into an institution stretching all over Europe, there had to be a structure to preserve its unity. Thus over the centuries the "priesthood" in the Church developed a second function: maintaining order, orthodoxy, and loyalty to the Church universal. Thus the priest also became an *official*.

The two roles of minister ("servant") and official ("manager") may conflict insofar as the first calls for empathy, vulnerability, a willingness to *be used* both by Christ and by the people. The other "official" sense is more assertive, decisive, directive.

In the beginning, when the Church was still suppressed, the "servant" side dominated. Gradually, though, as the Church grew larger and needful of organization, the "manager" aspect began to dominate in the life of the clergy and people. The clergy, the ordained, emerged as men "set apart," with certain civil privileges the laity, the nonordained members of church community, did not enjoy. The Church became less and less understood as the body of Christ in which all members had a role to play, or even as the People of God.

Christ Washing Peter's Feet
Ford Madox Brown (1821–1893)

CLERGY / LAITY

In the earliest church communities Christians did not divide themselves into two separate categories of Christians—one active, the "Church teaching" (the clergy); and one passive, the "Church taught" (the laity).

"By the imposition of hands

and through the words

of the consecration,

the grace of the Holy Spirit is given,

and a sacred character is impressed

in such wise that bishops,

in an eminent and visible manner,

take the place of Christ himself,

teacher, shepherd, and priest,

and act as his representative. . . ."

"By virtue, therefore,

of the Holy Spirit

who has been given to them,

bishops have been

constituted true and authentic

teachers of the faith

and have been made

pontiffs and pastors."

Catechism of the Catholic Church, 1558

Unfortunately, that division did happen when the persecution of Christians ended, Christians were openly accepted in society, and Christianity became the official religion of the Roman Empire.

In A.D. 318, the Roman emperor Constantine (306–337) appointed all bishops to the post of imperial judges; and the episcopacy, the office of bishop, began to seem more like a jurisdiction than a sacramental ministry. What is more, both in the Empire and after the barbarian invasions, lesser clerics were most often literate, disciplined, and trained to keep confidences. As a result, bishops and priests also became valuable civil servants—*clerici,* "clerks"—in a strictly secular way. They began to dress, live, and act in a manner similar to their secular counterparts. They became a kind of elitist "gentry."

Also, as the Empire became Christian most adults were already baptized, and their children were routinely baptized in infancy. Christianity seemed to be simply "passed on" (like an ethnic heritage might be passed on today) without any need to appropriate it personally and to undergo a personal conversion from the world's values to the kingdom's values. Christians "wore" their Christianity as routinely and unreflectively as putting on a yarmulke or a dashiki.

As "Church" became nearly coterminous with civil "society," bishops could no longer have hands-on (literally) contact with people in a large diocese. They had to devolve onto assistant priests many of the functions bishops had performed in the earliest church communities. Bishops became more involved in church governance than in worship outside their cathedrals.

Priesthood

*Y*ou are the chosen race, the King's priests, the holy nation, God's own people, chosen to proclaim the wonderful acts of God, who called you out of darkness into his own marvelous light.

1 Peter 2:9

Those words were written not for those who have undergone the rite of ordination but for those who have undergone the ritual washing, anointing, and imposition of hands at baptism.

THE PRIESTHOOD OF THE LAITY

We, the body of Christ, simply cannot lay all the responsibility for proclaiming the Gospel and ministering with others as Jesus commanded on our ordained priests.

There are many tasks of Christian service that cannot be "left at the priest's door."

If there is a crisis in priestly vocations, perhaps the Holy Spirit is "speaking" through that lack. Perhaps the Spirit is telling us that the laity must take up a more active role in the priestly people, and not go on expecting the priest to "take care of everything." There are people in the pews whose skills—gifts— are different from the pastor's. Some are better organized; others have more savvy about financial matters, roofing, floods, grouting in the school showers. Nor can lay Christian service stop within the parish.

The apostolate of the social milieu, that is, the effort to infuse a Christian spirit into the mentality, customs, laws, and structures of the community in which a person lives, is so much the duty and responsibility of the laity that it can never be properly performed by others. In this area the laity can exercise an apostolate of like toward like.

Decree on the Apostolate of the Laity

Special Olympics.

Jesus' concern was not merely for his own family, for the Jewish people. Jesus extended himself to Romans, Greeks, and others. He reached out to self-righteous Pharisees—though they refused to listen. He spoke out against the injustice of burdening others with hardships that one did not share, and he whipped the money changers from the Temple. In fact, his criticisms became so threatening to the leaders of the establishment that they had him executed.

Mercy Ships: A Ministry of Youth with a Mission, Senegal, West Africa.

THE MINISTERIAL PRIESTHOOD

The priest is a *member* of the body of Christ, not its head; Christ is its head. "There are different ways of serving but the same Lord is served" (1 Corinthians 12:5). The ordained priesthood is one ministry among many in the body of Christ. The priest stands *within* the Church, not above it.

Then how is the priest's ministry in the Church different from that of any other genuine Christian's?

During the ordination of a priest, the bishop addresses all present, saying:

> By consecration he [the candidate] will be made a true priest of the New Testament, to preach the Gospel, sustain God's people, and celebrate the liturgy, above all, the Lord's sacrifice.
>
> *Ordination of a Priest*

The bishop then addresses the candidate, saying in part:

> You must apply your energies to the duty of teaching in the name of Christ, the chief Teacher. . . . Meditate on the law of God, believe what you read, teach what you believe, and put into practice what you teach. . . .
>
> In the same way you must carry out your mission of sanctifying in the power of Christ. Your ministry will perfect the spiritual sacrifice of the faithful by uniting it to Christ's sacrifice. . . .
>
> Finally, conscious of sharing in the work of Christ . . . seek to bring the faithful together into a unified family and to lead them effectively, through Christ and in the Holy Spirit, to God the Father. Always remember the example of the Good Shepherd who came not to be served but to serve, and to seek out and rescue those who were lost.
>
> *Ordination of a Priest*

The ordained priest is a *person-symbol* whose purpose is to awaken faith in the community, to body-forth Christ: "It is no longer I who live," as Paul said, "but it is Christ who lives in me" (Galatians 2:20). The priest's very presence at least ought to be a reminder that reality has a dimension larger than the everyday. His inner motivation is a felt need to serve people in a more intense way than the nonordained baptized person is called to serve. It is a conscious identification with the priesthood of Christ.

Presiding at the Eucharist does not mean "playing the role" of Jesus, but—as jazz "takes over" the musician—the priest allows Christ to "take him over" and "play him." Christ alone is the source of all priesthood, the true celebrant. Other priests can join in that priesthood only insofar as Christ empowers them.

The priest acts *in persona Christi* and *in persona ecclesiae*, "in the person of Christ" and "in the person of the Church," whenever he proclaims the word of God, transforms the bread and wine, forgives sins. At those moments, the power of Christ and the power of the People of God is "focused" into him as if he were a lens.

The American bishops compare the priest's role to that of an orchestra conductor:

> The conductor succeeds when he or she stimulates the best performance from each player and combines their individual efforts into a pattern of sound, achieving the vision of the composer. The best leader is one who can develop the talents of each staff person and coordinate all their efforts, so that they best complement each other and produce a superior collective effort.
>
> *As One Who Serves*

The purpose of any parent or teacher is, ironically, to render themselves unnecessary, so that children and students can go out on their own. So, too, the priest—just as Jesus did—prepares disciples and then sends them out on their own. Neither Jesus nor Paul was a presider. They were persuaders.

Priesthood is one thing; priests are another. Just as Baptism does not "bestow" faith, and Confirmation does not "bestow" the wisdom of the Spirit, the sacrament of Holy Orders does not "bestow" knowledge, purity, gentleness, open-mindedness, or a universally appealing personality.

Pope John Paul II, World Youth Day, 1993, Denver, Colorado.

As with any sacrament, what is bestowed in Holy Orders is the Spirit's challenge to develop those potential virtues and the individual's commitment to try. Just as the Church commits itself at Baptism to support the Christian growth of the newly baptized, so too at ordination the church community commits itself to support the continued death-and-rebirth of a man's priesthood.

During the prayer of consecration which immediately follows the laying on of hands, the bishops prays:

> Almighty Father,
> grant to this servant of yours
> the dignity of the priesthood.
> Renew within him the Spirit of holiness.
> As a co-worker with the order of bishops
> may he be faithful to the ministry
> that he receives from you, Lord, God,
> and be to others a model of right conduct.
>
> *Ordination of a Priest*

DIFFERENT QUALITIES / DIFFERENT PRIESTS

In the Old and New Testaments, God chose individuals to "inspire," to speak in God's name. But God chose *this* individual, who is sometimes angry, like Jeremiah; sometimes grim but relenting, like Hosea; sometimes as welcoming as a forgiving mother, like Luke.

God chooses prophets and priests as an artist chooses brushes, some for the broad strokes, some for the fine lines. It is a wondrous thing about the Church: that there are priests who can bring the kingdom of God to dockworkers; there are priests who write poetry, to bring the kingdom into drawing rooms; there are priests who are recovering alcoholics, priests who are wounded just as those they seek out are wounded. We need them all. As long as their wounds are engrafted into the wounds of Jesus Christ.

There is a piece of advice one crusty old priest gives to students:

> "If a priest ever bawls you out in confession, say to him, 'Father, I came here to find Jesus Christ. And I didn't.' Then walk away, having reminded the priest of the One he has allowed to use him as a means of grace."

Ideally, as John Oliver Nelson puts it:

> A priest ought to be a "gracious, unassuming, joyful, completely *honest* and dependable servant of God and common folk.
>
> At least he must try. And it is consoling that priests go to confession like the rest of us.

*God chooses
prophets and priests
as an artist chooses brushes,
some for the broad strokes,
some for the fine lines.*

CHRIST'S UNIQUE PRIESTHOOD

How, then, is a Catholic priest *different* from any cultic priest? Any minister?

Jewish priests were of the tribe of Levi, "Levites." By the time of Jesus the high priest had become a political appointment, and the levitical priesthood had become an elitist "priestly caste." Jesus demanded that his priests reject the arrogance both of pagan rulers and of the self-righteous Pharisees.

Unlike the levitical power elite, the Son of God became high priest of the New Covenant, first by humbling himself to become fully human and then by his humiliating suffering and death:

> *Let us then hold firmly to the faith we profess. For we have a great High Priest who has gone into the very presence of God—Jesus, the Son of God. Our High Priest is not one who cannot feel sympathy for our weaknesses. On the contrary, we have a High Priest who was tempted in every way that we are, but did not sin.*   Hebrews 4:14–15

The Crucifixion
Vladimir Mazuranic (1910-   )

Jesus showed in a most dramatic and sacramental way what he believed the nature of true priesthood was:

So he rose from the table, took off his outer garment, and tied a towel around his waist. Then he poured some water into a washbasin and began to wash the disciples' feet and dry them with the towel around his waist. . . .

"I, your Lord and Teacher, have just washed your feet. You, then, should wash one another's feet. I have set an example for you, so that you will do just what I have done for you."   John 13:4–5, 14–15

To the mind of the Son of God, *that* is what it means to be a priest: to serve, to touch, to teach.

The classical explanation of the priesthood of Christ (and by analogy, of all priests who share in the priesthood of Christ) is given in the Letter to the Hebrews. The key to Christ's priesthood is that, by the Incarnation, the Son of God fused himself with humanity, the lightning rod, the channel connecting the divine energy of God with the human energy in our souls. Since we "are people of flesh and blood, Jesus himself became like [us] and shared [our] human nature" (Hebrews 2:14).

Those profoundly felt ties with humanity are what make Christ the Priest (and all priests) not distant and judgmental but compassionate and faithful.

And so [Jesus] is able, now and always, to save those who come to God through him, because he lives forever to plead with God for them.   Hebrews 7:25

The model of all priests' ministry is Jesus' dealing with his own small group of followers. He taught them, served them, even to the point of getting down on his knees and washing their feet.

He was patient with their doubts, their skepticism, their wrongheaded ideas of what is important. He even forgave their desertion. The priesthood of Jesus, then, was in *response* to *their* needs—both the ones they openly brought to him, and the needs they did not even realize they had.

Protestant ministers as well as priests strive to model themselves on that ideal, and some try and fail. But what separates the two forms of serving others most dramatically is that priests are celibate.

In the ecclesial service
of the ordained minister,
it is Christ himself
who is present to his Church
as Head of his Body,
Shepherd of his flock,
high priest of the redemptive sacrifice,
Teacher of Truth.
This is what
the Church means
by saying that the priest,
by virtue of the sacrament
of Holy Orders,
acts in persona Christi Capitis.

Catechism of the Catholic Church, 1548

CELIBACY

After Jesus arrived in the territory of Judea on the other side of the River Jordan, he discussed the teaching of the Law of Moses about marriage and divorce with a group of Pharisees. When Jesus finished, the disciples said:

> *"If this is how it is between a man and his wife, it is better not to marry."*
>
> *Jesus answered, "This teaching does not apply to everyone, but only to those to whom God has given it. For there are different reasons why men cannot marry: some, because they were born that way; others, because men made them that way; and others do not marry for the sake of the Kingdom of heaven. Let him who can accept this teaching do so."*
>   Matthew 19:10–12

It is interesting that, immediately after that, people bring children to Jesus to be blessed. And then immediately after that, the rich young man happens along. He has done everything that he thinks the Law expected of him—he obeyed all the commandments. In reply, "Jesus looked straight at him with love" and loved him (Mark 10:21).

But the young man wanted more; he wanted "perfection," that is, to have the most human fulfillment of which he was capable. Then Jesus offered him a vocation:

> *"You need only one thing. Go and sell all you have and give the money to the poor, and you will have riches in heaven; then come and follow me."*   Mark 10:21

This was not the call to ordinary discipleship, the call each of us receives in Baptism. It was to something *more*.

> *When the man heard this, gloom spread over his face, and he went away sad, because he was very rich.*
>   Mark 10:22

The important thing is that Jesus loved the man even if he "only" kept all the commandments! That is enough! What Jesus offered was a vocation to serve in a more intense way: to be a disciple like the Twelve. But the man simply could not bring himself to do that. Yet Jesus *still* loved him.

A very well-to-do Jewish agnostic once asked a priest why he was celibate, and the priest answered:

> "I know that love is not quantifiable, but my energy is very much quantifiable. I figure that if I were married, my wife and kids would deserve my *best* loving. But loving three or four or five people that intensely is not enough for me. So I keep my ability to love 'unfocused,' so that whoever shows up gets the full shot."

Surely a celibate priest has more time, mobility, and freedom from legitimate family entanglements in order to serve. Yet how can a celibate empathize with the problems of married people when he has never been married?

In the first place, a celibate priest is a human being. He has himself suffered what most human beings have had to suffer in living out their relationships. He knows and has experienced what it is like to struggle against selfishness—in himself as well as in others, with people who refuse to change for their own good, with being taken advantage of.

Second, by taking the vow of celibacy a priest has not surrendered his sexuality. He has wrestled with the mystery of sexuality as married people do, again not only in himself but also with many others. And, one supposes, if marital difficulties are a large part of the problems brought to him, he has made the effort as most married people have to study and understand marriage. What is more, most marital problems are not problems with "sex" but problems with relationships between people. And the priest is a "people."

One might argue that the celibate priest has never had the chance to share a real body-and-soul relationship with another person, to experience the everyday problems of dealing not only with one another but with children for whom parents have ultimate responsibility for twenty-plus years. Yet it is those very married people who have in fact suffered and enjoyed that relationship who come to an outsider, the celibate priest, for advice. Having had the experience, they come to reflect on the experience and understand its implications. People come to a priest for advice not because he is an adept sexual practitioner but because supposedly the Church has sent him off for a very long time to become "wise." As one priest writes:

It is at least arguable that the basis of people's trust in the priest stems in large part from his celibacy, which is a *sign of his commitment* to them.

George McCauley, S.J.

The Rites of Ordination

All three ordination rites—"Ordination of a Bishop," "Ordination of a Priest," "Ordination of a Deacon"—take place during the celebration of the Mass and should take place on a Sunday or holy day when a large number of the faithful can take part in the celebration.

LAYING ON OF HANDS/ PRAYER OF CONSECRATION

The most basic symbol of ordination is the laying on of hands. The bishop alone lays his hands on the deacon, but at the ordination of a priest all priests present impose hands on their new brother priests. At the ordination of a bishop all bishops present lay their hands on the heads of bishop candidate)—signifying their brotherhood in this power to sanctify.

Then with hands extended over the candidates for the priesthood, the bishop sings aloud:

> Almighty and eternal God, . . .
> you shared among the sons of Aaron
> the fullness of their father's power,
> to provide worthy priests in sufficient
>   number for the increasing rites
>   of sacrifice and worship.
> With the same loving care
> you gave companions to your Son's
>   apostles to help in teaching the faith:
> they preached the Gospel to the whole
>   world. . . .
> May he be faithful in working with the
>   order of bishops,
> so that the words of the Gospel may
>   reach the ends of the earth,
> and the family of nations,
> made one in Christ,
> may become God's one, holy people.
> *Ordination of a Priest*

INVESTITURE/ANOINTING

After the prayer of consecration, the head of the new bishop is anointed with chrism. Again, the oil *seals* the candidate, as in "signed and sealed." The bishop is *confirming* the ordination. The new bishop is then presented with and accepts the Book of the Gospels, and is vested with a ring, a mitre, and his pastoral, or shepherd's, staff.

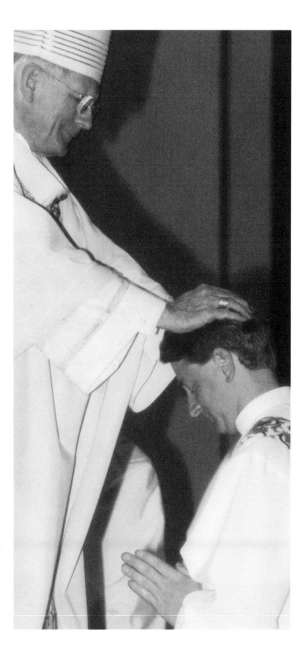

In the ordination of a deacon, the newly ordained deacon is vested with stole and dalmatic and presented with the Book of the Gospels. As the bishop presents the deacon with the Book of the Gospels, he says:

> Receive the Gospel of Christ,
> whose herald you now are.
> Believe what you read,
> teach what you believe,
> and practice what you teach.
> *Ordination of a Deacon*

In the rite of the ordination of a priest, the newly ordained priest is vested with stole and chasuble. The bishop then anoints the palms of the hands of the new priest with perfumed chrism, and the newly ordained priest receives bread on a paten and wine and water in a chalice as the instruments by which he will serve the community.

Like the white garment given to newly baptized, the vestments are a dramatic visual symbol of a whole new life. The bread and wine and dishes that the bishop offers to the new priest have been given to him *by the people*. Again, the ordaining bishop acts *in persona Christi* and *in persona ecclesiae*. It is Christ and the people of his Mystical Body who empower this new priest.

As he presents the gifts the bishop says:

> Accept from the holy people of God the
> gifts to be offered to him.
> Know what you are doing, and imitate
> the mystery you celebrate:
> model your life on the mystery of the
> Lord's cross.
> *Ordination of a Priest*

All three rites of ordination conclude with the kiss of peace, which is followed by the Liturgy of the Eucharist.

ORDINATION OF A PRIEST

The ordination of a priest begins after the gospel.
The bishop, wearing his miter, sits at his chair.

LITURGY OF THE WORD

ORDINATION OF A PRIEST

Calling of the Candidate

Let [Name] who is to be ordained priest please come forward.

Presentation of the Candidate

The candidate is presented to the bishop with the words:

After inquiry among the people of Christ and upon recommendation of those concerned with his training, I testify that he has been found worthy.

Election by the Bishop and Consent of the People.

The bishops says,

We rely on the help of the Lord God and our Savior Jesus Christ, and we choose this man, our brother, for priesthood in the presbyteral order.

All give their assent to the choice, saying,

Thanks be to God.

Homily

Examination of the Candidate

Are you resolved, with the help of the Holy Spirit, to discharge without fail the office of priesthood in the presbyteral order as a conscientious fellow worker with the bishops in caring for the Lord's flock?

Are you resolved to celebrate the mysteries of Christ faithfully and religiously as the Church has handed them down to us for the glory of God and the sanctification of Christ's people?

Are you resolved to exercise the ministry of the word worthily and wisely, preaching the Gospel and explaining the Catholic faith?

Are you resolved to consecrate your life to God for the salvation of his people, and to unite yourself more closely every day to Christ the High Priest, who offered himself for us to the Father as a perfect sacrifice?

Promise of Obedience

Kneeling before the bishop, the candidate places his joined hands between those of the bishop and promises obedience to the bishop and his successors.

Invitation to Prayer

Litany of the Saints

Laying On of Hands

The bishop lays his hands on the candidate's head, in silence. Next all the priests present, wearing stoles, lay their hands upon the candidate in silence.

Prayer of Consecration

Investiture with Stole and Chasuble

Anointing of Hands

The bishops anoints the palms of the newly ordained priest, saying:

The Father anointed our Lord Jesus Christ
through the power of the Holy Spirit.
May Jesus preserve you to sanctify the Christian people
and to offer sacrifice to God.

Presentation of the Gifts

The deacon brings the paten and chalice to the bishop, who hands them to the new priest, saying:

Accept from the holy people of God the gifts
    to be offered to him.
Know what you are doing, and imitate
    the mystery you celebrate;
model your life on the mystery of the Lord's cross.

Kiss of Peace

LITURGY OF THE EUCHARIST

"Ministry" is, as John Futrell points out, "human services performed in response to the human needs of people." Ministry is not profit oriented or power oriented, but rather offers the self to serve. Ministry comes from bonding with others, yielding to their needs, cajoling, outfoxing, luring to a larger life. It is love of God expressed *through* love of the neighbor.

Ministry is not a process in which something is "done to" others, with the minister in a higher position than the one served. Rather it is a process of healing and growth that is done *with* others. It goes on within the one served, with the minister serving as a facilitator, like a midwife at a birth.

Reflection

Mull over what has been said about the priesthood in this chapter, especially what was said about the priesthood of the laity. Women feel, rightly, underused by the Church they profoundly care for. But all the faithful—men and women, adults and youth—are "priestly" in a very real sense.

- *Why do we say that?*
- *In what ways are all the faithful "priestly"?*
- *In what ways can you live out your "baptismal priesthood"?*

Two other sacraments,

Holy Orders and Matrimony,

are directed towards the salvation of others;

if they contribute as well to personal salvation,

it is through service to others that they do so.

They confer a particular mission in the Church

and serve to build up the People of God.

Catechism of the Catholic Church, 1534

Understanding Holy Orders

Review

1. How did the priesthood function in the early Church? What factors gradually divided the Church into an often elitist clergy (Church teaching) and a subservient laity (Church taught)? How did Vatican II set about alleviating that division?

2. How is a priest different from a lay person? What two sometimes conflicting roles must the priest balance? What does it mean to say the priest acts only *in persona Christi* and *in persona ecclesiae* when he presides at the sacraments?

3. What is the root of the word *minister?* How did Jesus at the Last Supper demonstrate what ministry really means?

4. Explain the symbols that embody the ordination of priests: the people applauding consent, laying on of hands (by the bishop and all priests present), vesting, anointing the hands, touching the vessels used at the celebration of Mass. Which two are the key symbols?

5. Vatican II has a long section called *Decree on the Apostolate of the Laity*. What does that mean for the doctor, the businesswoman, the cab driver, the hair stylist?

Discuss

1. Discuss the advantages and disadvantages of a celibate clergy. Perhaps another way to the point at issue is to pool the group's knowledge about Protestant ministers, their wives, their children.

2. List the places that are hospitable to you but where a priest would be unwelcome or at least made to feel uncomfortable.

3. This question is (for now) restricted to boys, though girls can join in. Are there any challenges involved in the priesthood, other than celibacy, that would keep you from considering it as a legitimate career option?

4. Ordination does not "cure" human weakness. We all know priests who are grumpy, cold, boring, or bossy. What would a good Christian do for such a suffering fellow Christian? Who ministers to the minister? Would you talk to another priest about it?

5. Jesus said, "I've come that you may have life, and have it more abundantly." List the people you know—at home, school, work, neighborhood—who do not appear to be living life as abundantly as they could. Now what.

Activities

1. Christ sent his disciples out to bring the liberation of the Gospel to every corner of the world and of human life. You are a disciple of Christ. Talk to your pastor and come up with a list of ways you can serve others. Choose one and invite your pastor to be your "mentor" and "guide" to help you serve in that way.

2. At the ordination of a priest the bishop tells the candidate to "put into practice what you teach." In some ways, you are a teacher too. The things you do, the things you "put into practice" teach others. With your group draw up an outline of the things your group does at school. Then, list what these things teach others.

3. Interview a priest and a deacon. Ask each to describe three qualities of a good leader and a good "minister." Have them tell you why these qualities are important. Share your findings with your group.

4. Imagine that you are the bishop of your diocese or archdiocese. "As bishop" watch several news broadcasts. What are some of the hardest tasks you face as the leader of the people of your diocese? How would you go about facing those tasks?

Scripture Readings

Skim the passages. Pick one that appeals to you and (1) summarize its main point, (2) tell how it relates to the chapter, and (3) list one or two thoughts that entered your mind as you read it.

- Genesis 14:18–20   Melchizedek offered bread and wine to God

- Deuteronomy 6:3–9   Keep these words in your heart

- Isaiah 61:1–3   The Lord has anointed me

- Matthew 5:13–16   Lights in the world
- Luke 22:14–20, 24–30   One who serves
- John 20:19–23   Receive the Holy Spirit
- John 21:15–17   Tend my sheep
- Romans 12:4–8   Gifts differ

✎ Journal

Paul encouraged Timothy, "Do not neglect the spiritual gift that is in you" (1 Timothy 4:14). What spiritual gifts has God given to you? Are you neglecting to use them to serve others? Explain. How can you use them more generously?

While the common priesthood of the faithful is exercised by the unfolding of baptismal grace— a life of faith, hope, and charity, a life according to the Spirit—, the ministerial priesthood is at the service of the common priesthood. It is directed at the unfolding of the baptismal grace of all Christians.

Catechism of the Catholic Church, 1547

Chapter 10

Matrimony: A Partnership of the Whole of Life

"For this reason a man will leave his father and mother and unite with his wife, and the two will become one." There is a deep secret truth revealed in this scripture, which I understand as applying to Christ and the church.

Ephesians 5:31–32

MARRIAGE

Survey

This survey is not an exercise for a grade, but a means to stir up interest and get an idea of varying opinions in your group. Some of the statements are matters of objective fact; others are merely subjective opinions. On the rating scale under each statement circle the number that best reflects your current opinion about that statement.

> +2 = strongly agree,
> +1 = agree,
> 0 = cannot make up my mind,
> −1 = disagree,
> −2 = strongly disagree.

Then share the reasons for your opinion.

1. A wedding is rite of conversion from independence to partnership.

   +2 +1 0 −1 −2

2. The key to marriage is a paradox: each spouse belonging totally to another yet remaining a unique self.

   +2 +1 0 −1 −2

3. A married couple is a lot "more married" after ten years of marriage than they were on their wedding day.

   +2 +1 0 −1 −2

4. In a marriage, the husband can supply the *animus* that his wife lacks.

   +2 +1 0 −1 −2

5. Like all sacraments, marriage is both a gift and a challenge.

   +2 +1 0 −1 −2

6. Two people who have never formed a self (soul) are not likely good risks for intimacy and partnership.

   +2 +1 0 −1 −2

7. At its most basic dimension, a Christian marriage is a bilateral contract between two adults.

   +2 +1 0 −1 −2

8. Two people who sign a premarital financial agreement have already invalidated their marriage.

   +2 +1 0 −1 −2

9. People with no long-term connection to the Catholic Church should still be allowed a Catholic marriage.

   +2 +1 0 −1 −2

10. A marriage is forever, no matter what.

    +2 +1 0 −1 −2

A Puzzlement

In the second act of *The Skin of Our Teeth* by Thornton Wilder (1948), Maggie Antrobus tells her husband, George, who is ready to leave her:

> I didn't marry you because you were perfect, George. I didn't even marry you because I loved you. I married you because you gave me a promise. That promise made up for your faults. And the promise I gave you made up for mine. Two imperfect people got married, and it was that promise that made the marriage. . . . And when our children were growing up, it wasn't our love that protected them—it was that promise.

■ *What does Maggie mean?*

Intimacy and Partnership

Marriage is probably the easiest sacrament to understand because the reasons people marry are easiest to understand. A wedding—even outside a religious context—is very clearly a change, a rite of conversion, from independence to partnership. A marriage is the basic human experience of what creative, life-giving, redemptive love *means*: you are not alone, you are not meaningless, you and I *are* "home."

The key to a successful marriage is a paradox: finding the healthy balance between belonging totally to each other and yet maintaining a unique individuality that will keep each spouse an interesting person, a continued gift for whom each day each partner is grateful. How does a man and a woman become a "we" while each one still remains an "I"? How can "I love you" mature into "We love us"?

"And they become one" (Genesis 2:24). How can they both be absorbed in the other and yet each still be an autonomous self? Picture a dogwood tree, white or pink. A canny old gardener painstakingly grafts a branch of the opposite color into the tree. After some years, no one can tell whether the original tree was white or pink. They have become one and are now one tree, pink and white. That is what happens in a good marriage.

In Genesis we read:

That is why a man leaves his father and mother and shall cleave to his wife, and they become one.   From Genesis 2:24

The word *cleave* has two contradictory meanings. One is "to sever, to part or disunite," just as the gardener had "cut" a white (or a pink) branch from another dogwood. But the other, opposite meaning of the word *cleave* is "to join, to fuse," as the gardener grafted the one branch into the other living tree. And the two became one tree. But neither part changed color. The white stayed white, and the pink stayed pink. That is what happens in a marriage: a man and a woman "cut" themselves off— with no small sense of loss—from their families and years of habits that they have become comfortable with and fuse them- selves into a single, new reality: a marriage, a new family. But this "cutting" is done without each spouse losing a sense of being a unique self.

> *Marriage is union,*
> *a total gift of the self,*
> *without losing a sense of*
> *still being a unique*
> *human being.*
> *It is a fusion of life stories.*

Matrimony, or Christian marriage, like every sacrament, is a rite of conversion. But, as with every other sacrament, the moment of the sacramental celebration of a marriage is only the focal moment in a very long series of moments that have led up to it, prepared for it, and also stretch outward before the couple into the unfathomable future. These two people now giving witness to their marriage promises have been becoming married for quite some time. And they will become more and more married every day of their married life.

Every married couple is a *lot* more married today than on the day they first promised responsibility for each other for the rest of their lives, no matter what.

Like the engrafted dogwood tree described earlier, marriage is a union. It is a total gift of the self, and yet—ironically— without losing a sense of being a unique human being. It is a fusion of life stories, and yet there are still two quite different voices telling it.

On the anniversary of a marriage (or at least on the fifth anniversary) it is a good custom for a couple to renew those marriage promises in the presence of the family and friends with whom the couple daily renews their story:

- To remember again, explicitly, the moments of happiness and trial, success and sadness.

- To pledge again fidelity and commitment.

Marriage is a gift only insofar as its promises are accepted again and again.

Some dewy-eyed romantics say a marriage is not a 50 percent–50 percent but a 100 percent gift from both spouses. Such a view is far too simple and naive. Even in a fusion as intimate as a marriage, spouses need to have "a room of their own," a place to which each can retreat and *be* a self. Otherwise, each spouse becomes *absorbed* in the other, and by that very fact will have nothing left to give.

> *One of the major difficulties people*
> *who are married have in loving each*
> *other is that they have never learned*
> *to love—or even know—themselves.*

Part of the paradox of a healthy marriage is each spouse giving the other spouse the freedom to be an integral part of who-I-am and yet not-me. If either spouse absorbs the other, the marriage is through. As the poet Rainer Maria Rilke said, the greatest gift two spouses can give each other is "to love the distance between us." You can be pink. I can be white. We are still one tree.

A Rite of Conversion

As with all seven sacraments, marriage is a rite of conversion. It is the movement from death to rebirth—from *death* to complete independence, to *rebirth* to a life in which, "no matter what," you never have to face life alone.

There is a purpose to each of the natural crises of human growth, crises that result from leaving something very good behind for something better. Obviously, birth is such a crisis, but without it we have no life. What the changes of adolescence are intended to produce is an *identity*: a personally validated *adult* self, understood and accepted, not just a personality but inner character.

That "self," in the natural order of things, should prepare one for the intimacy and partnership of marriage. The tragedy is that too many young people today are not being helped to focus their attention on the very purpose of their adolescence. As a result too many people who do not even know their own selves come together and offer those inadequately known selves to each other— forever. Too many marriages are like joining hands with a near stranger and jumping off a cliff. One of the major difficulties people who are married have in loving each other is that they have never learned to love—or even know—themselves.

Nor can one spouse expect the other to make up for what he or she never got around to developing in his or her character during adolescence. A wife cannot "supply" her husband's undeveloped "feminine" side, providing all the empathy, vulnerability, and inclusiveness that he lacks. Nor can a husband "supply" his wife's undeveloped "masculine" side, providing all the decisiveness, determination, and calculation. If spouses have such expectations, the marriage might last, but it is a caricature of two inadequate people: "Oh, 'the little woman' takes care of all that religion business," and "Oh, my husband does all that checkbook stuff."

One of the better images of a healthy marriage is the picture of the Chinese Tao: a circle cut in half by a wavy line, one half white, the other half black. But in each half of the circle there is a smaller circle of the other color. Stereotypically, a man is decisive, hard-nosed, aggressive; and a woman is yielding, inclusive, peacemaking. But a wife has that small circle within her that demands that she also be decisive, hard-nosed, aggressive; and a husband has within him the need to be yielding, inclusive, peacemaking.

Contract / Covenant

Until the new 1983 Code of Canon Law of the Catholic Church, the word used to describe marriage was *contract*. Since then, the word *covenant* has been substituted for *contract*. This substitution points to a dramatic shift in our understanding of what a marriage is. Paul Palmer, S.J., summarizes that shift:

> Contracts deal with things, covenants with people. . . . Contracts are best understood by lawyers, civil and ecclesiastical; covenants are best understood by poets.
> . . . Contracts are witnessed by people with the state as guarantor; covenants are witnessed by God with God as guarantor. Contracts can be made by children who know the value of a penny; covenants are made only by adults who are mentally, emotionally, and spiritually mature.

OLD TESTAMENT

When the Israelites tried to understand their relationship with Yahweh, they looked around for a human counterpart, and the most obvious approximation was marriage. On Sinai, Yahweh took the people of Israel to wife, and no matter how promiscuous Israel became, Yahweh remained an ever faithful "spouse." The prophet Hosea, in a crazily symbolic gesture, took the prostitute Gomer as his wife, to show how relentlessly faithful God is to people:

> *Israel, I will make you my wife;*
> *I will be true and faithful;*
> *I will show you constant love*
> *   and mercy*
> *and make you mine forever.*

> *The Lord said to me, "Go again and show your love for a woman who is committing adultery with a lover. You must love her just as I still love the people of Israel, even though they turn to other gods."*   Hosea 2:19–20; 3:1

NEW TESTAMENT

In the New Testament gospel parables, Jesus pictures himself as a bridegroom:

> *"At that time the Kingdom of heaven will be like this. Once there were ten young women who took their oil lamps and went out to meet the bridegroom. Five of them were foolish, and the other five were wise . . . The bridegroom was late in coming, so they began to nod and fall asleep.*
> *   "It was already midnight when the cry rang out, 'Here is the bridegroom! Come and meet him!' . . . The five who were ready went in with him to the wedding feast, and the door was closed."*
> Matthew 25:1–2, 5–6

And in the Book of Revelation heaven is described as a wedding feast in which the Son of Man takes humankind as his bride.

> *Then there came from the throne the sound of a voice, saying, "Praise our God, all his servants and all people, both great and small, who have reverence for him!" Then I heard what sounded like a crowd, like the sound of a roaring waterfall, like loud peals of thunder. I heard them say, "Praise God! For the Lord, our Almighty God, is King! Let us rejoice and be glad; let us praise his greatness! For the time has come for the wedding of the Lamb, and his bride has prepared herself for it. She has been given clean shining linen to wear." (The linen is the good deeds of God's people.)*   Revelation 19:5–8

MARRIAGE COVENANT

Both the Old and New Testaments express our relationship with God, using language taken *from* an understanding of an ideal marriage. This in turn helps us understand marriage from God's ideal love of us.

———

A covenant says,
"I am with you,
regardless.
No ifs, or buts,
or conditions."

———

HAVRIETIS AQVAM 7 VERTETVR ĨSANGVINEM · ESODI · IIII · CAP ·

VOX DOMINI ĨTONVIT SVPER AQVAS · P̃S · XXVIII · C̃ ·

DESCĒDIT 7 LAVIT SEPTIES INIORDANE · III · R̃ · V · C̃ ·

Wedding at Cana

Fra Angelico (1400–1455)

A contract is carefully worded, and everybody knows exactly what is involved. But a covenant is open-ended, and is a total commitment of self to the other. A covenant, unlike a contract, is a pledge of personal loyalty no-matter-what. Which makes it obvious that couples who draw up "premarital agreements" about who gets what in case of a break-up have—by that very fact—denied what their marriage promises.

A contract is always bilateral and conditional. It spells out, "I will do this if you will do that, and if you do not, you have violated the agreement and I am released from my obligations to you." A covenant, on the other hand, says, "I am *with* you, regardless. No ifs, or buts, or conditions. There is only one rule: We can work it out."

Christian marriage is an image of the covenant of Yahweh with Israel and the covenant of Christ with his Body, the Church. Christian spouses must promise the same commitment to love without end that God has for us—Yahweh, for Israel, and Christ, for his Body. Self-sacrificial love, embodied in the crucifix, is the touchstone of Christian identity and therefore of Christian marriage.

"Conjugal love involves a totality, in which all the elements of the person enter—appeal of the body and instinct, power of feeling and affectivity, aspiration of the spirit and of will. It aims at a deeply personal unity, a unity that, beyond union in one flesh, leads to forming one heart and soul; it demands indissolubility and faithfulness in definitive mutual giving; and it is open to fertility.

Catechism of the Catholic Church, 1643

Marriage Preparation

A very delicate and often painful situation sometimes arises in the marriage preparation process. The person exploring Christian married life with a couple may develop strong concerns about the couple's readiness for Christian marriage at this time. What might cause such doubts?

- Conversations might have revealed that the couple has little if any "genuine" commitment with the Catholic Church community.

- A couple might also want a "church" wedding simply for the externals surrounding it, such as the music and the dress-up rather than for making a genuine "religious" commitment to each other, calling the People of God to witness it.

- The engaged couple has come to the Church, requesting to be married "in the Church" solely because their parents are practicing Catholics and the couple simply wants to pacify them and avoid dealing with the consequences of not getting married in the Church.

IMMEDIATE PREPARATION

In his apostolic exhortation *On the Family*, Pope John Paul II acknowledged the "natural right" of a man and woman to marry. But, in the same letter, he speaks of a couple's immediate preparation for marriage as a moment on their "journey of faith, which is similar to the catechumenate," that the Christian family and the whole of the church community should become involved in.

The word *religion* comes from Latin roots that mean "to bind strongly." Without a serious *connection* to the Catholic eucharistic community, is there real "religion" in the lives of the couple? Just as you may be human but not act humanly, you may be Catholic but not act Catholic.

When a couple ask a priest to preside at and witness the exchange of their consent, the first question he ought to ask the engaged couple is whether they "practice" their faith. Do they at least "come home" fairly often?

It must not be forgotten that these engaged couples by virtue of their baptism are already sharers in Christ's marriage covenant with the church, and that, by their right intention, they have accepted God's plan regarding marriage and therefore, at least implicitly, consent to what the church intends to do when she celebrates marriage.   *On the Family*

A DECISION

When an engaged couple admit they do not practice at all, the priest ask may them separately to write him a letter saying honestly why they want a priest to witness at their marriage—not this priest as their friend, but any priest, even a stranger, even if their parents are not going to be there.

The faith of the person asking the church for marriage can exist in different degrees, and it is the primary duty of pastors to bring about a rediscovery of this faith and to nourish it and bring it to maturity. . . .   *On the Family*

The letters are quite honest. Sometimes, they result in one or both of the partners seriously reassessing their laxity in religious practice for the first time since high school or college—as adults.

All too often, though, their letters—quite sincere and on the surface seemingly Christian (if not exactly "Catholic")—reveal a "Christianity" that is more tinged with memories of a Catholic childhood than with a present relationship with God and that is, beneath the surface, little more than a genuine, profound, and laudable-if-limited ethical humanism.

One prospective groom wrote that no one could live in any big city without being aware of Christ in agony—the homeless, the disenfranchised, the dead-ended. A moving letter. Though the young man did not take part in the celebration of Mass and, in fact, deferred to his future wife to bring up the children as Jews ("more for ethnic and family reasons than religious ones"), the priest asked if the man himself at least prayed occasionally, tried to sustain a connection to God.

The man said, "Not really."

Yet he still sincerely maintained he was in a very real sense a "practicing Christian" and at least radically Catholic. He was using those words in the same blithely self-deceptive way characters on soaps use the words "making love," when love hasn't the slightest thing to do with the relationship. It was impossible to convince him that being Catholic—or even Christian—means more than just being a good human being.

> When in spite of all efforts engaged couples show that they reject explicitly and formally what the church intends to do when the marriage of baptized persons is celebrated, the pastor of souls cannot admit them to the celebration of marriage. In spite of his reluctance to do so, he has the duty . . . to make it clear to those concerned that in these circumstances it is not the church that is placing an obstacle in the way of the celebration that they are asking for, but themselves. *On the Family*

Reflection

Consider the situation at the end of this segment: the young man asking for a Catholic priest to witness his wedding when he did not practice his faith and intended to bring up his children Jewish.

- ■ *If you were the priest or deacon he approached, would you accept? Why?*

- ■ Anyone baptized Catholic is a Catholic Christian; that "seal" does not go away. But is there a "limit" to those the Church should admit to the celebration of the sacrament of Matrimony? Where does one "draw the line"—if at all? To pose the question in another way:

The entire Christian life bears the mark of the spousal love of Christ and the Church. Already Baptism, the entry into the People of God, is a nuptial mystery; it is so to speak the nuptial bath which precedes the wedding feast, the Eucharist. Christian marriage in its turn becomes an efficacious sign, the sacrament of the covenant of Christ and the Church.

Catechism of the Catholic Church, 1617

BECOMING MARRIED

Survey

This survey is not an exercise for a grade, but a means to stir up interest and get an idea of varying opinions in your group. Some of the statements are matters of objective fact; others are merely subjective opinions. On the rating scale under each statement circle the number that best reflects your current opinion about that statement.

+2 = strongly agree,
+1 = agree,
 0 = cannot make up my mind,
−1 = disagree,
−2 = strongly disagree.

Then share the reasons for your opinion.

1. Like all sacraments, a wedding is only one focal moment in a long-time process.

   +2   +1   0   −1   −2

2. Like any act of faith, marriage is a calculated risk. The more calculation, the less risk.

   +2   +1   0   −1   −2

3. Marriage is the surrender of something good in the hope of something better.

   +2   +1   0   −1   −2

4. Florists, photographers, musicians, and caterers can make everyone forget the core of a marriage.

   +2   +1   0   −1   −2

5. Like a formal funeral, a formal wedding can help those left behind "let go" more easily.

   +2   +1   0   −1   −2

6. The actual wedding is quite brief and can get swallowed up by the fuss and frills.

   +2   +1   0   −1   −2

7. The priest is a "lens" through whom the marriage vows go to the Church, the people in the pews.

   +2   +1   0   −1   −2

8. In a marriage, the partners have "power" over one another only insofar as they serve one another.

   +2   +1   0   −1   −2

9. It's not sex that keeps a marriage together; it's a promise.

   +2   +1   0   −1   −2

10. The words *trial marriage* are a contradiction in terms.

    +2   +1   0   −1   −2

The Engagement

As we have seen, the wedding ceremony is only one climactic moment in a long process of *becoming* married. That process begins when the couple began dating, getting gradually to know each other, easy with each other, friendly, testing to find out if this person just might be Mister or Miss Right.

When the relationship begins to become exclusive, the couple reach another stage that is evolving into a deeper commitment to each other. This can be very precarious when the feelings are overpowering and the commitment is not—because of schooling, finances, unreadiness to take lifelong responsibility for another human being— and when one or the other partner has yet to take full responsibility for her or his self.

When a man and woman finally make the resolve to become engaged and make their intention to commit to each other public, the commitment deepens further. And as in all love relationships the more one invests in the other, the more painful betrayal can be. That does not mean that betrayal, that "little death," cannot be turned into a rebirth (just as after the wedding). If the couple can get through those trials—and still love each other—the "little death" has only made the love stronger. Scar tissue is toughest.

"Who is this arising like the dawn, fair as the moon, resplendent as the sun, terrible as an army with banners?"

Song of Songs 6:10 (*The Jerusalem Bible*)

The Wedding

The wedding itself is a death to the old and a rebirth as a new composite self, and it can be a wrenching experience. In the Steve Martin remake of *Father of the Bride*, it's the night before the wedding and he and his daughter are shooting baskets in the driveway, and she says:

> I just kept thinking about how this is my last night in my bed and like my last night as a kid. I mean, I've lived here since I was five—and I feel like I'm supposed to turn in my key tomorrow. It was so strange packing up my room. I couldn't throw anything away, so I have all these yearbooks and ratty stuffed animals, my old retainer, all my old magic tricks. I mean, I know I can't stay, but I don't want to leave.

But the comfortable, well-known objects and habits two people surrender to get married are "necessary losses."

PREPARATIONS

Just as the media and advertisers have taken over Christmas, the wedding industries (florists, photographers, musicians, limousine services, caterers) have taken over marriage—or at least the focal symbols in marriage. Many couples "register" patterns for dishware and silver so friends can give them as presents.

Picking gowns for the bride and bridesmaids (never worn again) occupies weeks. The morning of the wedding itself is frequently chaotic (vs. cosmos): one of the bridesmaids has the wrong shoes; the florist forgot to put baby's breath in the bouquets; the white runner down the main aisle snags and looks wrinkled; a huge spray of gladioli in the front of the church screens off the priest; the country-club reception just about impoverishes the bride's family.

Another triumph for the trivial. A woman and a man are pledging their lives to each other, yet a great many of the people present are fretting over stuffed cream puffs and the proper drapery of the bridal train. Still, a formal church wedding makes it easier for the parents of the couple to "let go," to realize—however painfully—that a new era has begun, a new "little church" is forming. And it involves the whole family and their friends, a community sharing a momentous event and approving it.

THE RITE OF MARRIAGE

Whether the celebration of the sacrament of Matrimony takes place within or outside the celebration of Mass, the ceremony is remarkably chaste and simple. After the homily, the priest or deacon speaks to the couple about Christian marriage and asks them to state their intentions. Then the couple join their right hands and, either in response to the celebrant's questions or repeating the promises after him, they each declare their consent. The bridegroom promises:

> I, [Name], take you, [Name], to be my wife. I promise to be true to you in good times and in bad, in sickness and in health. I will love you and honor you all the days of my life.

The bride promises:

> I, [Name], take you, [Name], to be my husband. I promise to be true to you in good times and in bad, in sickness and in health. I will love you and honor you all the days of my life.   *Rite of Marriage*

Then the couple exchange the wedding rings the priest has blessed.

> [Name], take this ring as a sign of my love and fidelity. In the name of the Father, and of the Son, and of the Holy Spirit.   *Rite of Marriage*

And it's done.

How can I ever express
the happiness of the marriage
that is joined together
by the church,
strengthened by an offering,
sealed by a blessing?
How wonderful the bond
between two believers,
with a single hope, a single desire,
a single observance,
a single service.
They are . . . both servants;
there is no separation
between them in spirit or flesh.

Tertullian, *Ad Uxorem*

RITE OF MARRIAGE DURING MASS

Christ the Lord raised this union to the dignity of a sacrament so that it might more clearly recall
and more easily reflect his own unbreakable union with his Church.   *Rite of Marriage, "Introduction"*

ENTRANCE RITE

*The priest, vested for Mass, meets the bride and groom at the door
of the church and greets them in a friendly manner, showing that the
Church shares their joy.*

LITURGY OF THE WORD

*There may be three readings, the first of them from the Old Testament.
After the gospel, the priest gives a homily.*

Rite of Marriage

*The priest questions the couple about their intentions.
Each answers the questions separately.*

> My dear friends, you have come together
> in this church so that the Lord may seal
> and strengthen your love in the presence
> of the Church's minister and this community.
> Christ abundantly blesses this love. He has already
> consecrated you in baptism and now he enriches
> and strengthens you by a special sacrament so that
> you may assume the duties of marriage in mutual
> and lasting fidelity. And so, in the presence of the
> Church, I ask you to state your intentions.

> [Name] and [Name], have you come here freely
> and without reservation to give yourselves to each
> other in marriage?

> Will you love and honor each other as man and wife
> for the rest of your lives?

> Will you accept children lovingly from God, and bring
> them up according to the law of Christ and his Church?

Consent

The priest invites the couple to declare their consent.

> Since it is your intention to enter into marriage,
> join your right hands, and declare your consent
> before God and his Church.

*The couple join hands and declare their consent (see page 237).
Receiving their consent, the priest says,*

> You have declared your consent before the Church.
> May the Lord in his goodness strengthen your consent
> and fill you both with his blessings.
> What God has joined, men must not divide.

Blessing and Exchange of Rings

The priest says:

> May the Lord bless † these rings
> which you give to each other
> as the sign of your love and fidelity.

The bride and groom exchange rings.

General Intercessions

LITURGY OF THE EUCHARIST

Nuptial Blessing

*After the Lord's Prayer . . . the priest faces the bride and bridegroom and,
with hands joined, says:*

> Father, . . .
> Give them the strength which comes from the gospel
> so that they may be witnesses of Christ to others. . . .
> And, after a happy old age,
> grant them fullness of life with the saints
> in the kingdom of heaven.

Blessing at the End of Mass

*Before blessing the people at the end of Mass, the priest blesses the
bride and groom, praying in part:*

> May the peace of Christ live always in your hearts
>   and in your home.
> May you have true friends to stand by you, both in
>   joy and in sorrow.
> May you be ready and willing to help and comfort all
>   who come to you in need.
> And may the blessings promised to the compassionate
>   be yours in abundance.
> Amen.

SYMBOLS OF MARRIAGE

Despite all the hoopla and folderol that clutter up so many modern weddings, the symbols of marriage are quite simple too.

Now many priests stand *between* the couple and the people to emphasize that it is the couple who are the primary ministers of this sacrament, bestowing the sacrament on each other and receiving it. And it is the *Church* who ratifies their declaration of consent. The priest ministers as the lens through which the declarations of consent are offered to the people and through whom the people express their approval. Often the priest invites those present to symbolize their approval of the new marriage by their hearty applause. At a wedding, no one is merely a spectator.

What do rings "say," symbolize? A senior ring, a bishop's ring. Rings bespeak both constriction and empowerment. Before this moment each was free to choose from all the single members of their opposite sex. But that freedom could not activate until *expended* on the one person, rejecting all the rest. The exchange and wearing of a wedding ring is a reminder that one is never free of responsibility for the other. It is also a reminder that one is never alone.

In the Christian story, "gift, power, honor" are not bestowals but challenges. Grace does not "happen" without our rising to the challenge. Jesus constantly told his power-hungry disciples that the true leader is one who *serves*:

> *An argument broke out among the disciples as to which one of them should be thought of as the greatest. Jesus said to them, "The kings of the pagans have power over their people, and the rulers claim the title 'Friends of the People.' But this is not the way it is with you; rather, the greatest one among you must be like the youngest, and the leader must be like the servant. Who is greater, the one who sits down to eat or the one who serves? The one who sits down, of course. But I am among you as one who serves."*
>
> Luke 22:24–27

Christian couples . . . nourish and develop their marriage by undivided affection, which wells up from the fountain of divine love, while, in a merging of human and divine love, they remain faithful in body and in mind, in good times as in bad.

Rite of Marriage, "Introduction"

A husband has "power" over his wife only insofar as he serves her; a wife has "power" over her husband only insofar as she serves him. Yet very often, true service says, "Thus far, and no further." Marital love *is* loving your "neighbor"—your spouse—with as much love as you love yourself.

"Take this ring as a sign of my love and fidelity." Most people seem to think that these words are restricted to "sexual fidelity," and only in the negative "thou shalt not." On the contrary, these words are a pledge of faithfulness to the other's entire being: to stay with you, to forgive you, to understand you—no matter what. As Maggie Antrobus said, it wasn't their love that made their marriage but the marriage promise that made the love possible.

Marriage is not a feeling. It is an act of will that takes over when the feelings fail.

THE EARLY YEARS

Herbert Anderson and Robert Fite call the period of adjustment after the wedding "When the Ordinary Gets Complicated."

Differences

No problem if both spouses like rock music, but if he loves to play the bagpipes, she ought to know that long before she accepts an engagement ring. What happens if he's messy and she's a neatness freak? If he's always ten minutes early and she's always ten minutes late? Whose family do we have Christmas dinner with? Do we eat liver? And a very tough one: who holds the remote control for the TV? Do we insert the toilet roll overshot or undershot? "Well, my *mother* always used to . . ." Especially when conflicting habits are weighed down with family loyalty, spouses can become like two little kids arguing about who insulted whose mother.

None of those little spats is about a genuine "fault," but each is a *difference*. And by communicating and compromising, "we can work it out."

Sexual Relations

The sexual relationship in marriage is now a "sacramental" relationship, a source of grace for the married couple:

> *A man should fulfill his duty as a husband, and a woman should fulfill her duty as a wife, and each should satisfy the other's needs. A wife is not the master of her own body, but her husband is; in the same way a husband is not the master of his own body, but his wife is.*   1 Corinthians 7:3–4

God created us as sexual beings. And sexual relationships in marriage are unassailably *good*.

Which might provide an occasion to speak of premarital sex. The ideal honeymoon is delirious, and it lasts longer than just the week or two during which the couple go off by themselves. In most cases the relationship is highly sexual, intoxicating, out-of-this-world, and it is often the sex that puts all the little spats into perspective. But if the couple has had a serious sexual involvement for a couple of years before the marriage, they have already had their honeymoon. That is the tragic result of living in our society that takes a reality so wondrous and precious as sexual intercourse and makes it commonplace. For a good marriage a genuine friendship is necessary. Sexual activity before marriage can easily prevent the building of a marriage on the foundation of friendship.

The words *trial marriage* are an oxymoron, a two-word contradiction. You cannot "try out" a lifelong promise.

"Sexuality, by means of which man and woman give themselves to one another through the acts which are proper and exclusive to spouses, is not something simply biological, but concerns the innermost being of the human person as such. It is realized in a truly human way only if it is an integral part of the love by which a man and woman commit themselves totally to one another until death."

Catechism of the Catholic Church, 2361

Spiritual Intimacy

Nor is the intimacy in marriage merely sexual. Marriage is not merely a union of two bodies. It is a union of two entire selves—body, mind, and soul. Far more important in marriage is the deepening of a married couple's *emotional, spiritual* intimacy—which many males confuse with sexual intimacy.

Emotional, spiritual intimacy involves being willing to be *vulnerable*, not just physically but with one's whole *self*, which, ironically, takes a great deal of inner self-confidence. It means letting one's hair down, letting the other wander around those dark caverns in the soul. Which in turn takes courage based not only on one's own lovability and faith but also on the love one is certain the other spouse has for him or her. Oddly, such emotional honesty is a burden both spouses need to share—a sharing that bonds them more closely. Being understood and accepted is more important than being right—or perfect.

Each spouse has to have the freedom to be a self as well as the inner freedom to *reveal* that self to the other spouse. Even after that free commitment is celebrated in the marriage rite, the couple can still remain unfree, hiding their true selves from each other as Eros hid himself from Psyche, coming to her only at night, an adolescent sexual relationship waiting for hardships to rebirth it into love. Like the fallen Adam and Eve, the couple hide their "nakedness" with fig leaves because they themselves are uncomfortable with who they are.

That is why the sacrament of Matrimony is—or can be—a continual redemption from enslavement to self-doubt, self-distaste, self-deception. Freely and unashamedly, a man or woman has allowed someone else to come into his or her innermost self, to walk around and see all the scars, the ghouls and demons, the fears and weaknesses. And he or she says, "So what? You're still mine. I'm still yours."

As the early years progress, the intoxication of romance slowly neuters down because of the intrusions of reality. The couple begin to learn the difference between being-in-love and loving. There are not many real love songs. The only one that comes to mind is "Do You Love Me?" from *Fiddler on the Roof*, when after twenty-five years of a prearranged marriage, Tevye asks his wife, Golde, if she loves him. All that time, they have just been too busy even to think about it. And she answers:

> For twenty-five years I've lived with him,
> Fought with him, starved with him.
> Twenty-five years my bed is his.
> If that's not love, what is?

All the other songs, in my opinion, are romantic songs, being-in-love songs: "You are the promised touch of springtime; I can't live without you; you're my everything."

Romance is a wonderful, exhilarating, transforming feeling. But it is only a feeling. Genuine, or real, love has little, if anything, to do with palpitations of the heart and heavy breathing. Real love is an act of the will; it takes over when the feelings fail, when the beloved is no longer even *likable*. Real love is very undramatic, sharing the very down-to-earth chores: living within a budget, putting out the garbage, getting up to change a diaper in the middle of the night. Not poetry, just prose: providing, encouraging, giving pleasure, conversing, planning—and giving us the grace to laugh at ourselves.

The process of the early years of becoming married is *bonding*, facing not only the challenges of intimacy but the challenges of partnership. The bonds that web the early marriage relationship form in all kinds of small ways: going to a garage sale, refinishing furniture, doing the dishes, making love, visiting each other's families, buying Christmas presents, trying to balance the checkbook together, going to church.

Many mature couples want to postpone marriage until they are both very well established in their careers and have a nice tidy sum in the bank. But older married couples say that the struggles to make it in the early years, together, was the solid foundation of their later life.

> *Romance is a wonderful, exhilarating, transforming feeling. But it is only a feeling. Genuine love has nothing to do with palpitations of the heart and heavy breathing.*

Part of becoming well married involves each spouse's letting go of all unrealistic expectations of the other spouse, of living not with an idealized Cinderella or Prince Charming but with a flawed-but-loved human being. Married life is also, however, a commitment to keep each another growing, which means change, moving through each "little death" to a "rebirth." Married life necessarily involves creating a climate of acceptability in which, if one spouse wants to go back and get a degree, the other will find some way to empower it; and if one spouse wants to take a year off and write a novel, the other will find a way to show support of that choice.

In an marriage that is alive and growing, a husband or wife ought to be able to say as Saint Paul said of the Philippians, "I thank my God for you every time I think of you" (Philippians 1:3).

INTERRELIGIOUS MARRIAGES

Couples living in mixed marriages—marriages between a Catholic and another baptized person, or between a Catholic and a nonbaptized person—have special needs.

If two spouses come from different religious traditions and each is important to them, or if one spouse has a radical intolerance for religion while it is important to the other and they simply go ahead thinking "things will work themselves out," they have very unrealistic ideas about what married love can accommodate.

There must be borne in mind the particular difficulties inherent in the relationships between husband and wife with respect for religious freedom; this freedom could be violated either by undue pressure to make the partner change his or her beliefs or by placing obstacles in the way of the free manifestation of these beliefs by religious practice. *On the Family*

Children of a Interreligious Marriage

In the view of the 1917 Code of Canon Law, the marriage partners were either Catholic or not. The non-Catholic either signed a form that said he or she promised to raise the children Catholic, or a Catholic marriage could not take place. But in 1967, Pope Paul VI removed that barrier and only the Catholic party in a mixed marriage needed to sign a form, promising to do "all in my power to share the faith I have received with our children by having them baptized and reared as Catholics." The non-Catholic spouse needs to be aware of that promise, but is not bound by it.

Before the marriage, the couple should be made aware that all future decisions about the faith life of children must be made jointly. This capacity to make a good marriage commitment should really be a norm of whether they can honestly enter into a marriage commitment. If one or the other partner has a serious conscience problem on that point, it is a clear indication that they ought to rethink whether their decision to marry at this time is a good decision.

Some couples dodge this responsibility by telling themselves they will let their children make their own faith decisions when the children grow old enough to choose. But:

■ first, when does that age come?

■ second, how will children even come to realize that a relationship with God is important, if their parents fob off the responsibility on them?

■ and, third, how will they decide among all the religions which one to choose? And if it becomes a matter of choosing between the father's religion or the mother's religion, it becomes an agonizing choice, forcing the child to choose between the mother and the father.

A child is not something owed to one, but is a gift. The "supreme gift of marriage" is a human person. A child . . . possesses genuine rights: the right "to be the fruit of the specific act of the conjugal love of . . . parents," and "the right to be respected as a person . . . from the moment of . . . conception."

Catechism of the Catholic Church, 2378

Celebration of an Interreligious Marriage

If the marriage is to be celebrated in a Catholic church, the Catholic priest or deacon is the "minister of record," serving as the official witness of the couple's giving their consent and signing the marriage certificate. If the marriage is celebrated in a non-Catholic church or synagogue or mosque, the priest can take an active part in the celebration, for example, by reading the Scriptures, giving the homily, giving the nuptial blessing, and so on. But the non-Catholic minister or rabbi receives the marriage vows.

Canon 844 of the 1983 *Code of Canon Law* allows a Catholic minister to permit other Christians to share in the sacraments of the Eucharist, Reconciliation, and the Anointing of the Sick if they:

- spontaneously request the sacraments,

- are unable to receive them from their own minister,

- are aware of what they are doing.

Marriages between a Catholic and a non-Catholic partner can be a marvelous experience, not only for the couple but for their families and for all the people present witnessing the marriage. A marriage between a Catholic and a baptized partner can give witness to the truth that we are all Christians; a marriage between a Catholic and a nonbaptized partner gives witness to the truth that at least we are all believers in a dimension larger than the merely earthly.

That, surely, is not the last word on the sacrament of marriage. But perhaps the last word of all regarding Christianity and Catholicism and marriage is one word: forgive, "Love never gives up; and its faith, hope, and patience never fail."

The books of Ruth and Tobit bear moving witness to an elevated sense of marriage and to the fidelity and tenderness of spouses. Tradition has always seen in the Song of Solomon a unique expression of human love, a pure reflection of God's love— a love "strong as death" that "many waters cannot quench."

Catechism of the Catholic Church, 1611

Reflection

Not too many of you reading these pages are about to get married. But all of us are—or ought to be—in love.

- Read what Saint Paul says about loving and test out your most ardent love against what he says:

  Love is patient and kind; it is not jealous or conceited or proud; love is not ill-mannered or selfish or irritable; love does not keep a record of wrongs; love is not happy with evil, but is happy with the truth. Love never gives up; and its faith, hope, and patience never fail.

  1 Corinthians 13:4–7

Understanding Matrimony

Review

1. How can two become "one flesh" yet remain two souls? How does the image of the dogwood help to understand that biblical teaching? Why should each partner still have a self?

2. What is the purpose of the natural crisis of adolescence? What should it produce in the soul? Why should that task have been taken care of *before* two people commit themselves to the intimacy and partnership of marriage?

3. What is the difference between a contract and a covenant? How does a marriage mirror Yawheh's commitment to Israel and Jesus' commitment to the Church?

4. What relationship should at least one partner have to the eucharistic community to ask for a Catholic wedding legitimately? What is the root of the word *religion?*

5. Throughout the book, we have considered having a healthy soul, a good philosophy of life, participation in the sacraments as being at "home." How is that particularly true of a marriage?

6. Explain: A wedding is only a climactic moment in a lifelong process.

7. Just as ad agencies have co-opted Christmas, how have the wedding industries co-opted weddings? How have they—like the media— made the trivial important and the important trivial? Which is more important: the vows or the videotape?

8. Explain the meaning of the simple symbols in a wedding: holding hands, words, rings. When you "give your word," what are you giving?

9. As the bishop at an ordination, the priest or deacon who witnesses a marriage often asks those assembled—the Church—to symbolize their approval by applauding. Why is that significant?

10. What does *fidelity* mean? Surely it is not merely sexual monogamy.

Discuss

1. What happens to a marriage when one partner submits 100 percent to the other? Consider the woman who completely defines her *self* as "this man's wife, those children's mother." What might happen when the husband dies and the children all move away to begin their own families?

2. Many marriages break up because one partner says, "I've got to find myself." When should a person do that?

3. Sometimes a couple in a troubled marriage decide to have a child, thinking it will heal their relationship. How wise is that?

4. What different attitudes do a couple bring to a marriage when they consider it a contract, not a covenant?

5. What kinds of things does one give up in order to become married—not just material goods but spiritual goods? Why is it worth the loss?

6. Why is the morning of the wedding usually chaos (vs. cosmos)?

7. Sometimes the family of the bride spends $20,000 or more on a wedding. Is that reasonable? How much could that cash mean to a couple just starting out? Would the reception be any less fun, any less meaningful, if it were held in a church hall?

8. The early years are "when the ordinary gets complicated." Why? In what ways? What does it mean in a marriage to "have a room of one's own"?

9. Today many couples live together for a couple of years before commitment to marriage. But statistics show that most couples who do that break up later. Why? Why is a "trial marriage" a contradiction in terms?

Activities

1. Interview members of your parish's marriage preparation team. Find out how your parish prepares a couple to make their final decision to marry and to celebrate the sacrament of Matrimony.

2. Brainstorm in small groups how young people "give their word" to others. Then list the ways that "Giving one's word" prepares young people for their future exchange of marriage promises.

3. Work in small groups to identify several movies and television sitcoms in which marriage is portrayed. In one column list those shows that reflect the Bible's and Church's teaching on marriage; in another column list those that do not. Then draw up a portrait of "marriage" as it is portrayed by the media.

4. Debate: Living together before marriage weakens a relationship between a man and woman and does not prepare them for marriage.

5. Consult with three long-time married couples and ask them to list the ingredients of a lasting marriage, in no particular order. Then have them pick the most important. Report back to the group.

Scripture Readings

Skim the passages. Pick one that appeals to you and (1) summarize its main point, (2) tell how it relates to the chapter, and (3) list one or two thoughts that entered your mind as you read it.

• Tobit 7:9–10, 11–15	May God fill you with blessings
• Tobit 8:5–10	May old age bring us together
• Song of Songs 2:8–10, 14, 16; 8:6–7	Love is strong as death
• Matthew 5:13–16	A house built on rock
• Matthew 22:35–40	The greatest commandment; the second is similar to it
• Mark 10:6–9	They are no longer two
• John 2:1–11	The wedding at Cana
• 1 John 4:7–12	God is love

✎ Journal

Marriage, like all relationships, is built on fidelity. Reflect on your relationship with your family. Your peers. In what ways are you faithful to others? What happens when others are unfaithful to you? Describe your feelings.

Epilogue

Some Methods of Praying

No runner gets onto a track, no soccer player goes onto a field, no actor or dancer makes an entrance on a stage without warming up. They are not only limbering up their bodies and voices but psyching themselves out of one life into a completely different one. So too with praying. Anyone wanting to pray should follow the same preparation exercises, no matter what method of praying proves most conducive to the individual.

Preparing

1. ***Time.*** Make an interior commitment of the next ten or fifteen minutes or half-hour. It's set aside from the everyday into the sacred. At least for that time, the world can get along without you. And have *no expectations!* You're letting God do the work. Perhaps all that will happen is that you experience peace. Isn't that enough? Perhaps you have the exhilarating sense of not being alone, of being in another Presence. Isn't that enough? Expect no lights or revelations.

2. ***Place.*** This will depend on the individual. Some find a church or chapel best; others prefer sitting in a park; some like walking. The important thing is to find a place with the fewest distractions to break the "connection."

3. ***Position.*** If you are staying in one place, the configuration of the body is important. If you sprawl, you'll fall asleep for sure. Sit on a chair or pillow, back straight, legs crossed Indian style, your hands opened upright on your knees. You are focused and comfortable, and your whole body "says" receptivity. Most keep out distractions best by closing their eyes.

4. ***Letting Go.*** It is important—physically and psychologically—to let go, to stop trying to control what happens, to dominate God or manipulate God's will. Roll your head around your neck; many of us can feel the muscles grinding against one another. Let all the tension and concerns drain out of your head into your shoulders. Imagine them as something physical or like waves of energy draining down your back and arms, into your legs and seat, and out into the chair. Now you are ready—not passive, but receptive.

The Mantra

To use a mantra (a constantly repeated phrase), focus your attention on your breathing. Breathe very deeply, in for five counts, hold it, out for five counts. Over and over until you get an easy, steady rhythm.

The most famous mantra is "AUM," repeated over and over, feeling the vibrations in one's chest, mouth, arms. I have no idea what it means, if it has any meaning at all, but it works. "The Jesus Prayer" mentioned in Salinger's *Franny and Zooey* is another: on the intake, "Jesus, Son of David," and on the exhale, "Have mercy on me, a sinner." But you could use any words repeated over and over: "Father," "Mother," "Love."

The purpose of a mantra is to short-circuit the calculating intelligence that keeps to schedules, balances budgets, figures things out. It opens up—in males or females—what Jung called our "feminine" dimension: receptive, nurturing, conceiving. The object is to be like Our Lady at the Annunciation: "Be it done unto me as you will." To conceive Christ in us.

Many people say they no longer pray the rosary because they can't keep their attention on the words. But the whole *purpose* of the rosary is that you *don't* concentrate on the words, that they set up a rhythm in your mind and soul that goes *beyond* words. It sets up a "being-with," a connection.

Scripture: Mulling Ideas

After preparing yourself, open the Scriptures at any place and center the focused inner powers of yourself on what God is trying to say. (Best to start with the New Testament; the Old Testament can provoke too many problems for the beginner.) Make the section small, no more than a few verses. "What are these strange words trying to say to *me?*" Don't probe the words. Let them manipulate *you*. Roll them over in your mind and soul.

If you are unfamiliar or uneasy with Scripture, try these:

Isaiah 6:6–8	Romans 7:4–6
Matthew 25:37–40	I Corinthians 13:8–13
Mark 8:31–33	Ephesians 3:14–19
Luke 14:12–14	Philippians 2:5–11
Luke 1:1–5, 9–14	Hebrews 5:1–4

"And the word of God came to me saying. . . ." What does it *mean?* How do I translate this to the people around me?

Scripture: Controlled Daydreaming

The difference is in mulling over the *ideas* in the Scriptures and *reliving* the Scriptures. What Jesus said and did "speak" today more movingly than his words or actions.

Relax, let go of the world, read the Scripture passage, and then in your imagination slip into the scene—as any one of the participants. Earlier we spoke of becoming Jesus at the Last Supper, going from one to the other on our knees, washing their feet—then looking up and seeing the people in our class or office or faculty peopling the table.

Taste the herbs in the food; *smell* the sweat, the dry reeds on the floor, the candle wax; *feel* the textures of the tablecloth and sandals and the benches; *hear* the words not only in your ears but in the stirrings of the hair on the back of your neck; *see* the drab colors, and Jesus etched against that background. Now go through the scene not as an observer but as a participant.

We are all no more than matchmakers, trying to make God an appealing friend.

I have done my best. I now withdraw.

Index

Acknowledgments

Scripture quotations are taken from or adapted from the Good News Bible text, Today's English Version. Copyright © American Bible Society 1966, 1971, 1976, 1992. Used by permission.

Excerpts from the English translation of the *Catechism of the Catholic Church* for the United States of America copyright © 1994, United States Catholic Conference, Inc.—Libreria Editrice Vaticana. Used with permission.

Excerpts from the English translation of *The Roman Missal* © 1973, International Committee on English in the Liturgy, Inc. (ICEL); excerpts from the English translation of *Rite of Penance* © 1974, ICEL; excerpts from the English translation of *Rite of Baptism for Children* © 1969, ICEL; excerpts from the English translation of *The Ordination of Deacons, Priests, and Bishops* © 1969, ICEL; excerpts from the English translation of *Rite of Confirmation*, © 1972, ICEL; excerpts from *Pastoral Care of the Sick: Rites of Anointing and Viaticum* © 1982, ICEL; excerpts from the English translation of *Rite of Christian Initiation of Adults* © 1985. All rights reserved.

The poem by Gerard Manley, S.J. on page 23 is from *Poems of Gerard Manley Hopkins*, 3d ed.,edited by W.H. Gardner (New York and London: Oxford University Press, 1948).

The poem by John Donne on page 37 is from *The Complete Poetry and Selected Prose of John Donne*, edited by M. H. Abrams (New York and London: W. W. Norton and Co., 1979).

"The Twelve Steps" are reprinted with permission of Alcoholics Anonymous World Services, Inc. Permission to reprint this material does not mean that AA has reviewed or approved the contents of this publication, nor that AA agrees with the views expressed herein.

Excerpts on pages 24, 67, 103, 140, 144, 149, 203, and 209 are from *The Documents of Vatican II,* Walter M. Abbott, S.J., Gen. Ed. Copyright © 1966 by The America Press.

Excerpts on pages 232, 233, and 244 are from *On the Family* Copyright © 1982 by UNITED STATES CATHOLIC CONFERENCE.

Excerpt on page 5 is from *Hard Times* by Charles Dickens, Afterword Copyright © 1961 by the New American Library of World Literature, Inc.

Excerpt on page 125 is from *The Man on a Donkey: A Chronicle* by Hilda Frances Margaret Prescott, Copyright © 1952 by H.F.M. Prescott (The MacMillan Company).

Excerpts on pages 106, 135, 167 are from *The Meaning of the Sacraments* by Monika Hellwig, Copyright © 1981 by Pfaum/Standard.

Excerpts on pages 141, 183, and 228 are from *The New Dictionary of Sacramental Worship*, Peter E. Fink, S.J., Ed.. Copyright © 1990 by The Order of Saint Benedict, Inc., Collegeville, Minnesota (A Michael Glazier Book, The Liturgical Press, Collegeville, Minnesota).

Excerpt on page 211 is from *As One Who Serves,* Copyright © 1977 by UNITED STATES CATHOLIC CONFERENCE.

Excerpts on pages 155 and 216 are from *Sacraments for Secular Man* by George McCauley, S.J., Copyright © 1969 by Herder and Herder, Inc., New York, New York.

Excerpt on page 225 is from *The Skin of Our Teeth* by Thorton Wilder, Copyright © 1952 by Thornton Wilder.

Excerpt on page 41 is from *Sleep with Angels* by Mary Fisher, Copyright © by 1994 by Moyer Bell, Wakefield, RI.

Photo Credits

Bill Aron   134

THE BETTMANN ARCHIVE   16, 127–128

Jennifer Bindhammer   210

Dennis Brack/BLACK STAR   40, 55

Robert Brenner/PHOTO EDIT   245

David Butow/BLACK STAR   180

Catholic News Service   83

Philip Coblentz   13, 23, 27, 50, 107, 129, 130

Rick Friedman/BLACK STAR   61

Robert M. Friedman   206

Dennis Full   5–7, 12, 14, 26, 28, 34–35, 38–39, 42, 49, 52, 56, 62, 64, 66, 67, 75–82, 87, 90–95, 97, 103, 105, 111, 115, 117, 118–122, 136–151, 153–154, 158, 162–172, 182, 184, 188, 209, 211, 215–216, 225, 227, 232, 240

Galleone Photography   212

Jeff Greenberg/PHOTO EDIT   51

Dennis Hallinan/FPG   84

Richard Hutchings/PHOTO EDIT   11, 53

Erica Lansner/BLACK STAR   8

Richard C. Leach   112

Mark Link, S.J.   109

Edward J. Lynett, III   217–219

MacDonald Photo/PHOTO EDIT   189

John Neubaur/PHOTO EDIT   193

Michael Newman/PHOTO EDIT   36

Alan Oddie/PHOTO EDIT   187, 191, 192

Lisa Quinones/BLACK STAR   179

James Shaffer/PHOTO EDIT   196, 228

SCALA/ART RESOURCE/van Gogh   157

SCALA/ART RESOURCE/E;l Greco   89, 205

SCALA/ART RESOURCE/Madox Brown   207

SCALA/ART RESOURCE/Michelangelo   25

SCALA/ART RESOURCE/Rembrandt   59

SCALA/ART RESOURCE/Titian   65, 106

SCALA/ART RESOURCE/da Vinci   132

SCALA/ART RESOURCE/Carracci   160

SUPERSTOCK   108, 159, 235, 242

SUPERSTOCK/Fra Angelico   230

SUPERSTOCK/Ferrari   31

SUPERSTOCK/El Greco   195

SUPERSTOCK/Mazuranic   213

SUPERSTOCK/Murillo   161

Telegraph Colour Library/FPG   47

Uniphoto   152

Woody Woodworth/SUPERSTOCK   242

John A. Zierten   104